WALLACE STEGNER'S UNSETTLED COUNTRY

Ruin, Realism,
and Possibility in
the American West

Edited by MARK FIEGE,
MICHAEL J. LANSING,
and LEISL CARR CHILDERS

University of Nebraska Press
Lincoln

© 2024 by the Board of Regents of
the University of Nebraska

All rights reserved
Manufactured in the United States of America

The University of Nebraska Press is part of a land-
grant institution with campuses and programs on the
past, present, and future homelands of the Pawnee,
Ponca, Otoe-Missouria, Omaha, Dakota, Lakota, Kaw,
Cheyenne, and Arapaho Peoples, as well as those of the
relocated Ho-Chunk, Sac and Fox, and Iowa Peoples.

Publication of this volume was assisted by the Wallace
Stegner Chair in Western American Studies and the
Ivan Doig Center at Montana State University.

Library of Congress Cataloging-in-Publication Data
Names: Fiege, Mark (Mark T.), editor. | Lansing,
Michael, editor. | Carr Childers, Leisl, editor.
Title: Wallace Stegner's unsettled country: ruin, realism,
and possibility in the American West / edited by Mark
Fiege, Michael J. Lansing, and Leisl Carr Childers.
Description: Lincoln: University of Nebraska Press,
[2024] | Includes bibliographical references and index.
Identifiers: LCCN 2023013863
ISBN 9781496236173 (paperback)
ISBN 9781496238375 (epub)
ISBN 9781496238382 (pdf)
Subjects: LCSH: Stegner, Wallace, 1909–1993—
Criticism and interpretation. | Western stories—
History and criticism. | West (U.S.)—In literature. |
BISAC: LITERARY CRITICISM / American / Regional |
NATURE / Environmental Conservation & Protection
Classification: LCC PS3537.T316 Z96 2024 |
DDC 813/.52—dc23/eng/20230628
LC record available at https://lccn.loc.gov/2023013863

Designed and set in Minion Pro by L. Welch.

CONTENTS

Realism

Possibility

ILLUSTRATIONS

ACKNOWLEDGMENTS

Bringing together an anthology composed of the work of a dozen authors is no small feat. We thank each of the authors for their contributions and appreciate all their efforts in collaborating with each other and with us through the revision process. They persevered despite facing disruptions caused by a global pandemic. We thank Mary Murphy and Susan Kollin for their hard work in bringing these authors together for the first time in Bozeman, Montana, in May 2019. We appreciate the support of the Ivan Doig Center for the Study of the Lands and Peoples of the North American West as well as everyone who contributed to and participated in that symposium. We especially thank Susan Heyneman, John Heyneman, Corky Brittan, and other benefactors and supporters of the Wallace Stegner Chair in Western American Studies. Bridget Barry at the University of Nebraska Press was supportive, thoughtful, tolerant, and responsive throughout the publication process. Finally, we are grateful for the support of each other. It was a privilege and a pleasure working with two other scholars whose thoughts and ideas brought fascinating perspectives to the intellectual framing and construction of this anthology. The product of that process is more than this body of work alone. It also is a set of relationships that we treasure.

Wallace Stegner's Unsettled Country

Prologue

Wallace Stegner in
His Time and in Ours

MARK FIEGE,
MICHAEL J. LANSING,
AND LEISL CARR CHILDERS

> I really only want to say that we may love
> a place and still be dangerous to it.
> —Wallace Stegner, "Thoughts in a Dry Land"

In May 2019 the Ivan Doig Center for the Study of the Lands and Peoples of the North American West, in partnership with the Wallace Stegner Chair in Western American Studies (both at Montana State University), invited scholars to Bozeman to consider Wallace Stegner's legacy and its meaning for our times. It was fitting for Montana State to host such an event. Stegner held important ties to the university, and nearly thirty years after his death—despite growing attention to Indigenous and other writers whose work expressed the vast range of human experience in North America—this long gone white male author still seemed to have enduring interest for readers whose understanding of the West he had shaped. What was at stake in the symposium, however, was less the beauty of Stegner's prose, his ability to tell a good story, or his powerful evocations of the western landscape, and more what he and his work might do for readers—white readers especially—who live in a moment of accelerating regional, national, and planetary turmoil and the profound precarity and uncertainty that comes with it.

Stegner was familiar with disorienting change, and he rode its unsettled currents across most of the twentieth century. He was born in Lake Mills, Iowa, in 1909, and his childhood was marked by a family constantly on the move, to North Dakota, Washington, Saskatchewan, Montana, and Utah. He earned degrees at the University of Utah (1930) and the University of Iowa (1932, 1935) before teaching literature and writing at Utah, Wisconsin, and Harvard. In 1946, he moved to Stanford University, where he established a creative writing program that attracted talent from across the country. As an author, he focused on the American West, first gaining fame for his novel *The Big Rock Candy Mountain* (1943) as well as for nonfiction books such as *Mormon Country* (1942), *One Nation* (1945), *Beyond the Hundredth Meridian* (1953), and *This Is Dinosaur* (1955). One of the leading writers of post–World War II America, especially his fiction, Stegner in his prime won the Pulitzer Prize for *Angle of Repose* (1972) and the National Book Award for *The Spectator Bird* (1977). When he passed away in 1993 from injuries suffered in a car accident in New Mexico, he stood out for his commitment to, and critique of, the American West.

Before and after Stegner's death, scholars summarized, contextualized, and assessed his life, work, and significance. Numerous interviews, biographies, and compilations explored the range of his experiences, thought, and work. Many commentators could not help but memorialize, even in touching personal terms, the influence of an author who wrote so beautifully about the West and the sense of place that he found in it.[1] Yet even the encomiums expressed a sense of difference, of friction, of more troubled, conflicted, and darker sides to the man. After his death, Jackson Benson, one of Stegner's former students, published a biography that delved deeply into the author who spent his career "constantly cast in the role of outsider," writing against the grain and taking on "the role of a realist who is to tell us disagreeable truths."[2]

More recently, *New York Times* critic A. O. Scott—the type of eastern literary arbiter who irritated Stegner—noted the overlooked richness of Stegner's work, how it resists easy pigeonholing and how it often leads many readers into uncertain, thought-provoking terrain. "Stegner's books abide in an undervisited stretch of the American canon," Scott observed, "like a national park you might drive past on the way to a theme park or ski resort. If you do visit, you find a topography that looks familiar at first glance—as if from an old postcard—but becomes stranger and more deeply shadowed the longer you stay."[3]

Scholars who remained for long stretches in that bypassed national park recognized a part of Stegner's work that rises like a ridgeline from dark canyons into light. Historian Charles Rankin saw Stegner as an "optimist, truth-seeker, pragmatic realist," and "dreamer of a better society" who "forever felt an acute deficiency for having never 'stuck' in a western place long enough to become part of it." Stegner "championed adaptation" to the limitations of the western environment and, despite his bitterness towards his fellow human beings' exploitative and prejudicial behavior, believed that people "have the capacity to do right."[4] Scott similarly pointed out Stegner's fondness for the word "solidarity," an ideal incompletely achieved by settlers and their descendants.

Stegner was not without his critics. In *Why I Can't Read Wallace Stegner and Other Essays: A Tribal Voice* (1996), Elizabeth Cook-Lynn (Crow Creek Sioux), a scholar we acknowledge and honor, asserted that Stegner egregiously adhered to frontier and vanishing Indian myths and thereby created "the potential to cut off dialogue and condemn to oblivion or absurdity Indian writers who want to continue the drama." Stegner's myopic claim of indigeneity, she wrote, obfuscates the reality that the settler "invasion of the New World was never a movement of moral courage at all; rather, it was a pseudoreligious and corrupt socioeconomic movement for the possession of resources."[5] In Stegner's search for belonging and understanding of the places he held dear, he used concepts and language current among white European American writers and intellectuals of his time to reify national myths that emphasized the primacy of the settlers who colonized the continent and who, along with their descendants, benefited from national policies that privatized land and enabled the ruthless extraction of resources from it.

Yet, as Scott noted, Stegner also raged against some of the consequences of settler myths and the exploitation they justified, whether or not he fully recognized the origins of the damage. In doing so, Stegner took the first step toward peeling back the mask of the settler perspective and rethinking the region's and nation's past, present, and future. As Scott stated, we should assess Stegner critically while engaging his work: "To hold Stegner exempt from criticism seems to me as shortsighted as refusing to read him."[6] Building on the criticism of Cook-Lynn and others, yet following Stegner through the shadowed canyons of his work, challenges us to unsettle the western American past in its fullness with the objective of finding a better way forward.

Montana State University proved to be a useful setting to rethink both the author and his beloved region. In 1987 the institution awarded Stegner an honorary doctorate, inaugurating a warm, intense relationship with the noted author. A few years later, shortly before his death, Stegner returned to deliver an address that, in retrospect, became the foundation for the annual Wallace Stegner Lecture, a series that continues to this day. Soon after Stegner's passing, faculty, staff, and friends of Stegner—including philosophy professor Gordon "Corky" Brittan and benefactor Susan Heyneman—established the Wallace Stegner Chair in Western American Studies, the first occupant of which was T. H. Watkins, Stegner's friend and protégé as well as a prominent journalist, historian, and conservationist. Some three decades later, there seemed to be good reason to build on Montana State's connection to Stegner by convening a gathering in which to reflect on his intellectual, artistic, and political legacy and his relevance to an uneasy present and difficult future.

Using Stegner to think about the American West in the twenty-first century means unsettling—the double meaning is intentional—the author and the region. The 2019 symposium organized by Mary Murphy, Susan Kollin, and Mark Fiege focused on "reimagining" the American West "in an era of instability." Asked to "revisit and reinterpret" Stegner and to consider "the political, economic, and ecological tumult of our times," the scholars who gathered in Bozeman engaged in intense conversation. Over three days, they grappled with the present even as they examined the complicated ways in which Stegner imagined the West's past and future. Climate change, postcolonialism, racial strife, patriarchy, inequality, and other issues took their rightful place alongside public lands controversies and conservation. By the end, participants and the editors of this volume came to believe that Stegner would advise settlers to sort through the wreckage of our time to find ideas, tools, and resources with which to build something new, a society still flawed and an environment still damaged but more fair, just, and healthy than what we live with now.

The resulting volume unsettles Stegner and the West in new ways. Following Stegner's example, these essays emerge from a collective commitment to confronting ruin, thinking realistically, and seeing possibilities even in especially difficult times. Mark Fiege's opening essay recovers the ways that Stegner's work reminds us to acknowledge the brokenness of settler colonialism and its residue of anger and grief while urging us to reimagine a more modest, grounded, sustainable, cooperative future rising from the wreckage.

The first section, "Ruin," grapples with Stegner's failings, flaws, and blind spots. It also seeks to reimagine a region often taken for granted. Alexandra Hernandez reminds us that the inclusion of stories from diverse communities and cultures—stories that Stegner rarely put front and center—are critical to an accurate representation of the region's history. Michael J. Lansing shows that defining the region according to environmental characteristics allowed Stegner to ignore the ways that the commodification of landscapes and nature perpetuated settler colonialism. As Flannery Burke shows, two literary lions—Stegner and his good friend Bernard DeVoto—envisioned the West with gendered assumptions that limited their support for western writing and western places to those they knew best and often claimed as their own. Finally, Michael Childers opens a shadowy, underexamined side of Stegner and his politics: his use of the national park ideal to bludgeon Ronald Reagan's efforts to reverse decades of federal environmental policy.

Taking its cue from Stegner's blunt assessment of his own time, the second section, "Realism," questions myths and tropes that Stegner and his admirers perpetuated. Nancy S. Cook revises and expands the list of Stegner's students to include women novelists and poets, editors as well as authors. She reminds us that if the Edward Abbeys and Wendell

Berrys who passed through his workshops and seminars advanced one perspective on the American West in their writings, others unsettled that perspective. Michael A. Brown challenges readers to see in the pages of Stegner's writing an unexpected nugget hiding in plain sight: a moral philosophy rooted in magnanimity and points it toward the development of a new political economy of land ownership and stewardship. Lastly, Leisl Carr Childers and Adam M. Sowards examine the evolution of Stegner's famous phrase, the "geography of hope," and the way in which we contend with its application to the public lands today.

As Stegner showed, the West contains the seeds of alternative futures arising from the ruin that characterizes much of the region. Within the wreckage are sources of potential transformation. In the final section, "Possibility," Melody Graulich employs memoir and Stegner's writings to explore the contradictory definitions of what constitutes a usable education in today's world. Robert B. Keiter considers the ongoing debates over the creation, expansion, and reduction of national monuments and the opportunities those debates open to enshrine a more powerful Indigenous presence on public lands. Finally, two essays close the volume with a reconsideration of Stegner's most enduring and promising theme—hope. Paul Formisano calls on the "geography of hope" to reimagine the ways that people might bridge their differences to address and resolve the pressing challenges of our time. Robert M. Wilson concludes by noting that although Stegner never wrote about climate change, he thought deeply about adaptation and hope. Adapting to the climate-changed West will be a great environmental test, but maintaining hope in the face of so much loss will be an equally significant spiritual, moral, and political challenge.

By itself, this book cannot bring about the alternative future that many imagine. It can, however, help people think differently about a storied but damaged region and recognize the potential in it for more peaceful, just, and democratic ways of living and being. To borrow from Kim Stanley Robinson and Raymond Williams, it can help shift the "structure of feeling" for the West that many people share.[7] Though the dominant settler order is deeply entrenched, we see its injustice and unsustainability as it falls apart before our very eyes. This book can help to collectively unsettle the region and point us in the direction of the better future that is possible.

Notes

1. The following list is thorough but hardly exhausts the range of work on Stegner: Forrest G. Robinson and Margaret G. Robinson, *Wallace Stegner* (Woodbridge CT: Twayne, 1977); Wallace Stegner and Richard W. Etulain, *Stegner: Conversations on History and Literature* (Salt Lake City: University of Utah Press, 1983, rev. ed. 1990; rpt., Reno: University of Nevada Press, 1996); Nancy Colberg, *Wallace Stegner: A Descriptive Bibliography* (Lewiston ID: Confluence, 1990); Page Stegner and Mary Stegner, eds., *The Geography of Hope: A Tribute to Wallace Stegner* (San Francisco: Sierra Club Books, 1996); Page Stegner, ed., *Catching the Light: Remembering Wallace Stegner* (Stanford CA: Stanford University Libraries, 1996); Charles E. Rankin, ed., *Wallace Stegner: Man and Writer* (Albuquerque: University of New Mexico Press, 1996); Jackson Benson, *Wallace Stegner: His Life and Work* (New York: Viking, 1996); Curt Meine, ed., *Wallace Stegner and the Continental Vision: Essays on Literature, History, and Landscape* (Washington DC: Island Press, 1997); Wallace Stegner and James Hepworth, *Stealing Glances: Three Interviews with Wallace Stegner* (Albuquerque: University of New Mexico Press, 1998); John L. Thomas, *A Country in the Mind: Wallace Stegner, Bernard DeVoto, History, and the American Land* (New York: Routledge, 2000); Los Altos History Museum, *Wallace Stegner: Throwing a Long Shadow* (Los Altos CA: Los Altos History Museum, 2005; exhibition catalog), https://www.losaltoshistory.org/exhibit/wallace-stegner/; Page Stegner, ed., *The Selected Letters of Wallace Stegner* (Berkeley CA: Counterpoint, 2007); Philip L. Fradkin, *Wallace Stegner and the American West* (New York: Knopf, 2008); David Gessner, *All the Wild That Remains: Edward Abbey, Wallace Stegner, and the American West* (New York: Norton, 2015); Matthew D. Stewart, *The Most Beautiful Place on Earth: Wallace Stegner in California* (Salt Lake City: University of Utah Press, 2022).
2. Benson, *Wallace Stegner*, 6–7, 15.

3. A. O. Scott, "Wallace Stegner and the Conflicted Soul of the West," *New York Times*, June 1, 2020, https://www.nytimes.com/2020/06/01/books /review/wallace-stegner-west-angle-of-repose-big-rock-candy-mountain -crossing-to-safety.html.

4. Rankin, *Wallace Stegner*, 4, 5.

5. Elizabeth Cook-Lynn, *Why I Can't Read Wallace Stegner and Other Essays: A Tribal Voice* (Madison: University of Wisconsin Press, 1996), 31, 33. See also Eve Tuck and K. Wayne Yang, "Decolonization Is Not a Metaphor," *Decolonization: Indigeneity, Education & Society* 1, no. 1 (2012): 1–40.

6. Scott, "Wallace Stegner."

7. Kim Stanley Robinson, *The Ministry for the Future* (New York: Orbit, 2020), 123–24; Raymond Williams and Michael Orrom, *Preface to Film* (London: Film Drama, 1954), 21–23. See also Joshua Rothman, "Best-Case Scenario: The Climate-Change Sci-Fi of Kim Stanley Robinson," *New Yorker*, January 31, 2022, 30–39.

Openings

It is perfectly clear now that we can destroy ourselves . . .

—Wallace Stegner, "Conservation Equals Survival"

1

Wallace Stegner's
Unsettled Country

Ruin, Realism,
and Possibility in
the American West

MARK FIEGE

In *The Big Rock Candy Mountain* (1943), Wallace Stegner tells a small story, one among many in the book, that is emblematic of his vision of the American West. Drawn from personal experience, it centers on deception, betrayal, ruin, heartbreak, and death. Anyone who wonders about Stegner's enduring relevance should reread that passage and numerous others in his work. Vivid and emotionally compelling, it is an aesthetic gem, a beautiful example of the storyteller's art. Yet the passage also offers something other than beauty—and maybe something more important. Like many of Stegner's writings, it offers us a means to begin making sense of the West in our own troubled times.[1]

It is 1919, and the Mason family—Bo and Elsa and their boys, Chet and Bruce—are preparing to leave their failed wheat farm on the Saskatchewan prairie. Always in pursuit of the main chance, "the big rock candy mountain," Bo already has scoped out his next get-rich-quick scheme, running whiskey over the border into Prohibition-era Montana. The easy wealth of the resource frontiers—gold, grass, timber, fish, and now grain—is gone, and perhaps the trade in illicit alcohol is the best he can do. As the departure day nears, the Masons shed their animals, including Bruce's disabled but beloved horse, Socks. Bruce's momentary, absent-minded neglect helped cause Socks's damaged legs, and the boy feels immense responsibility and affection for the animal. Bo reassures Bruce that Socks will go to a caring wrangler, but behind Bruce's back, Bo negotiates the sale knowing that the man will slaughter the horse for its hide. The scene is set; the tension builds. Leaving for Montana in Bo's new automobile, the family passes the town dump. The reek of decay reaches them first. Dread and loathing rise in Bo and Elsa as they see what lies ahead, and they grimly endure Bruce's screams and sobs as they pass the skinned carcass of Socks, still wearing his steel leg braces. "Wherever you go," Elsa thinks to herself, "whenever you move and go away, you leave a death behind."[2]

Wallace Stegner's writing again and again offers a powerful lesson to those of us who live in the West and have roots in the colonization, settlement, and exploitation of the region. The first thing we settlers must do in assessing our moment in the panorama of western American history, Stegner tells us, is to acknowledge the brokenness of the region and the wreckage, debris, and residue of anger and grief that fills its spaces. The precursor to action is first to admit the ruin and corruption and give voice to the pain.[3] Stegner did that brilliantly, and in doing so, he left a powerful literary legacy that is worth revisiting. In his framework of meaning, he experienced the end of the frontier, a soul-crushing collapse that created an intellectual and artistic opening for him to cry out. We might consider the value of such grief-stricken testimony as we survey the ruins that surround us now. In the form of climate change, unbearable heat, megafires, dying forests, dwindling rivers, collapsing fisheries, rampant exploitation, profound inequality and intensifying poverty, staggering piles of waste, fearsome political reaction, racist brutality, and broken, diseased bodies, the wreckage accumulates, the hurt magnifies, the wounds weep, and the scars thicken. Like Stegner, let us acknowledge the brokenness of this land and honor the anguish that we feel. All of us have stories of big rock candy mountains, grand illusions, failed dreams, bitter defeats, and deaths left behind. Let us tell those stories. More than ever, we need them.

Acknowledging ruin and honoring pain will enable us to take inspiration from even more useful and compelling features of Stegner's literary, intellectual, and political legacy. *The Big Rock Candy Mountain* is relentlessly bleak and concludes with an adult Bruce standing at the graves of his father, mother, and brother. Characteristic of Stegner's work, desolation and death engender an appreciation for the lessons that the West's painful past offers. Sunlight and an expansive vista—a common motif in Stegner's stories—moves Bruce to reflect. Recalling the time when his father killed a snake that then disgorged a gopher it had eaten, two more deaths left behind, Bruce thinks that it was good to have experienced life with his family and learned things that no one can take from him. He wonders if his parents' virtues, not just their flaws, combined and recombined in his life and across generations, might at last yield "a proper man."[4] The theme of destruction creating the conditions for wisdom and a more stable and enduring way of life recurred with increasing vigor in Stegner's writings after 1943, and it is a theme of great significance to us now. Our ruin, our pain, our anger and grief, can open our eyes to the possibility of a wiser, more durable, just, democratic, inclusive, cooperative, and better future, a future not just of proper men and proper women but, more important, of proper citizens and proper human beings.[5]

Wallace Stegner was hardly a perfect person or writer, especially by today's standards. There is good reason why feminists, Native people, and other writers and intellectuals find his work objectionable.[6] For such a humane, liberal-minded man, he sometimes wrote things that have made readers cringe, then and since. And always at the center of his stories, always at the center of his imagined western American experience—as if there were such a singular thing—was a white man much like himself. The universal "we" and "our" in his sweeping statements seem to have been white Americans. Stegner, in sum, was imperfect in his time and in ours. But if those of us who take Stegner seriously are honest, and honesty was a trait that Stegner prized, we also must acknowledge that he was, more often than not, tolerant, open, generous, inclusive, fearless, and, above all, blunt. "No one who has studied western history," he wrote in 1962, "can cling to the belief that the Nazis invented genocide. Extermination was a doctrine accepted widely, both unofficially and officially, after the Civil War."⁷ And again and again, he returned to his vision of a durable, distinctively western culture growing from the ruins of the extractive excesses that scarred the region, in places where people retain a meaningful connection to the land, to history, and to each other. Such places, he said toward the end of his life, "are likely to be there when the agribusiness fields have turned to alkali flats and the dams have silted up, when the waves of overpopulation that have been destroying the West have receded, leaving the stickers to get on with the business of adaptation."⁸

It is the exceptional writer who ventures into the darkness and retrieves kernels of wisdom and a vision of an alternative future. The well of defeat and ruin offers powerful medicine to those who partake of its bitterness. The theologian Reinhold Niebuhr once observed that the people who come closest to living in God's grace are those who are so badly beaten that they have little if any ego left with which to delude themselves and detract from their ability to lead lives of moral clarity and selfless generosity.⁹ Wallace Stegner was not necessarily one of those people. He was a proud and sometimes surprisingly thin-skinned man who privileged his writing over virtually everything else, who nursed petty resentments, who hungered for recognition, prizes, and money—and who was stung when he did not get them.¹⁰ He was at his best, however, when he sat down at his desk, not as a great writer but as one of the beaten on whom shone a ray of God's saving grace. Ruin enabled Stegner to see the world clearly and realistically, and to recognize that defeat and pain are the means to envision an alternative existence in which people live more fairly and justly with one another in a more stable, right relation to the land. The unsettled Stegner—the destabilized, beaten Stegner—identified a path to another West, not a West of egoism, self-absorbed individualism, domination, and wealth-seeking greed but of modesty, cooperation, community, democracy, and decency. That is the Stegner who calls to us now; that is the Stegner for our troubled times.

Here is an alternative story about Wallace Stegner. It is mostly a twentieth-century story of loss, of searching, and of recognizing possibility. It draws on a range of events in Stegner's life and a range of his books and essays, but mostly *The Big Rock Candy Mountain*, *Wolf Willow*, *The American West as Living Space*, and *Recapitulation*. It is Stegner's story, but it is my story and your story—our story—too. It might offer us some means to escape the bleak and desolate ground on which we now find ourselves trapped.

To begin seeing Wallace Stegner's relevance and usefulness, it is worthwhile to survey the historical context of his life and the events that provoked and sharpened his acute awareness of ruin and loss. His eighty-four years spanned some of the most tumultuous and destructive events of the modern world. Born in 1909, he experienced, as the child of a grain-growing settler family in Saskatchewan, the final phase of a centuries-long process—the "great land rush," as one historian called it—in which European nations colonized vast areas of the Earth and reorganized them for capitalist production.[11] In the Great Depression of the 1920s and 1930s, he lived through the catastrophic collapse of that planetary colonial movement and the industrial capitalist exploitation that was integral to it. He witnessed two world wars and a third struggle for global supremacy, all of which cost the lives of untold millions. He benefited from the post–World War II maturation of the mass extraction-production-consumption economy and the social and geographic mobility that it engendered, but he objected to the system's excesses, especially its environmental destructiveness and social dislocations and alienations. In the final period of his life up to his death in 1993, he witnessed the stirrings of protest against the modern order—call that order what you will—and, to a degree, participated in the protest.

Stegner still speaks to us because the sources of the ruin and loss that concerned him never went away completely and actually have grown. The problems he saw, experienced, and lamented were the beginnings of our problems today. Liberal historiography depicts the Great Depression as the supreme crisis of modern industrialization from which the New Deal rescued the country.[12] In effect, historians represent the Great Depression and New Deal as the end of the beginning of modern corporate capitalism and its rocky coming of age. But things are different now, and thus the past appears different. The passage of time, the dismantling of the New Deal's political and economic legacy, and the intensification of the Earth System crisis demand that we reframe if not overturn the old liberal interpretation. The crises and wrenching changes through which Stegner lived and about which he wrote can be viewed, not as the end of the beginning but as the beginning of the end.

Despite the New Deal, indeed in part because of its destructive environmental interventions, dams and highways foremost among them, our problems have not been ameliorated but have intensified.[13] We are not in an end-time in a biblical sense, just yet, but we are facing the catastrophic end of things as we have known them. We are now facing the end of a reasonably stable climate, the end of resources easily plucked like low-hanging fruit, and the end of seemingly limitless terrestrial, atmospheric, and oceanic open space. Planetary reality is closing in on us, and we can no longer sustain the illusion that the Earth is both a cornucopia of wealth and an infinite sewer or a bottomless garbage pit that can absorb a perpetual stream of waste, whether plastic or carbon dioxide or anything else.

In retrospect, in the collapse of the planetary great land rush followed by the Great Depression, Stegner witnessed the first shocks to the advanced modernist program. And he lived long enough to be present at the start of still more. In 1988, five years before Stegner passed away, scientist James Hansen testified before Congress about the threat of climate change and the Earth System crisis now destabilizing our world.[14] The collapse of the frontier, as Stegner saw and described it, was the beginning of the end of one way of living and the opening of a path to another. His close ties to us and his ability to give voice to feelings of ruin and loss make him more relevant and useful than ever.

Stegner was born and came of age at the beginning of the end, and the book that best depicts the collapse and its losses is *The Big Rock Candy Mountain*, an intimate, heartbreaking, epic family tragedy and perhaps his greatest piece of writing. Although primarily a work of fiction, the story tracks closely with the difficult first decades of Stegner's life, and he later admitted that parts of it were painful to compose and written through his tears.[15] The struggles of the Mason/Stegner family—its cruelties and violence, its setbacks, defeats, humiliations, illnesses, and deaths—and the yearning of Bruce/Wallace to achieve a stable life connected to people and place dramatize the pathologies of the great land rush and its final collapse. Here in stark detail is the human cost of what Stegner called the frontier but what today some call settler colonialism.[16] Disturbing events pile one atop the other as they build toward the brutal murder-suicide at the climax of the book's narrative arc.

It might be going too far to assert that *The Big Rock Candy Mountain* is a postcolonial novel, but we should entertain that possibility because of what it suggests for our contemporary struggles. The psychiatrist and revolutionary ideologist Frantz Fanon, in *The Wretched of the Earth* (1961), summarized the self-centered, domineering confidence of the typical settler story. "The settler makes history," Fanon wrote; "his life is an epoch, an Odyssey. He is the absolute beginning: 'This land was created by us'; he is the unceasing cause: 'If we leave, all is lost, and we will go back to the Middle Ages.'"[17] Although Fanon had in mind French and British colonialists, his description fit well enough what Stegner in North America labeled the frontier myth and in which words such as "savagery," "barbarism," and "night" stood in for the Middle Ages. Stegner wrote the opposite of such a fantasy. In *The Big Rock Candy Mountain*, settlers do not make history; they are unmade by it. Their lives are tragic, not heroic and glorious; their corruptions, pathologies, and defeat mark a sad end. If not a postcolonial novel, conventionally defined, *The Big Rock Candy Mountain* at least ruptured the frontier myth and described in excruciating detail the reality behind the illusions and pretensions of settler colonialism. Stegner's world broke apart, and from the shattered pieces of unsettled settlers, he composed a novel of considerable authenticity and emotional power. We live amid those fragments yet, and their number and mass have grown. Stegner's spirit summons us to acknowledge and grieve for the shards and give voice to the truth that the world we have known and imagined is wrecked and gone.[18]

If we heed Stegner's call and build from his legacy, we will find ourselves in the company of more than just Bruce and Wallace, good and worthy as they are in their own right. For all the loneliness and alienation that *The Big Rock Candy Mountain* conveys, Stegner was and is not alone—he and his work are strands in a larger collectivity that speaks to brokenness and ruin and that remains worthy of our engagement and solidarity. In 1935 Mari Sandoz published *Old Jules*, another richly imagined, beautifully written, postfrontier, postcolonial work gritty with authenticity. It might be read as a feminist counterpoint—or counterpart—to *The Big Rock Candy Mountain* and its masculine perspective, although Sandoz's grim depiction of her violent, profane father and his exploits and failures in the Sand Hills of Nebraska illuminates the pathologies of patriarchy against which Stegner, too, struggled.[19] In the twinned characters of Jules Sandoz and Bo Mason, we confront the brutal but precarious patriarchal heart of settler colonialism.

The patriarchal ruin that unfolds in the pages of Sandoz and Stegner echoes in the more recent writings of William Kittredge and the story that he told numerous times of his family's ranch situated in the vast sagebrush- and bunchgrass-covered landscapes of the Great Basin in southeast Oregon. One piece of the story, "Owning It All," offers a stunning sketch of ranch patriarchy and its corruption. Every day someone drives the grandfather down to the corrals, where he raises his shotgun and, at close range, annihilates magpies caught in a trap. When asked to explain, the old man replies, "Because they're mine."[20] The quest to dominate and control the land, revealed no less powerfully in Kittredge's other versions of the story, eventually degrades and rends the family and destroys its hold on the ranch. Kittredge likened his serial memoir to a kind of therapy in which a person tells his or her story over and over until it resolves itself in the person's mind.[21] That element of storytelling also is present in Stegner's work, and its importance to us today is manifest.[22] Storytelling as therapy, as healing, as truth telling, as a step toward reconciliation, is a necessary precondition to finding a way forward. Only until we confront the wreckage in our land and in our lives, only until we acknowledge the trauma and consciously hold its pain in our bodies and allow ourselves to feel its power, can we leave it behind and learn to live with its legacy but without its crippling paralysis.[23]

Kittredge's notion of storytelling as therapy is reminiscent of Fanon's treatment of the sick and deranged people who appear in *The Wretched of the Earth* and whose stories Fanon recorded in his case files. One of settler colonialism's primary products is wretchedness, of the colonized, of the colonizers, and of the animals—horses, snakes, gophers, magpies, and more—that the colonizers dominate, exploit, and destroy. Fanon treated French Algerian colonists whose mental disorders and suffering resulted from their role in colonialism's dehumanizing violence. His greatest sympathy, however, was for the Algerians he doctored and whose side he took in their resistance to French rule. In a western American setting, the mental disorders and wretchedness of the colonized is unforgettably expressed in the haunting novel by James Welch, *The Death of Jim Loney* (1979). Stegner knew and admired Welch—"Jimmy," Stegner called him—and was aware of other Native writers, although not to the depth that we expect today of a major white western American intellectual and artist.[24] Nonetheless, Welch's book is comparable to the work of Stegner as it unfolds a story of ruin characteristic of *The Big Rock Candy Mountain* and other books. Isolated, forsaken, helpless, alienated in his Native land, the mentally ill Jim Loney spirals downward to a sad, violent, suicidal end.[25]

Fanon mused at length on colonialism and the causes and consequences of its traumas and mental disorders. He noted that its dislocations, disorientations, contradictions, and terrifying predicaments often induced feelings of vertigo in colonizers and colonized alike. He wondered if it evoked or expressed a condition common to humankind. "In other words," he observed, "we are forever pursued by our actions. Their ordering, their circumstances, and their motivation may perfectly well come to be modified *a posteriori*. This is merely one of the snares that history and its influences sets for us. But can we escape becoming dizzy? And can we affirm that vertigo does not haunt the whole of existence?"[26]

Wallace Stegner, in effect, had an answer to Fanon's questions. By the time Fanon published his treatise, Stegner had given a fair amount of thought to human actions and their ordering, their circumstances, and their motivations, and how they can trap people or be reinterpreted in light of events after the fact. The modern condition, it might be said, is to feel disoriented—to feel alienated, unmoored, lost, anxious, nauseated, dizzy. Stegner's response was to return to the past and sort through its ruins and its debris, and from those remains find a way forward to a life more grounded, stable, connected, and whole. We can learn much from Stegner's project that can help us as we struggle to move beyond the constraints of the past and the present to reimagine the future. To escape the snares that history sets, revisit the history.

Wolf Willow: A History, a Story, and a Memory of the Last Plains Frontier, published in 1962, was Stegner's strange and beautiful effort to recover a useable past authentic to his life and his circumstances as he entered middle age, and which pointed to an escape from the trap that history had set. Stegner traveled back to the site of his boyhood years in Saskatchewan, and from observations, conversations, and research, he explained the one place that he believed most defined him and gave him a feeling of grounded connection. "I may not know who I am," he famously wrote, "but I know where I am from." Moving effortlessly between genres—history, fiction, memoir—he drew a kind of "deep map" of the small town, grassland, and cypress-covered hills that shaped him so powerfully.[27] Beginning with his desire to find a meaningful past beneath the domed expanse of the Saskatchewan sky—"the question mark in the circle"—he guided the reader through a series of chronological chapters infused with striking autobiographical insights that culminated in a stunning climax and resolution. Stegner interrogated his past and his memories of it; *Wolf Willow* narrated answers useful to him then and of enduring value to us now.

Stegner's yearning to revisit and reclaim his personal history was part of a broader movement among modern writers and intellectuals to recover lost worlds. In the immediate aftermath of the Great Depression and World War II and their upheavals, and in the midst of postwar economic and demographic booms and their social dislocations and environmental disruptions, people of all kinds sought to reconnect to forgotten pasts that offered grounding in the face of relentless change. In particular, scholars and writers turned their attention to older patterns of family, village, and community life. The British historian Peter Laslett, for example, authored *The World We Have Lost: England before the Industrial Age* (1965), which influenced the American historian Kenneth Lockridge and his *A New England Town* (1970), one statement in a vast dialogue about the lost ways of life in the colonial period and across American history generally. The conversation pulled in nearly every group, including African Americans; in the generational turn that followed the great Black migrations from the South, Alex Hailey published *Roots: The Saga of an American Family,* in 1976, the bicentennial of the American republic, and which aired in miniseries form on television the following year.[28] Stegner participated in this broad effort to recover meaning and identity in the face of disaggregating social forces and the erosion of memory. He originally intended to trace his family's story from Denmark to North America but abandoned that project to focus on the Saskatchewan episode. *Wolf Willow* was his rediscovery of the world that he had lost, a reclamation of his roots and of the origins of his very self.

Wending his way through the past, from early Native history through European settlement, Stegner pauses again and again to reflect on the disorientation and psychological fracturing that characterized his life and the lives of fellow settlers. His "disjunct, cellular family" could not see completely "our place in a larger movement." His experience of the tail end of the great land rush in a remote pocket of Canada put him "through processes of deculturation, isolation, and intellectual schizophrenia," much of it stemming from the history of European civilization that he learned in school but that could not explain his local, grassroots, personal experience of place. The settlers' confusion similarly arose from their ignorance of Native history, the evidence of which lay directly under their feet, and which presented an "uncrossable discontinuity." The border compounded the problem of the fractured, split self: "The 49th parallel ran directly through my childhood, dividing me in two." The local past, and the meaning and direction it could give, was there for Stegner and his cohorts to find if they searched for it, but "the first generation of children to grow up in a newly settled country do not ordinarily discover their history, and so they are the prime sufferers from discontinuity."[29]

*Dis*orientation, *dis*juncture, *dis*continuity, *de*culturation—the problem that Stegner identified was characteristic of colonial systems and the people who bore their burdens and suffered their contradictions and derangements. It resembled the predicament of American Indians caught between their Native cultures and the disorienting forces of Euro-American society.[30] It was similar to the classic problem of "double-consciousness" described by the great African American historian and intellectual W. E. B. Du Bois.[31] It was comparable to the condition that Frantz Fanon observed, that colonialism's negation of the colonized person's humanity and true self constantly forced the colonized to ask the question, "In reality, who am I?"[32] The fractured consciousness of the white settler, of course, differed from that of the colonized. Stegner's predicament did not result from an inferior, subordinate position on the other side of a racist color line but from his conflicted experience of nationality, geography, social class, place, chronology, and history. Such was the insidious power of colonialism, however, that it spread its corruptions and mental disorders into the lives of settlers, too, beginning with the subordinated generations of its children.[33]

*Re*cover, *re*call, *re*member, *re*construct—Stegner's solution to the problem was to sift through the historical evidence to fashion a meaningful story essential to his sense of self—to make himself whole. In the essay "The Dump Ground," he begins the process by revisiting a place filled with the debris of settler colonialism and thus a repository of the memories and the local history that he sought to gather and restore. A site of childhood magic and wonder, the town dump taught important lessons. It was not an end but a beginning, an opening. It "was the very first community enterprise, the town's first institution. . . . The place fascinated us, as it should have. For this was the kitchen midden of all the civilization we knew. . . . The town dump was our poetry and our history." As such, it was a first-order source of clues that would help answer the question mark in the circle: "If I were a sociologist anxious to study in detail the life of a community I would go very early to its refuse piles. For a community may as well be judged by what it throws away—what it has to throw away and what it chooses to—as by any other evidence."[34] It is telling—and offers an important lesson for us today—that Stegner grounded his search for meaning in his memory of the dump and its accumulations. To understand ourselves and our predicament in history and to assess our future, we would do well to begin with our castoffs—our garbage, wreckage, and ruin.

Sorting through the detritus and residue of the past, Stegner at last arrives at an icon with special meaning for him, the cowboy—although with emphasis on a subtle but crucially important side of cowboy life buried in the mythic stereotype he often ridiculed. "Specifications for a Hero" opens with a description of the cowboy code and its prized traits—courage, toughness, competence, self-reliance, stoicism—but also the traits that lurked in its dark id: cruelty, callousness, reckless-ness, prejudice. Ever the divided self, Stegner recalls his childhood failure to live up to the code, for he was, he says, a coward and a cry-baby, a sensitive boy better suited to the female schoolroom than to the masculine corral. Still, the cowboy code shaped him, and its effects "remain in me like the beach terraces of a dead lake."[35] He is impa-tient with weakness, pity, incompetence, affectations, bragging, and pretentious talk. Although he could not be a cowboy, he recalls how the overlap between the settler homesteaders and the cowboys who preceded them enabled him to observe the cowboys' work habits, their ethnic makeup, their code, and their reserved, laconic style. In the rich mix of cowboy culture, Stegner identifies a key trait: their solidarity—

their "comradeship"—and their unstated expectation that each of them, without comment or praise, would uphold their shared values.[36]

In that understated but crucially important communal component of the cowboy code, Stegner recognizes the seed of an alternative world, a different and better future, and it is here that *Wolf Willow* takes a dramatic turn. Stegner's research impresses upon him that the bitter winter of 1906–7 was a decisive moment in Saskatchewan history. By destroying the open range livestock economy, it cleared the way for settler farmers such as the Stegners. "Almost as suddenly as the disappearance of the buffalo," Stegner writes, the catastrophe "changed the way of life of the region. A great event, it had the force in the history of the Cypress Hills country that a defeat in war has upon a nation." He remembers hearing a few cowboy stories as a child, and he refers to a few uncovered while "digging in the middens where historians customarily dig," but otherwise the cowboys revealed little.[37] To imagine the terrifying moment when disaster laid bare what the cowboys valued most—and what Stegner values most—Stegner transitions from history and memoir into fiction.

Page Stegner, Wallace's son and an accomplished scholar and writer, believed that "Genesis," the novella at the heart of *Wolf Willow*, was the best piece of short fiction his father ever wrote.[38] Raw, stark, and savage, it is a story of how nature's fury demolishes pretensions and leaves behind tougher, more resilient values and commitments that might become the core of an alternative way of life. Rusty Cullen, a young, green Englishman, heads out with the other cowboys on a fall roundup. At first all goes well enough, and despite a smoldering conflict with the testy Ed Spurlock, Rusty is swept up in the beauty and adventure of riding the range. Then, as the cowboys nearly complete the job, an icy blizzard catches them off guard. They manage to gather several hundred head, but as snow and bitter wind scatters their horses and forces them to turn the cattle loose, they realize that their own lives are not guaranteed. Without their mounts and on foot—in that sense, no longer cowboys, only desperate, vulnerable men—they set off for a cabin at a cow camp several miles away. As they stagger onward, the wind turns eerie, haunted, and hallucinatory, the collective voice of all people—women, children, and men, Native and settler—who had suffered and died in that unforgiving country. "*Qu'appelle? Qu'appelle?*" cries the wind. Who calls? Who calls? Terrified, near death, the cowboys set aside personal differences and help each other keep moving. Their faces, hands, and feet freezing, their energy running out, they barely make it to the cow camp. Morning brings a painful but powerful reckoning. As he endures the agony of warm blood bringing numbed appendages back to life, Rusty thinks that never would he "want to do anything alone again, not in this country." And he realizes that nothing that he or the other cowboys had done to survive their harrowing journey was particularly excellent or noteworthy, for what passes "for heroics in a softer world was only chores around here."[39]

"Genesis" is very nearly the antithesis of the settler narrative that Fanon described. Rusty Cullen and the other cowboys are beaten survivors, not heroes. Their loss of animals and their confrontation with death comes close to an experience of the lethal violence that the colonized wanted to inflict on the colonizers. "For the native," Fanon wrote, "life can only spring up again out of the rotting corpse of the settler."[40] Stegner cannot allow the spirit of the country to kill the cowboys—the settlers—but he comes close. What endures beyond the near-death experience of the cowboys, the die-up of the cattle and horses, and, come spring, the animals' rotting corpses, is everything that Stegner imagined for the American West: an acceptance of human limitations in the face of nature's power, the need for community—solidarity and comradeship—as a means of survival, a humble commitment to shared values and living small, and a willingness to engage in self-deprecating humor. The genesis of Stegner's alternative West is not birth, a heroic conquering advance into unsullied country, but death and its legacy of ruin. Defeat and destruction are the precursors to a better way of life adapted to the realities of place. New life, as Fanon observed, arises from the rot.

"Genesis" offers sobering lessons with obvious relevance to our own time. By standing settler mythology on its head—by turning the world upside down and showing the cowboys to be not heroes but beaten men with little if any ego intact—Stegner subverted a classic western American story and gave us a model of how to think about ourselves as we struggle to escape the snares that history has set for us. Our defeat, our ruin, strips away our pretenses and gives us an opportunity for a bracing reality check, an agonizing reappraisal, that we must undergo if we are to imagine a way forward for ourselves and for everyone and everything we care about. Sometimes events shatter illusions and despite our pain, give us a chance to dream the world anew.[41]

If we are to benefit fully from Stegner's courage and creativity, however, we also need to confront the shortcomings and limitations of what he wrote, for those can instruct us, too. Stegner never fully escaped the legacy of the settler colonialism that he could not kill completely. Traces of it persisted in him, as he said, like the relict beach terraces of a dead lake in the Great Basin. It is telling that Stegner's effort to know himself by returning to his boyhood home remained fractured and incomplete. He confirmed where he was from, as he said, but he left open the question of who, exactly, he really was.

Stegner's struggle to know himself exemplified a profound dilemma inherent in the settler experience. Settlers desire an identity derived from deep connection to place—to be of and from a place. Yet it is virtually impossible for them to attain that goal. The settler origin story is one of migration and appropriation, of traveling to a new place and taking and developing the land. In contrast, the origin story of Natives most often is one of emergence from the Earth, even from a specific place on the Earth, or from an animal ancestor. Even when a settler feels connected and proudly asserts himself to be, for example, "a fifth-generation Montanan" or one of Stegner's "stickers," such boasts are diminished if not negated by the mere presence of a person from a nearby Indian reservation whose ancestry dates back dozens and perhaps hundreds of generations.[42] The yearning of settlers for connection and fulfillment in response to the restless conditions and hardships of their lives is evident in Stegner's *Wolf Willow* and much American literature. Disconnection, dissociation, disorientation, and the circumstances that caused them inspired stories in which the unmoored and the bewildered struggle and almost always fail to find their way. Even when Stegner kills the cattle and nearly kills the cowboys, as a defeat of a nation in war, he still cannot make himself whole from the surviving fragments. Always a side of himself remains incomplete, unintegrated, lost.

Good portions of Stegner's life and work, in contrast to the transformational possibilities expressed in *Wolf Willow*, convey an enduring sense of alienation, loneliness, even sadness. For all Stegner's devotion to the American West and his deeply personal identification with the region, he never found a permanent place there. Although he traveled widely through the West and formed lasting friendships and associations with many westerners, and despite that he admired Mormon communalism and felt affection for Salt Lake City, he never again lived in Montana, Utah, or Saskatchewan.[43] He enjoyed his home in the Los Altos Hills of California, but his residence there was marginal to the deep interior that most inspired him. When he departed from Stanford University, he did so in disillusionment tinged with alienation and bitterness.[44] For all Stegner's love of the West, the place he felt most at home and connected to the land was his summer residence in Vermont. He took special satisfaction in his house made of lumber from trees felled on the site and around which he would have his ashes scattered.[45] In the end, the admirer of arid landscapes and their expansive vistas found his place, not on open plains, below rocky peaks, or among canyon country monuments but in the Green Mountain State.

Ever a prime sufferer from discontinuity, Stegner reprised the themes of disconnection, alienation, and loss in *Recapitulation* (1979), his sequel to *The Big Rock Candy Mountain*. The story finds Bruce Mason, years later, back in Salt Lake City ostensibly to oversee the funeral of an aunt but really to reckon with his past in that place. He imagines that he will reacquaint himself with old adolescent friends, especially his beloved buddy Joe Mulder, but he cannot summon the will, the sense of purpose, to follow through. He realizes that the past is dead to him now, including the younger self he left behind long ago. Once more he ends at the family burial plot, this time not in sunlight and an expansive vista but in storm clouds and a downpour. "According to the best traditions of American mobility," he thinks, "and in conformity to his own status as an orphan," his mortal remains "would end up somewhere else, probably scattered out beyond the Golden Gate somewhere," with no family member to decide otherwise or even to remember him. Heading back to his hotel room before the long drive back to California, he is "busy in his head with one final check-off. Around Bruce Mason as he once was, around the thin brown hyperactive youth who had so long usurped space in his mind and been a pretender to his feelings, he drew a careful rectangle, and all the way up on the elevator to pack his bag he was inking it out."[46]

Perhaps the most poignant example of Stegner's lingering alienation concerns *Wolf Willow*. Despite the book's strong declarative sentences and optimism, pieces of it are tantalizingly enigmatic and convey traces of the emotions Stegner later expressed in *Recapitulation*. Why, for example, did Stegner impose the pseudonym "Whitemud" on Eastend, the actual name of the town in Saskatchewan where the Stegner family lived? Why the disconnect? And why, when Stegner returned to Eastend to recover his past, did he decide to go incognito as "Mr. Page"? He claimed that he did not want to be judged in light of townspeople's memories of his disreputable father, but Corky Jones, his old cowboy friend and the model for Rusty Cullen, reassured him that his fears were groundless. The biographer Philip Fradkin quoted an Eastend memory of his visit and his evasiveness, which is as revealing as it is sad: "Everybody was trying to figure out who that man was, and then old Mrs. So-and-So said, 'I know who it is! It's Wallace Stegner.' And the next day he was gone."[47]

It remains for us to reimagine ourselves and the American West in ways that Wallace Stegner was unable to do in his lifetime. A twentieth-century man, he experienced the modern world's statist and capitalist achievements but also its instability and contradictions and the first signs of its collapse. In the midst of increasing ruin, he squarely faced reality and produced a body of written work that gave voice to the pain of discontinuity, dislocation, marginalization, alienation, loss, and defeat. And he did more: he gave voice to the values that he believed must inform an alternative way of life in the West that would transcend and outlive the destructive forces that had shaped the region. That he could not completely free himself from settler colonialism and its snares is no knock on him and his work; it is up to us, now, to emerge on the other side of his many pages and find ways to say what he could not say, to go where he could not go, and to build what he could not build. Stegner pointed to an alternative and better future; it is up to us to go there and begin creating it.

Such is the purpose of the essays in this anthology. Each author uses Stegner as a means to an end: to envision something beyond him in a world more just, fair, and stable than the one in which he lived and died and which we are rapidly leaving behind. Not every contributor likes Stegner, likes him with the same intensity, or agrees on his legacy and his enduring utility. All acknowledge his blind spots and failings. Most important, all take him seriously as a means to organize a critical view of the American West and its past and future in the context of our troubled present. The ideas that course through every essay, finally, do not just come from intellectual, professional, and political work; they also arise from the heart of each author and the wells of emotion that feed it and keep it pumping.

When I first read *The Big Rock Candy Mountain* a long time ago, I had no clue that it would affect me so deeply. Like a gut punch, it caught me off guard, bewildered me, forced me to confront unpleasant realities. I had read *Angle of Repose*, Stegner's other great western novel, and *Beyond the Hundredth Meridian*, his history of western exploration and science. I expected *The Big Rock Candy Mountain* to offer more of the same. How wrong I was. From the bleak scene depicted in its opening pages, it grabbed my attention and fed my imagination. The deeper I went, however, the more my engrossment stoked my unease. The story of the Mason family was too much like the story of my own unsettled family, of my westering parents and the problems, pathologies, and violence that dragged us down. Unease turned to anguish, and anguish soon became grief. I recall reading the book at night, lying on my back, then sliding it under the bed and turning out the light. I wanted so badly for the story to go away, but it would not go away, would not leave me alone, would not let me sleep. In another instance, my wife remembers me throwing the book to the floor; I remember sitting in a chair and abruptly throwing it across the room, not because it was bad but because it was so good, so close to home, so true. The outcome of my encounter with the book was inescapable: Stegner left me no choice but to reorder my understanding of the past and my place in it.

A book can do that for you. It can change your life. It can show you that history is not distant and abstract but in you, and you in it. A book can reveal past patterns manifest in your life, and how those patterns have systemic sources rooted in particular ways of thinking, acting, and organizing power. A book can make you recognize and resist silence and the injustice, inequality, and violence that it perpetuates. A book can give you a new story more meaningful and motivational than the one you once told. A book can make you want to change, and to change the world. That is what reading Stegner's *The Big Rock Candy Mountain* did for me.

Wallace Stegner wanted his readers to see that the ruins of the present could give rise to a better future, and he urged us to imagine the future as he imagined it, as a vast field of possibility. Time and again, he expressed that belief in visual, spatial, atmospheric terms—as sunlight, as openness, as a virtually endless expanse capable of inspiring and enriching human creativity and decency: the American West as living space, the geography of hope, the open space of democracy. When Rusty Cullen and the cowboys headed out for the roundup, they "burst out onto the great glittering plain. . . . It was tremendous, like a plunge over a cliff. The sun looked them straight in the eyes, the earth dazzled them. Over and under and around, above, below, behind, before, the Englishman felt the unfamiliar element, a cleanness like the blade of a knife, a distance without limits, a horizon that did not bound the world but only suggested endless space beyond."[48]

It is fair to criticize Stegner's description of vast western space, especially the public lands, in such open-ended, universal terms because it might seem to overlook and disregard the specific sovereign claims of Native people to its geographies.[49] Yet it is equally fair to point out that Stegner's depiction of western space and its possibilities does not necessarily preclude the acknowledgment of Native interests. The national parks and protected areas of the American West never have expressed a single purpose, use, or meaning; rather, those have shifted and evolved over time.[50] Stegner's imagination of western public lands speaks to a physical, cultural, and political flexibility and capaciousness that enables us to envision a postcolonial American West in which Native cultures reclaim and redefine landscapes in terms that are culturally grounded and culturally specific but, in their own way, no less universal.[51]

The process is well underway. Alaska national parks, Sand Creek Massacre National Historic Site, Bears Ears National Monument, the National Bison Range, and other public land units recognize the historic claims of Native people, who comanage the areas. Native people have pressed the federal government to remove offensive place-names and restore Indigenous toponyms. In 2021 Deb Haaland (Laguna Pueblo) became secretary of the interior and Chuck Sams (Cayuse and Walla Walla) the director of the National Park Service, the first Native people to hold those offices. Proposals to "re-Indigenize" Yellowstone and other national parks are on the table.[52] It is not a fantasy to imagine a new conservation—even a radical peoples' conservation—shorn of its colonial encumbrances and aligned with the highest ethical commitments of the people most directly descended from the land's first human inhabitants. In light of Stegner's generosity, magnanimity, and expansive vision, it is difficult to believe that he would have opposed the trend—indeed, to the contrary.[53]

We have a choice. We can stand with the old, world-weary Bruce Mason as he severs his ties to the past and inks out his name and his earlier self, the ultimate expression of cancel culture and an after-the-fact reordering of history that does not resolve but perpetuates his disconnection and alienation. Or, like the contributors to this volume, we can stand with the young Bruce Mason in the cemetery on the mountainside as the sun breaks through the clouds and realize that it was good to have been part of the struggle, that despite the deaths left behind and the wreckage all around, we still have a future, a region, and a world to win.

Notes

1. Wallace Stegner, *The Big Rock Candy Mountain* (New York: Doubleday, 1943; rpt., New York: Penguin, 1991), 298–308, 321–32.
2. Stegner, *Big Rock Candy Mountain*, 332.
3. See, for example, Malkia Devich-Cyril, "To Give Your Hands to Freedom, First Give Them to Grief," *In These Times* 45 (August 2021): 33–37; Will Griffiths, "Our Last Cast: The Future of Salmonid Angling in the American West" (MA thesis, Montana State University, 2021); Dahr Jamail, *The End of Ice: Bearing Witness and Finding Meaning in the Path of Climate Disruption* (New York: New Press, 2020); Roy Scranton, *Learning to Die in the Anthropocene: Reflections on the End of a Civilization* (San Francisco: City Lights Books, 2015); Ann Laura Stoler, ed., *Imperial Debris: On Ruins and Ruination* (Durham NC: Duke University Press, 2013), especially the richly imagined and suggestive 1–35.
4. Stegner, *Big Rock Candy Mountain*, 562–63.
5. Scranton, *Learning to Die*, 89–117. See also, for example, Stephen Pyne, "The End of the World," *Environmental History* 12 (July 2007): 649–53; Erik Olin Wright, *Envisioning Real Utopias* (New York: Verso, 2010); Terry Tempest Williams, *The Open Space of Democracy* (Eugene OR: Wipf and Stock, 2004); and the prescient novels of Octavia E. Butler, *Parable of the Sower* (New York: Four Walls Eight Windows, 1993; rpt., New York: Grand Central, 2019), and *Parable of the Talents* (New York: Seven Stories, 1998; rpt., New York: Grand Central, 2019). Stoler, *Imperial Debris*, 14, urges us to "turn to ruins as epicenters of renewed collective claims, as history in a spirited voice, as sites that animate both despair and new possibilities, bids for entitlement, and unexpected collaborative political projects."
6. See, for example, Philip L. Fradkin, *Wallace Stegner and the American West* (New York: Knopf, 2008), 255–72; Michael Cohen, "The Bob: Con-

fessions of a Fast-Talking Urban Wilderness Advocate," in *Wilderness Tapestry: An Eclectic Approach to Wilderness Preservation*, ed. Samuel I. Zevelikoff, L. Mikel Vause, William H. McVaugh (Reno: University of Nevada Press, 1992); Elizabeth Cook-Lynn, *Why I Can't Read Wallace Stegner and Other Essays: A Tribal Voice* (Madison: University of Wisconsin Press, 1996); Robert Vitalis, "Wallace Stegner's Arabian Discovery: Imperial Blind Spots in a Continental Vision," *Pacific Historical Review* 76 (August 2007): 405–37; Roxana Robinson, "Wallace Stegner and the Trap of Using Other People's Writing," *New Yorker*, June 1, 2022, https://www.newyorker.com/books/page-turner/wallace-stegner-and-the-trap-of-using-other-peoples-writing.

7. Wallace Stegner, *Wolf Willow: A History, a Story, and a Memory of the Last Plains Frontier* (New York: Viking, 1962; rpt., New York: Penguin, 2000), 73–74.

8. Wallace Stegner, *The American West as Living Space* (Ann Arbor: University of Michigan Press, 1987), 85–86.

9. Reinhold Niebuhr, *The Irony of American History* (New York: Charles Scribner's Sons, 1952), 151–74, especially 161–62.

10. See, for example, Fradkin, *Wallace Stegner*, 246–47, 250–52, 275–77.

11. John C. Weaver, *The Great Land Rush and the Making of the Modern World, 1650–1900* (Montreal: McGill-Queen's University Press, 2003).

12. See, for example, David Kennedy, *Freedom from Fear: The American People in Depression and War, 1929–1945* (New York: Oxford University Press, 1999). Kennedy's outstanding book is careful to address the complexities and failures of the New Deal but overall presents a positive interpretation that exemplifies liberal historiography.

13. See, for example, Donald Worster's prescient *Rivers of Empire: Water, Aridity, and the Growth of the American West* (New York: Pantheon, 1985).

14. Naomi Klein, *This Changes Everything: Capitalism vs. the Climate* (New York: Simon and Schuster, 2014), 73–75; Andrew Bacevich, *After the Apocalypse: America's Role in a World Transformed* (New York: Metropolitan Books, 2021), 82–103.

15. Wallace Stegner and Richard W. Etulain, *Stegner: Conversations on History and Literature*, rev. ed. (Salt Lake City: University of Utah Press, 1990; rpt., Reno: University of Nevada Press, 1996), 41.

16. On settler colonialism, see Margaret D. Jacobs, *White Mother to a Dark Race: Settler Colonialism, Maternalism, and the Removal of Indigenous Children in the American West and Australia, 1880–1940* (Lincoln: University of Nebraska Press, 2009), 1–11; Margaret D. Jacobs, *After One Hundred Winters: In Search of Reconciliation on America's Stolen Lands* (Princeton NJ: Princeton University Press, 2021), 1–17; Anthony W. Wood, *Black Montana: Settler Colonialism and the Erosion of the Racial Frontier, 1877–1930* (Lincoln: University of Nebraska Press, 2021), 1–25; and Lorenzo Veracini, *The World Turned Inside Out: Settler Colonialism as a Political Idea* (London: Verso, 2021), 1–26. The classic theoretical statement on settler colonialism and Native and Indigenous people is Patrick Wolfe, "Settler Colonialism and the Elimination of the Native," *Journal of Genocide Research* 8 (December 2006): 387–409.

17. Frantz Fanon, *The Wretched of the Earth*, trans. Candace Farrington (New York: Grove, 1963), 51. Fanon originally published his work in French in 1961. Bashir Abu-Manneh, "Who Owns Frantz Fanon's Legacy?" *Catalyst* 5 (Spring 2021): 10–39, makes the case for Fanon's commitment to universalism based on class, not a narrow identity politics based on race.

18. "To pretend otherwise serves no purpose. To escape from our era of ideological fantasy requires taking stock of the dismal consequences that American arrogance and misjudgment have yielded since we thought the world was ours." Bacevich, *After the Apocalypse*, 172.

19. Stegner and Etulain, *Stegner*, 42–43, 79–80. In a related context, see also, for example, Annie Pike Greenwood, *We Sagebrush Folks* (New York: D. Appleton-Century, 1934; rpt., Moscow: University of Idaho Press, 1988), especially 197: "The father of a sagebrush family is its god or its demon. There is no escape for the wife or children."

20. William Kittredge, *Owning It All* (St. Paul MN: Graywolf Press, 1987), 67.

21. William Kittredge, *Hole in the Sky: A Memoir* (New York: Knopf, 1992), 67; William Kittredge, *Who Owns the West?* (San Francisco: Mercury House, 1996), 48, 87, 157–68.

22. See, for example, Wallace Stegner, *Recapitulation* (New York: Doubleday, 1979; rpt., Lincoln: University of Nebraska Press/Bison Books, 1986), the sequel to *The Big Rock Candy Mountain*.

23. See, for example, Bessel van der Kolk, *The Body Keeps the Score: Brain, Mind, and Body in the Healing of Trauma* (New York: Viking Penguin, 2014; rpt., New York: Penguin, 2015); and Elizabeth Rosner, *Survivor Café: The Legacy of Trauma and the Labyrinth of Memory* (Berkeley CA: Counterpoint, 2017).

24. Stegner and Etulain, *Stegner*, 137–38.

25. James Welch, *The Death of Jim Loney* (New York: Harper and Row, 1979; rpt., New York: Penguin, 1987).

26. Fanon, *Wretched of the Earth*, 253n. On existentialism and Fanon, see Sarah Bakewell, *At the Existentialist Café: Freedom, Being, and Apricot Cocktails* (New York: Other, 2016), especially 1–34, 273–74.

27. Stegner, *Wolf Willow*, 23; William Least Heat-Moon, *PrairyErth: A Deep Map* (Boston: Houghton Mifflin, 1991).

28. Such studies were legion; see also, for example, Ronald Blythe, *Akenfield: Portrait of an English Village* (New York: Pantheon Books, 1969); and Richard Francaviglia, *The Mormon Landscape: Existence, Creation, and Perception of a Unique Image in the American West* (New York: AMS Press, 1978).

29. Stegner, *Wolf Willow*, 20, 22–24, 26, 28–29, 53, 81, 111. On Stegner's observation of the "uncrossable discontinuity," see Wolfe, "Settler Colonialism and the Elimination of the Native."

30. Compare the plight of Jim Loney, for example, in Welch, *Death of Jim Loney*. Or see Leslie Marmon Silko, *Ceremony* (New York: Viking, 1977).

31. W. E. B. Du Bois, *The Souls of Black Folk* (Chicago: A. C. McClurg, 1903; rpt., New York: Signet, 1969), 45. See also John P. Pittman, "Double Consciousness," in *Stanford Encyclopedia of Philosophy*, ed. Edward N. Zalta (2016; revised, February 16, 2023), https://plato.stanford.edu/entries/double-consciousness/. It is worthwhile to contemplate the similarities in the blended genres that characterize both *Souls of Black Folk* and *Wolf Willow*.

32. Fanon, *Wretched of the Earth*, 250.

33. Abu-Manneh, "Who Owns Frantz Fanon's Legacy?," 38, asserts that "the core activity of universalists is to identify what is common between separate identities rather than to inflate what is different." In this essay, I choose to identify what is common in the experience of colonist and

colonized without minimizing differences, especially differences in access to power, arising from racial distinctions.

34. Stegner, *Wolf Willow*, 31–36.

35. Stegner, *Wolf Willow*, 132–33. Stegner's geological metaphor corresponds to the geological metaphor that informs Ann Laura Stoler and her colleagues as they "attempt to track the uneven temporal sedimentations in which imperial formations leave their marks. Most important, we seek to ask how empire's ruins contour and carve through the psychic and material space in which people live and what compounded layers of imperial debris do to them." Stoler, *Imperial Debris*, 2.

36. Stegner, *Wolf Willow*, 125, 136.

37. Stegner, *Wolf Willow*, 137–38.

38. Page Stegner, introduction to *Wolf Willow: A History, a Story, and a Memory of the Last Plains Frontier*, by Wallace Stegner (New York: Viking, 1962; rpt., New York: Penguin, 2000), xix.

39. Stegner, *Wolf Willow*, 202–3, 215–19.

40. Fanon, *Wretched of the Earth*, 93. And see "Carrion Spring," the chapter that follows "Genesis" in *Wolf Willow*.

41. On this point, see, for example, Klein, *This Changes Everything*; Nick Estes, *Our History Is the Future: Standing Rock versus the Dakota Access Pipeline, and the Long Tradition of Indigenous Resistance* (London: Verso, 2019); Holly Jean Buck, *After Geoengineering: Climate Tragedy, Repair, and Restoration* (New York: Verso, 2019); Wright, *Envisioning Real Utopias*; and Fredrick C. Cuny, *Disasters and Development* (New York: Oxford University Press, 1983).

42. "Fifth-generation Montanan" is a common expression heard in daily speech and conversation in Montana. For the Native counterpoint, see, for example, Carl M. Davis, *Six Hundred Generations: An Archaeological History of Montana* (Helena MT: Riverbend, 2019); Colin Calloway, *One Vast Winter Count: The Native American West before Lewis and Clark* (Lincoln: University of Nebraska Press, 2003).

43. On Stegner, Mormonism, and Salt Lake City, see, for example, Wallace Stegner, "At Home in the Fields of the Lord," in *The Sound of Mountain Water: The Changing American West* (New York: E. P. Dutton, 1980), 157–69.

44. Fradkin, *Wallace Stegner*, 153–62.

45. Fradkin, *Wallace Stegner*, 322–23.

46. Stegner, *Recapitulation*, 276–78.

47. Fradkin, *Wallace Stegner*, 37.

48. Stegner, *Wolf Willow*, 142. See also Wallace Stegner, "Coda: Wilderness Letter," in *The Sound of Mountain Water: The Changing American West* (New York: E. P. Dutton, 1980); and the impassioned declaration of Stegner's friend and protégé Terry Tempest Williams in *Open Space of Democracy*.

49. Nick Serpe, ed., "Indigenous Resistance Is Post-Apocalyptic, with Nick Estes," *Dissent Magazine* online, July 31, 2019, https://www.dissentmagazine .org/online_articles/booked-indigenous-resistance-is-post-apocalyptic -with-nick-estes.

50. For an insightful, provocative articulation of this idea, see Paul Schullery, *Searching for Yellowstone: Ecology and Wonder in the Last Wilderness* (Boston: Houghton Mifflin, 1997), 1–5. For an elaboration on the idea, see Paul Schullery, *Past and Future Yellowstones: Finding Our Way in Wonderland*, 2014 Wallace Stegner Lecture, S. J. Quinney College of Law, University of Utah (Salt Lake City: University of Utah Press, 2015).

51. See, for example, David Treuer, "Return the National Parks to the Tribes," *The Atlantic*, May 2021, https://www.theatlantic.com/magazine/archive /2021/05/return-the-national-parks-to-the-tribes/618395/; and Kim Tall- Bear, "Caretaking Relations, Not American Dreaming," *Kalfou* 6, no. 1 (2019): 25–41.

52. See, for example, Kekek Jason Stark, Autumn L. Bernhardt, Monte Mills, and Jason Robison, "Re-Indigenizing Yellowstone," *Wyoming Law Review* 22, no. 2 (2022): 398–487; Jason Anthony Robison, "Indigenizing Grand Canyon," *Utah Law Review* 2021, no. 1, article 3 (2021): 101–83.

53. Ashley Dawson, *Extinction: A Radical History*, expanded ed. (New York: OR Books, 2022), 85–94, 121–31; and "A People's Manifesto for the Future of Conservation," September 2021, https://www.ourlandournature.org /manifesto.

Ruin

What is false within is enough to ruin almost any life.
—Wallace Stegner to Norman Foerster, 1957

2

The American West
as Exploited Space

From *One Nation*
to Poston

ALEXANDRA HERNANDEZ

On a blistering summer day in 2010, I ventured to the outskirts of Arizona's Parker Valley with fellow National Park Service colleagues and two former Japanese American incarcerees, Ruth Okimoto and Marlene Shigekawa. As we caravanned in our dusty rental cars to the former Colorado River Relocation Center (commonly known as "Poston"), Ruth looked out the window and recounted life as a young child while living there. Thick creosote bushes and sagebrush lined the road and seemed to dance across the windows as we traveled along Mohave Road. Ruth, still peering out the window, abruptly interrupted her story and asked us to pull over our vehicle. We complied, and she quickly exited the car and shuffled through thick brush. Naively, I followed her, not thinking about the Mojave Green rattlesnakes that could be nestled under the bushes ready to strike. We did not quite know where she was going, but she moved with purpose, and we could barely keep up with her. She stopped at a break in the vegetation and stood silently until we caught up. "This was once the hospital," she said. I looked around for some sign or resemblance of a building. But there were no buildings along the desert landscape in front of us, only dust.

Then, Marlene said the words that would last with me and pierce my soul. "I was born here," she said. The smell of the sun-bleached earth rose from the desert floor in dusty wisps, and I felt sweat bead against my forehead. A lone salty drop traveled slowly down my cheek. When I brushed it away, another followed into a gentle stream over the curve of my cheek. At that moment, I realized I was crying. It wasn't just sweat but tears. The weight of Marlene's words sank in, and my eyes continued to well up. We stood in the vast emptiness of the desert with the intense heat between us. But under the soles of my baked shoes, you could see the faint remnants of a foundation covered in sand. According to Ruth this was once the site of a former incarceration center that unjustly imprisoned nearly twenty thousand Japanese Americans during World War II. This is Poston.[1]

That day marked my first trip as a historian with the National Park Service's Japanese American Confinement Sites (JACS) Grant Program, a federal financial assistance program established to preserve and interpret World War II Japanese American incarceration history. My experience there is permanently seared into my memory, as much as the memory of the scorching heat. Our guides, Ruth and Marlene, served as representatives from the Poston Community Alliance, a nonprofit dedicated to preserving the history of Poston and organized by former Japanese American incarcerees.[2] They shared an experience of incarceration in their youth: their families torn from their homes on the West Coast, forcibly removed, and sent to remote areas of the American West to massive incarceration centers. This is their experience of discrimination in the West.

These sites imprisoned families, children, men, and women, the majority of whom were American citizens. These centers were in some of the bleakest landscapes of the country. The locations of all ten major

1. (*opposite top*) A bulldozer clears desert brush to make way for further site development at Poston. Prior to opening Poston, the landscape was extensively cleared, utilities installed, and barracks constructed. Photo taken by WRA photographer Fred Clark, 1942. Courtesy the National Archives at College Park, photo no. 210-G-A156.

2. (*opposite bottom*) View of the Poston Relocation Center showing barrack blocks. Photo taken by WRA photographer Fred Clark from the top of water tower facing southwest, 1942. Courtesy the National Archives at College Park, photo no. 210-G-A190.

3. Japanese American incarcerees providing labor to construct Poston's adobe school complex. Photo taken by WRA photographer Francis Stewart, 1943. Courtesy the National Archives at College Park, photo no. 210-G-A819.

War Relocation Authority (WRA) centers were intentionally situated in the rural West and designed to cage and contain families in remote patches of land; the many injustices against them were out of sight and out of mind. As for Poston, it became the third largest populated area in Arizona nearly overnight in 1942.[3] But this was not a free American city. It was a prison. A prison surrounded by barbed wire and under armed guard. The story of Poston is part of the American West's legacy

4. Vacant barracks in disrepair after Poston's closure. Original photo caption states, "The barracks were of cheap construction, rough lumber, and tar paper and few people thought they would be occupied for three years." Photo taken by Hikaru Iwasaki, 1945. Courtesy the National Archives at College Park, photo no. 210-G-K335.

and our shared national history, yet we rarely think of it that way. The history of removal and exploitation of people of color is the legacy of the West. As large-scale policies of discrimination and incarceration can manifest and transform the landscape, they can also erase and obscure. As a result, the history of Japanese Americans incarcerated during World War II is often overlooked, hard to recognize on the landscape, and underemphasized when examining the making of the West.

The Power of Words and Images in *One Nation*

Making sense of the past, especially the history of discrimination or the transformation of the American West, is no easy task. One of the most prolific American writers and historians who attempted to understand both was Wallace Stegner. During the war *Look* magazine commissioned Stegner to write a series of cutting-edge articles on prejudice against religious and ethnic minorities.[4] At the time *Look* editors had a concern for the "growing wave of intolerance and prejudice" that swept the nation and sought to offer insight into how the nation could promote equal opportunities and tolerance.[5] Excited by *Look*'s proposal, Stegner believed a journalistic series of this kind would "be the best possible way to reach a mass audience with a message about equality and fraternity."[6] For nearly a year and a half, Stegner traveled across the country with *Look* photographers documenting instances of discrimination against Jews, Asian Americans, Native Americans, Mexican Americans, and many others. Stegner recounted his exhaustive itinerary: "I did a lot more traveling all over the country, and in more intimate ways than I had in the past. We'd go down to Elizabeth City, North Carolina, and shoot Jim Crow, or we'd go out to Dubuque, Iowa, and shoot a lot of monasteries and Catholic institutions in the Middle West. Traveling all through the West doing Mexican barrios, Filipino pickers in Stockton, Indian reservations."[7]

When Stegner wrote his first piece for *Look*, editors hesitated to publish it for fear of upsetting and potentially losing subscribers. Instead of the intended multipart series of articles, *Look* editors settled on a single, photograph-focused article in the magazine. Following the article Stegner and his wife, Mary, advocated for and collaborated with *Look* editors to publish the book *One Nation* in 1945, which utilized Stegner's initial research to craft a series of vignettes on American discrimination and intolerance.[8] Beautifully edited and designed, *One Nation* captures the reader with poignant and striking photography to supplement Stegner's recounting of the nation's exclusionary and violent practices against minorities. Although the book aimed to shed light on the reasons for discrimination, Stegner tried to envision a more tolerant postwar American society in what he described as his "wartime patriotism" book. As in his other literary works, Stegner infused *One Nation* with values of hope and civic responsibility. To Stegner, the fate of American democracy depended on messages of unity among all citizens.[9]

In his opening chapter, Stegner sets the stage by describing dark episodes of discrimination across the country. He outlines patterns of exclusion such as poverty, segregation, property restrictions, disenfranchisement, subpar education, and violence suffered by African Americans, Native Americans, Japanese Americans, and Mexican Americans. The book is then divided into five parts, each focusing on specific cultures, religions, and racial groups: "Pacific Races," "Mexicans," "Oldest Americans," "Negroes," and "Culture and Creed."[10] Within the chapter "77,000 Innocent Bystanders: *The Uprooted Japanese-Americans*," Stegner brings the reader within the barbed wired confines of isolated compounds in the barren West. He articulates the tragic uprooting of Japanese Americans who resided there during World War II, focusing attention on the segregation of families. Stegner speaks to the hastily constructed assembly centers at fairgrounds and racetracks that temporarily housed thousands of Japanese Americans on the West Coast. He also spends considerable time analyzing the reasons for the forced incarceration of nearly 120,000 Japanese Americans and lambasts these as being racially motivated segregation policies of the time.

Although Stegner tried to bring national attention to large-scale discrimination against Japanese and Japanese Americans with a behind-the-scenes look at camp life, it was no journalistic exposé. While reading *One Nation* with a more modern lens, there are noticeable faults and blind spots in Stegner's interpretation of Japanese Americans and their experiences of prejudice. Rather than include the direct experiences of Japanese Americans themselves, the chapter was principally written from his perspective and observations. By doing so, he relies on generalizations and misleading language that creates a sanitary view of mass incarceration that, at times, overly simplifies a complex history of exclusion. For someone who is idolized for his ability to eloquently write about the human condition on the western landscape, it is hard to understand why he did not integrate original accounts of Japanese Americans into his chapter to connect more viscerally with the reader. According to biographer Jackson J. Benson in *Wallace Stegner: His Life and Work*, Stegner visited at least two Japanese American incarceration sites in central California while on assignment for *Look*; however, his direct encounters or interviews with incarcerees are not mentioned or included in *One Nation*. Instead, his narrative oscillates between highlighting the injustices perpetrated against Japanese Americans to sanitizing their experiences through euphemisms.[11]

The use of terminology to describe Japanese American incarceration remains a historically challenging and debated issue. Historian Cherstin M. Lyon, in her book *Prisons and Patriots: Japanese American Wartime Citizenship, Civil Disobedience, and Historical Memory*, explains the complexity of terminology during World War II. Selective terminology such as "evacuation," "detention," and "relocation" were the preferred euphemisms found in WRA records, government propaganda, and historical narratives of the time. According to Lyon, these euphemisms provide "administrative and ideological context for the wartime treatment of Japanese Americans." These words also illustrate how the government justified the harmful treatment of Japanese Americans to the public and minimized the impact of their exploitative, carceral, and unconstitutional practices. Although President Roosevelt referred to WRA sites in multiple public addresses as "concentration camps," the federal government avoided calling them prisons. The word "internment" was never used by the WRA and is only found in postwar narratives.[12] Today, accuracy and appropriateness of this terminology is carefully examined. In the last decade historians, social justice advocates, and Japanese American organizations have researched and weighed the implications of euphemisms on the Japanese American community and the constitutionality of wartime carceral practices.

Stegner follows the conventional trend of terminology used during the 1940s. Even so, his choice of language in *One Nation* can be misleading, even jarring at times, and demonstrates the continued need for careful review of historical narratives. For example, Stegner diminishes the trauma experienced by many Japanese Americans by describing it as an "unhappy evacuation experience" or temporary "relocation." As the National Japanese American Citizens League argued in the *Power of Words Handbook: A Guide to Language about Japanese Americans in World War II*, terminology is an important factor to consider when reading historical narratives of Japanese American incarceration. The terms "evacuation" and "relocation" sanitize the history of forced removal, making it "more acceptable to the public," as if Japanese Americans were saved, helped, or rescued by the government.[13] In another instance Stegner refers to the WRA, the agency tasked with operating the incarceration centers, as "fair and sympathetic" in a time when the constitutionality of operations was in question. Although Stegner described the centers as "America's dreariest waste lands," his offer of empathy for the WRA is improper, inaccurate, and euphemistic, to say the least.[14] The issue of terminology is an important one as it can significantly influence the perception of an event by an untrained reader.

In journalistic style the chapter's narrative is paired with vivid images that correspond to Stegner's interpretation of forced removal and incarceration. As the chapter progresses, written narrative slowly transforms into short captions alongside a collage of photos or full-page photographs. Taken by *Look* photographer Frank Bauman, some of the photos feature a desolate camp enclosed in barbed wire with an octagonal guard tower and several blocks of barracks in the background.[15] Another depicts an armed guard with his rifle aimed out a guard tower window. Although the name of the camp featured in these photographs is never mentioned, the octagonal guard tower is unique to the Granada Relocation Center, or "Amache," located in southeast Colorado.[16] A newspaper article from the *Granada Pioneer* confirmed Frank Bauman visited Amache to photograph life there in 1943.[17]

Stegner concludes his chapter with descriptions of life in these incarceration centers. He notes the scant furnishings found in the barracks and the rationing of food. He goes on to describe the many facilities provided at the center: laundry and shower facilities, flourishing adult schools, farm programs that supported the center, along with "excellent" health care made possible by Japanese American professionals.[18] Each description is matched with photographs that are slightly reminiscent of the staged and propagandized photographs taken by the federal government. Some photos showcase smiling Japanese American women carrying pails of water to their barracks, doing laundry, and other domestic duties. Another shows grinning men harvesting sugar beets, with the caption, "From the beginning, Japanese were allowed jobs outside the relocation centers, though their enemies clamored that they be kept behind barbed wire. Their labor saved the 1942 beet crop in Utah and Colorado."[19] Similar to other narratives, proponents of these sites justified the exploitation of Japanese Americans to support wartime labor shortages to save crops and feed the nation. However, Stegner does not allude to the inhumane conditions of camp life before the construction of these major facilities, the exploitation of labor for agriculture and infrastructure development, or the struggle for proper medical care and education.

Other scholars of race have criticized Stegner's failure to fully reflect on and incorporate the experiences of people of color in his descriptions of life, landscape, and history in the American West. One of his most vocal critics is Elizabeth Cook-Lynn, a tribal studies professor emerita and Crow Creek Sioux writer whose work exposes the effects of settler colonialism and Native American dispossession in American literature. In Cook-Lynn's critical assessment of Stegner, *Why I Can't Read Wallace Stegner and Other Essays: A Tribal Voice*, she asserts that Stegner's white perspective and "personalization of history" lends to the legitimization of dominant narratives that do not represent the point of view of Native Americans and people of color who experienced the same environment or history much differently.[20] Cook-Lynn argues that Stegner's imagining of people of color and their experiences in the West contributes to the politics of possession and dispossession of history on the western landscape.[21]

Some of Stegner's other critics came from those who admired and studied his work well, such as western historian Elliott West. In his essay "Wallace Stegner's West, Wilderness, and History," West critiqued Stegner for not fully recognizing Native American experiences or acknowledging their longstanding presence on the western landscape. West charged that Stegner described Native Americans in "historically flat terms."[22] However, with every flaw, West found lessons learned. Stegner touched on his cultural competency in *One Nation*, but West called for us to examine our understanding of western history by elevating the prominence of people of color.[23] This pattern is seen in *One Nation* where Stegner makes assumptions about Japanese Americans' incarceration experiences but fails to include their own firsthand accounts. By doing so, *One Nation* evokes a white male perspective and unconsciously claims possession of Japanese American experiences.

Uncovering Policies of Dispossession and Exploitation at WRA Centers

Stegner only scratched the surface when documenting discrimination against Japanese Americans in the United States, as well as the impact of carceral policies on the western landscape. Prejudice against Japanese Americans before and during World War II resulted in large-scale discriminatory policies of removal, dispossession, and exploitation. Because of this, discrimination against Japanese Americans goes much deeper than what is presented in *One Nation*. Stegner observed the systematic dispossession of Japanese American families across the West following Pearl Harbor in 1941, but his observations had limitations due to available research and sources of the time.

By the late twentieth century, scholars had a better understanding of the dispossession tactics that started shortly after the bombing of Pearl Harbor due to available governmental records, research, and Japanese American oral histories. For example, the Treasury Department actively confiscated Japanese- and Japanese American–owned ships, suspended produce licenses, and froze all assets. With large-scale sale, confiscation, and abandonment of Japanese American property and businesses, the forced removal process essentially became a policy-driven device to deprive Japanese Americans of good farmland and business opportunities in the West.[24] The federal government violated Japanese Americans' right to due process through coordinated dispossession strategies and unconstitutional imprisonment. Franklin Delano Roosevelt and his administration categorized Japanese Americans as essentially Japanese nationals during World War II, thereby dismissing their citizenship and labeling them as foreign to justify the evacuation policy. Historian Greg Robinson, in his reasoned and balanced analysis of Executive Order (E.O.) 9066, concluded the Roosevelt administration had a complex record of "othering" Japanese Americans and racializing citizenship. The diminishment and outright disregard of citizenship and property rights meant Japanese Americans had to leave their property behind, entrust it to white neighbors and friends, or sell it at rock-bottom prices, resulting in generational economic oppression.[25]

Although Stegner mentions the desolate conditions and locations of the WRA sites, *One Nation* also leaves out the complex reasoning for how and why the federal government selected land in remote areas of the West.[26] Like the segregation of Native Americans on reservations, Japanese Americans were scattered across the remote western landscape to weaken the perceived threat of Japanese influence.[27] Some WRA centers, such as Poston, were located on tribal land, which added a layer of complexity to the incarceration history and perpetuated cycles of trauma among multiple ethnicities. Poston became one of the epicenters of racialized spaces, where government programs limited the movement of, and systematically marginalized, people of color in the West. Poston demonstrates a repeated legacy of dispossession, exploitation, and segregation of both Native Americans and Japanese Americans, which is not typically at the forefront of American history. The longstanding colonialism against Native Americans thereby reinforced further marginalization and incarceration of Japanese Americans.

After years of unsuccessful attempts to colonize the Parker Valley with Native Americans—due to insufficient funding and infrastructure—the Office of Indian Affairs (OIA) envisioned plans for using mass incarceration as an opportunity to tap into wartime funding and labor. This proposal tossed Poston into a regional land and water dispute and created animosity among local tribal members who struggled to obtain water rights. John Collier, OIA commissioner, saw the Colorado River Indian Reservation as an ideal site for Poston due to the amount of undeveloped acreage and available water rights along the Colorado River. The site could supply Japanese American labor for the construction of irrigation systems, infrastructure, and public works that would benefit Native Americans after the war. The influx of Japanese Americans in the area would also increase water consumption of the reservation and aid the tribes in obtaining water rights.[28]

In *One Nation* Stegner praised John Collier's efforts to reverse detrimental Native American assimilation policies with long-range programs that focused on improving Native American standard of living, sovereignty, and self-government.[29] However, Stegner did not realize that these OIA policies and programs exploited other people of color to reach its goals and were rooted in settler colonialist strategies. Prior to Poston's construction the local Tribal Council rejected plans for the site, given the intended use as a prison. However, the OIA overruled the council, and construction of the site continued along with the cycle of trauma and injustice. Sadly, the establishment of Poston thereby made this site "a reservation within a reservation."[30] Construction of Poston required massive military coordination to transform the desert into 71,600 acres of a self-contained prison, operated jointly by the OIA and WRA.[31]

Miles away from their homes, Japanese Americans tried their best to sustain some resemblance of dignity behind barbed wire. Many sites established in-house newspapers such as the *Poston Chronicle* to document daily life, injustices, and wartime news.[32] These newspapers documented instances of labor exploitation as Japanese Americans worked at camouflage net factories for wartime military efforts. At

Poston, Japanese Americans received substandard educational services for their children. This is a stark contrast to *One Nation*'s images of happy Japanese American children reading books at flourishing schools. Incarcerees had to lobby administrators to receive approval for the construction of an educational complex. In 1943 a *Poston Chronicle* article noted that nearly seven hundred thousand adobe bricks were needed for construction of the complex. However, incarcerees had to provide the labor for construction.[33]

Japanese American incarcerees comprised the main labor source for the construction of the area's irrigation canal system and roads along the Colorado River, which ultimately transformed the valley from a dry bleak desert into arable farmland in the years to come. The OIA intentionally exploited the backbreaking work of Japanese Americans' labor for these infrastructure projects to support the agency's larger Native American assimilation plans.[34] If you were to visit Parker, Arizona, today, the agricultural fields are sustained by some of these historic irrigation canals. However, many locals are unaware that Japanese Americans provided the necessary labor for such a monumental task.

After the war and following the closure of Poston in 1945, Japanese Americans tried to rebuild their lives. Many left with emotional scars that could never be mended, some returned home but arrived with little to nothing, and others could not bear to return home due to the difficult memories of loss, so they migrated elsewhere. Stegner described the difficulties of resettlement exacerbated by the lingering resentment and prejudice against Japanese Americans. Stegner's solution to ending the cycle of prejudice relied on calls for tolerance. Stegner hoped for a future supported by these ideals, but he also feared that doing nothing could easily reignite exclusionary policies against people of color and lead to the downfall of democracy. For Stegner and many others, the nation rested on precarious ground in 1945.[35]

Reconciling the Legacy of Stegner and *One Nation*

In the context of the 1940s, biographers and contemporaries of Stegner believed the publishing of *One Nation* could have easily proved disastrous to his career. However, he persisted with the project, believing the cause to be important for the future of the nation. It is admirable that Wallace and Mary Stegner continued their steadfast effort to publish *One Nation*, and it demonstrates their commitment to social justice during such turbulent times. *One Nation* captivated the American public and catapulted Stegner onto the national scene. Following publication, Stegner achieved a longstanding professional goal by securing a job offer from Stanford as an assistant professor.[36] After receiving several awards for the book, Stegner became a popular speaker on issues of race relations and equal rights. For a short period of time, he even served on the board of a local American Civil Liberties Union chapter.[37] As historian Patricia Limerick reflected in her essay "Precedents to Wisdom," the publishing of *One Nation* demonstrated that "Stegner was just as dramatically ahead of his time in the matter of race relations as he was in environmental affairs."[38] However, despite its acclaim, Stegner did not continue to champion racial and social justice issues in his other major literary works.

There is a clear contradiction, or perhaps shortfall, between Stegner's postwar racial equity advocacy and the themes of his literary work. Given the national attention and persistence from Wallace and Mary to promote *One Nation*, it would be reasonable to assume Stegner produced subsequent literature on race relations. But that is not the case. Instead, much of Stegner's later work is focused on environmental and conservation activism. At times, even Stegner's own academic and literary circles included essays on the same themes and racial issues found in *One Nation*. Nearly two years after the publication of *One Nation*, Henry Tani wrote a piece for the *Pacific Spectator* on the repercussions of incarceration and Japanese American postwar settlement. Stegner, along with other contemporaries such as Bernard DeVoto, contributed to the same issue. However, Stegner's essay focused on the life and mythology of nineteenth-century labor activist Joe Hill, a prelude to his later biographical novel.[39] Nothing else in Stegner's vast list of literary works seems to compare to *One Nation's* messages of tolerance and racial equality.

It is interesting to compare *One Nation* to his later literature, such as *The American West as Living Space*, where Stegner attempted to articulate the essence of the West, including the people who transformed it. Stegner crafts a unique picture of the landscape through vibrant descriptions of life in the West that has lingered in the American consciousness for decades. He is known as an American writer who *defined* the West through his tireless efforts to understand myth-making and the connections between history, culture, and the landscape.[40] Written four decades after *One Nation*, Stegner published *The American West as Living Space* in 1987 following a series of lectures at the University of Michigan Law School. Stegner's commentary centers on the experiences of people who migrated to the West and their intentional transformation of the land to survive the effects of aridity. However, when viewed through more contemporary lenses, Stegner's assessment of the West ignores the dispossession and exploitation of Native and marginalized peoples that made Anglo settlement, and ultimately settler colonialism, possible. Historians such as Margaret D. Jacobs no longer mince words when identifying and describing the oppressive results of settler colonialism in the West. In her book *After One Hundred Winters: In Search of Reconciliation on America's Stolen Lands*, Jacobs writes, "It can be deeply uncomfortable for many settlers to face the illegitimate foundations upon which our settlement is based, to consider that what might have been progress for settlers was devastation for . . . other Indian nations. It's hard to acknowledge that we settlers are trespassers on Native land . . . that our histories of triumph are inextricably intertwined with Indigenous histories of theft."[41] Reading Stegner's *The American West as Living Space* shows how he understands the West through this dominant settler narrative of exploited resources and land rather than the exploitation of people.[42]

Stegner's central interpretation of the West comes with similar limitations and blind spots found in *One Nation*. In both books Stegner places white men as the social norm against which all other cultures and identities are weighed. *The American West as Living Space* is based on a white-oriented perspective, where the central characters are Anglo migrants and the federal government, who manage and exploit environmental resources such as land and water.[43] It largely ignores the even more visceral legacy of the West, the exploitation of *humanity* in addition to natural resources. Settler colonialism and the federal government alike managed nature and exploited, dispossessed, and erased people of color who did not fit their vision of the West, whether it be a productive agrarian farmland or an empty scenic landscape.[44] Through active removal and promotion of a specific cultural narrative, people of color became invisible on the land and in the national consciousness.[45] As Carolyn Finney asserts in *Black Faces, White Spaces*, our ability to imagine others, especially in history and on the landscape, is "*colored by the narratives, images, and meanings we've come to hold as truths in relation to the environment.*"[46]

Since many of Stegner's western characters are primarily identified as white, the depiction of the western landscape is a predominantly white space, absent of people of color. This is a stark contrast to *One Nation*, where people of color are the central focus. When people of color are mentioned in Stegner's *The American West as Living Space*, they are typically relegated to enclaves of their own, unable to survive or adapt to incoming pressures and violence from invading white settlers. Stegner further diminishes people of color by classifying them as "subcultures" to a dominant white culture, which promotes a colonial imagining of the West.[47] Missing from Stegner's depiction of the West is the long-standing presence and influence of people of color on the western landscape, before, during and after white settlement.[48] As a person of color, I found it difficult, at times, to read *The American West as Living Space*, especially when Stegner described people of color as lacking agency, when he disregarded their cultural resiliency, and when he fixed white society as the social norm.

The many contradictions and cultural insensitivities found in Stegner's literature are challenging to reconcile, especially when he so strongly promoted cultural diversity and tolerance in *One Nation* and even actively advocated for international writers. Stegner traveled abroad quite frequently following the publication of *One Nation*.

From 1950 to 1951, Stegner and his family went on a globetrotting adventure, financed by the Rockefeller Foundation. While in Japan, a fellow acquaintance introduced Stegner to an accomplished Japanese writer, Yasunari Kawabata. Inspired by his travels and Asian culture, Stegner promoted Asian literature and writers in the United States. Furthermore, Stegner became a close advocate for Kawabata and helped him with publication in *The Atlantic*. This is one of many instances in Stegner's life where he personally practiced the message of *One Nation* through racial collaboration in a postwar era.[49]

One Nation and *The American West as Living Space* are valuable in demonstrating Stegner's attempts to make sense of the world around him, including race relations and the making of the West. But it also shows clear contradictions between his personal advocacy for racial equality and how he ultimately wrote about people of color in his broader literature. What is surprising is that *One Nation*'s themes of cultural diversity and racial justice did not permeate his later literature on the West. Instead, much of his work is known for his stalwart conservationism, not racial justice issues. How is Stegner to be remembered these many decades later? On one hand he can be viewed as an individual who wrote a narrative of the West that largely ignores people of color, while on the other he was genuinely concerned about the widespread racism and prejudice against them.

Erasure, Recovery, and Lessons for the Future

Since *One Nation* was published in 1945, Stegner could not fully report on the closing of the WRA centers, including the environmental legacy and widespread cultural and physical erasure of these sites. Following closure, the WRA systematically razed or auctioned off the remaining buildings on each site. Officials completely cleared buildings and people from thousands of acres of land, swiped clean and returned to the vast emptiness of the West. At Poston the federal government demolished many of the administration buildings. However, per John Collier's original plans, the OIA transferred barracks to local Native

American families for housing. Today, if you have a keen eye, you can see the former barracks still in use, modified and covered with stucco, and dotting the landscape in the surrounding Colorado River Indian Reservation. The OIA expanded and continued use of the original roads and irrigation canals built by Japanese American incarcerees. The exploited work of Japanese Americans contributed to the viability of the area's agriculture and remain an enduring, but largely unknown, history of the Parker Valley. The original Poston Elementary School complex is the only remaining historic site left, designated as a National Historic Landmark in 2012, owned and preserved by the Colorado River Indian Tribes in partnership with the Poston Community Alliance. The elementary school complex is very small compared to the original size of the center, with much of the original land now used as farmland.[50] As you drive past the agricultural fields, you are unaware that Poston ever existed, the history erased except for the elementary school and a small local monument erected near the site by former Japanese American incarcerees to memorialize the history.

With the systematic erasure of all ten WRA sites, the Japanese American incarceration story of World War II remained invisible on the land for decades. Former Japanese American incarcerees left with emotional scars and financial loss, many reluctant to even share their stories of forced imprisonment until the redress movement of the 1980s. With redress and the passing of the Civil Liberties Act of 1988, the federal government provided an official apology and monetary compensation to former Japanese American incarcerees. However, it provided more than just that: it provided an opportunity for Japanese American incarcerees and their families to finally seek healing through their story and affirmation of their experiences. It also became a way to acknowledge and legitimize their history, memories, and experiences of incarceration in the West. More broadly, it served as an opportunity to educate the public about the weaknesses of the Constitution and the importance of safeguarding our shared civil liberties, so it never happens again. As part of a growing modern movement to recognize sites that embody struggles for human rights, the former WRA sites soon became known as sites of conscience and provide valuable lessons to future generations.[51]

Although Stegner's interpretation of the West has clear blind spots, he does offer hope and lessons in evaluating our shared history that can still be useful for historians today. Stegner attempted to *uncover* discrimination against people of color in the United States and promoted equality to create a better democracy. These ideals can be guiding lessons for historians and Americans today, especially as we try to reconcile the trauma and injustices of the past. We can move forward from there, by uncovering stories of injustice that were actively *erased* from public view, both in history and on the landscape. We can look for stories that *transformed* the western landscape or investigate further when there are obvious voids caused by erasure. As historian Margaret Jacobs describes in *After One Hundred Winters*, we have a responsibility to challenge outdated narratives of the West and seek opportunities for reconciliation and redress. We can take proactive steps by listening to, and amplifying, the stories of those who experienced and survived injustices firsthand.[52] Just as Japanese American survivor testimony provided a foundation for the redress movement of the 1980s, and Holocaust survivors before that, personal testimonies of survival aid in expanding investigative research and can correct false narratives or incomplete historical records. The process of recovery is essential to ensuring that stories of survival, resistance, and resilience are told, which adds to a more accurate interpretation of history and improves our potential for substantive redress. If he were alive today, Stegner may even consider this our shared civic responsibility.

Assessing *One Nation* and *The American West as Living Space* also reminds us that mindful use of terminology and the incorporation of firsthand experiences of people of color are critical to providing an accurate representation of history as well. As the National Japanese American Citizens League stated, it is our responsibility "to acknowledge and correct this misleading language of the past and focus on truth and accuracy for the future. The objective here is to suggest vocabulary that facilitates a more accurate understanding of events and actions experienced . . . during this tragic time."[53] It is clear that community and national efforts to uncover underrepresented stories of marginalized peoples are a source of healing and recovery for those who survived the West's legacy of exploitation and erasure. As historians, it is important to reconcile these experiences no matter how different they may be from more popularized or dominant narratives of the past. For the field of history, researching and examining more complex explanations of American history not only provides for a more inclusive understanding of the past, but it also sheds light on the reality of the West in all its beauty *and* tragedy. Through active practice, we can make invisible stories visible again.[54]

Notes

1. *Poston Chronicle* 20, no. 28 (October 5, 1944), shelf no. NP2452, reel no. 6, Ft. 71, Japanese Camp Papers, Arizona Collection, Phoenix Public Library, Microfilm. The newspaper noted the peak population of Poston as 17,942 occurring in August 1942. In the "Poston Elementary School, Unit 1" National Historic Landmark nomination, historians Laurie and Thomas Simmons note the overall population passing through the gates as 19,392.

2. The Poston Community Alliance is a nonprofit organization established and led by former Japanese Americans who were once incarcerated at Poston. The organization's mission is to preserve the stories, artifacts, and historic structures related to Poston in collaboration with the Colorado River Indian Tribes Reservation (CRIT). For more information visit the reservation website, www.postonpreservation.org.

3. R. Laurie Simmons and Thomas H. Simmons, "Poston Elementary School, Unit 1," National Historic Landmark nomination (Washington DC: National Park Service, U.S. Department of the Interior, September 2011), 18.

4. Phillip L. Fradkin, *Wallace Stegner and the American West* (New York: Alfred A. Knopf, 2008), 105.

5. Wallace Stegner and editors of *Look* magazine, *One Nation* (Boston: Houghton Mifflin, 1945), v.

6. Wallace Stegner and Richard W. Etulain, *Stegner: Conversations on History and Literature* (Reno: University of Nevada Press, 1996), 39–40.

7. Stegner and Etulain, *Stegner*, 40.

8. Jackson J. Benson, *Wallace Stegner: His Life and Work* (New York: Viking Penguin, 1996), 143–47. Benson credits Mary Stegner as a driving force in the effort to get *One Nation* published. He also credits Mary with holding strong values and concerns for social injustices perpetrated against Japanese Americans.

9. Stegner and Etulain, *Stegner*, 40.

10. Stegner and editors of *Look, One Nation*, 1–15.

11. Benson, *Wallace Stegner*, 148.

12. Cherstin M. Lyon, *Prisons and Patriots: Japanese American Wartime Citizenship, Civil Disobedience, and Historical Memory* (Philadelphia: Temple University Press, 2012), xi–xiii.

13. National Japanese American Citizens League, *Power of Words Handbook: A Guide to Language about Japanese Americans in World War II; Understanding Euphemisms and Preferred Terminology* (San Francisco: National JACL Power of Words II Committee, 2020), 1, 7–9. Generally, JACL recommends using more accurate terminology, such as "American concentration camps," "incarceration camps," or "illegal detention center," rather than "relocation center" or "internment camps." However, in certain contexts, exceptions apply to "relocation center" such as when referring to a camp by its historic name.

14. Stegner and editors of *Look, One Nation*, 47, 54.

15. Stegner and editors of *Look, One Nation*, 54, 338.

16. R. Laurie Simmons and Thomas H. Simmons, "Granada Relocation Center," National Historic Landmark nomination (Washington DC: National Park Service, U.S. Department of the Interior, 2004), 6.

17. "Look Photographer Shoots Amache Life," *Granada Pioneer* (Amache CO), April 28, 1943, https://www.loc.gov/item/sn83025522/1943-04-28/ed-1/. Incarcerees created internal newspapers, such as *Granada Pioneer*; however, many were censored by the U.S. government and WRA administrators. Although Benson states Stegner visited WRA sites in California, it is unclear if he traveled with Bauman to Amache.

18. Stegner and editors of *Look, One Nation*, 59.

19. Stegner and editors of *Look, One Nation*, 61.

20. Elizabeth Cook-Lynn, *Why I Can't Read Wallace Stegner and Other Essays: A Tribal Voice* (Madison: University of Wisconsin Press, 1996), 29–30.

21. Cook-Lynn, *Why I Can't Read Wallace Stegner*, 38–40.

22. Elliott West, "Wallace Stegner's West, Wilderness, and History," in *Wallace Stegner and the Continental Vision: Essays on Literature, History, and Landscape*, ed. Curt Meine (Washington DC: Island Press, 1997), 90.

23. West, "Wallace Stegner's West," 90–94.

24. Greg Robinson, *By Order of the President: FDR and the Internment of Japanese Americans* (Cambridge MA: Harvard University Press, 2001), 75, 105.

25. Robinson, *By Order of the President*, 144.

26. Simmons and Simmons, "Poston Elementary School," 22. As part of the WRA's site selection process, viable locations had to fulfill several criteria for suitability: encompass land large enough to sustain five thousand people; provide for agricultural development or employment opportunities for incarcerees; and be located away from exclusion zones and strategic installations.

27. Robinson, *By Order of the President*, 2.

28. Brian Masaru Hayashi, *Democratizing the Enemy: The Japanese American Internment* (Princeton NJ: Princeton University Press, 2004), 16–17, 88–89. Hayashi explains that Colorado River Indian Tribes struggled to secure water rights in Arizona because Reserved Rights and Prior Appropriation Doctrine did not apply. At the time, the only prospect for obtaining tribal water rights depended on increasing consumption.

29. Stegner and editors of *Look*, *One Nation*, 142–45.

30. Simmons and Simmons, "Poston Elementary School," 4, 23.

31. Simmons and Simmons, "Poston Elementary School," 5.

32. *Poston Chronicle* 8, no. 10 (December 22, 1942).

33. *Poston Chronicle* 9, no. 6 (January 13, 1943).

34. Simmons and Simmons, "Poston Elementary School," 18, 26.

35. Stegner and editors of *Look*, *One Nation*, 14–15.

36. Stegner and Etulain, *Stegner*, 40, 65; Benson, *Wallace Stegner*, 5.

37. Benson, *Wallace Stegner*, 152.

38. Patricia Limerick, "Precedents to Wisdom," in *Wallace Stegner: Man and Writer*, ed. Charles E. Rankin (Albuquerque: University of New Mexico Press, 1996), 109–10.

39. Henry Tani, "The Nisei since Pearl Harbor," *Pacific Spectator* 1, no. 2 (Spring 1947): 203–13.

40. Curt Meine, ed., *Wallace Stegner and the Continental Vision: Essays on Literature, History, and Landscape* (Washington DC: Island Press, 1997), xix–xx.

41. Margaret D. Jacobs, *After One Hundred Winters: In Search of Reconciliation on America's Stolen Lands* (Princeton NJ: Princeton University Press, 2021), 6–7.

42. Carolyn Finney, *Black Faces, White Spaces: Reimagining the Relationship of African Americans to the Great Outdoors* (Chapel Hill: University of North Carolina Press, 2014), 7.

43. Wallace Stegner, *The American West as Living Space* (Ann Arbor: University of Michigan Press, 1987), 9–12.

44. Robert T. Hayashi, *Haunted By Waters: A Journey through Race and Place in the American West* (Iowa City: University of Iowa Press, 2007), 5.

45. Finney, *Black Faces, White Spaces*, xvii.

46. Finney, *Black Faces, White Spaces*, xii.

47. Stegner, *American West as Living Space*, 67–68.

48. Cook-Lynn, *Why I Can't Read Wallace Stegner*, 36–38.

49. Benson, *Wallace Stegner*, 185–86.

50. Simmons and Simmons, "Poston Elementary School," 8, 73.

51. Mitchell T. Maki, Harry H. L. Kitano, and S. Megan Berthold, *Achieving the Impossible Dream: How Japanese Americans Obtained Redress* (Urbana: University of Illinois Press, 1999), 225–26, 240–41. For more information about sites of conscience, please visit the International Coalition of Sites of Conscience, https://www.sitesofconscience.org/en/home/.

52. Jacobs, *After One Hundred Winters*, 87, 209.

53. National Japanese American Citizens League, *Power of Words Handbook*, 1.

54. Patricia Nelson Limerick, "Making the Most of Words: Verbal Activity and Western America," in *Under an Open Sky: Rethinking America's Western Past*, ed. William Cronon, George Miles, and Jay Gitlin (New York: W. W. Norton, 1992), 157.

3

Creation
as Erasure

Wallace Stegner and
the Making and
Unmaking of Regions

MICHAEL J. LANSING

In his 1987 book *The American West as Living Space*, Wallace Stegner argued that his subject encompassed "not only a region but also a state of mind." He further declared that "both the region and the state of mind are my native habitat." Stegner went on to define the West by referring to what he called "its abiding unity"—an arid landscape.[1] In this and many other essays, stories, and novels, the man that *Newsweek* magazine once called "the dean of western writers" did more to define the West as a distinct region than anyone else in post–World War II America.[2] And he used an environmental feature to do it.

But the ghost of an earlier region haunts much of his earliest work.[3] A now-forgotten place called the Northwest stands like a specter behind Stegner's first decade of published prose. This regional label, encompassing the lands between today's Upper Midwest and the Rocky Mountains, rose and fell between the 1880s and 1950s. Geographer Donald Meinig deemed it the second of three distinct Northwests in U.S. history. The first encompassed the Ohio River Valley in the early nineteenth century. The second included the Upper Mississippi Valley, along with both Dakotas and Montana. The third is the area we know today as the Pacific Northwest.[4]

Economic relations defined the second Northwest. Capital demarcated the relationships and perceptions and identities that made up the place. In contrast, Wallace Stegner used environmental features to define an American West that superseded other regional monikers. In fact, Stegner's central role in the creation of a regional West required the erasure of other designations. Without a shared natural characteristic to hold it together, the second Northwest (which included deciduous forests, coniferous forests, tallgrass prairies, shortgrass plains, and the alpine reaches of the northern Rockies) gradually fell into disuse.[5]

The shift away from the earlier designation obscured North Dakota's, South Dakota's, and Montana's longstanding hinterland-metropole relationship with the Twin Cities.[6] By excluding places east of the hundredth meridian from what became the West, Stegner downplayed capital's role in shaping these newly settled spaces. Reclaiming those relations—and the struggles they spawned—matters. At a moment when capitalism rapidly degrades the climatic systems that support human life as we know it, the erasure of capital's role in placemaking proves especially problematic.[7]

Analyzing places can be a tricky business, especially when demarcating regions. Boundaries remain fuzzy. Debates develop around definitions. Some historians turn to studies of human perception. Others appeal to the physical world.[8] Geographers, of course, go further. They focus tightly on the constructedness of place and space. After all, the complex relations between people and things produce place. Contestation, overlap, and messiness persist.[9]

The region identified by Donald Meinig as America's second Northwest grew into existence after the Civil War. Writers began referring to the Upper Mississippi River Valley and points west as the Northwest. This shift away from using the term to describe the Ohio River Valley marked an important shift in regional vernacular.[10]

That shift depended entirely on European Americans securing the lands of the Upper Mississippi Valley. The expulsion of Dakota people after the 1862 U.S.-Dakota War followed lopsided treaty making with Ojibwe and Ho-Chunk peoples. In the years that followed—and despite fierce resistance—the Lakota horse empire astride the Missouri River (along with the river villagers with whom Lakota people traded and fought) also lost much of its political and economic independence.[11] Nonetheless, Indigenous people held their sovereignty and culture close despite long odds.[12]

Loosed by the sidelining of Native peoples, multiple manifestations of capital sprawled across the region. Boosters and government agents promoted the agricultural possibilities of the Upper Mississippi and Upper Missouri. The rise of flour milling at St. Anthony Falls on the Mississippi River not only created the city of Minneapolis but also shaped the creation of a wheat-growing hinterland that stretched west to the Rocky Mountains. By the 1880s this Northwest—an economy that bound together urban and rural spaces to produce the world's first factory-made grain-based carbohydrates—found a powerful voice in the flour milling industry's trade journal. Based in Minneapolis, it called itself the *Northwestern Miller*.[13]

Railroads provided the physical links in, through, and across these spaces. The placemaking power of railroads is well known. Transporting materials, media, and people, two lines—the Northern Pacific and the Great Northern—extended west from Minneapolis and St. Paul to the Pacific Coast during the 1880s. Financiers as far afield as Great Britain helped fund the costly ventures, transforming landscapes and binding together diverse spaces.[14]

Flour milling and railroading combined to make Minneapolis–St. Paul a metropole. In turn, the two industries created hinterlands. The rural spaces incorporated into the burgeoning new Northwest depended on extracting wealth from the soil. Generally, the transformation of ecological entities into economic resources begat financial prosperity. Capitalism itself depended on the transformation of landscapes for its sustenance and growth. Importantly, that wealth stayed in the hands of a few. Uneven development marked these economic processes.[15]

To be sure, ecological processes remained prominent. The kinetic energy of falling water at St. Anthony produced the power for Minneapolis's flour mills. The burning of fossil energy to power steam locomotives made railroading possible. But without any unifying natural or climatic features, the transformation of nature into commodities across a diverse landscape of forests, prairies, plains, and mountains—and the relationships spawned by those transformations—firmly defined the Northwest. The history of the Northwest is the history of industrial capitalism enveloping the center of the continent.

Indeed, the intense development of capital-intensive extractive enterprise in this Northwest marked it as a crucial location in the American economy.[16] In 1913 the federal government created federal reserve banks with corresponding districts of economic activity. After a protracted campaign by Minneapolis's businessmen and bankers, the government recognized the metropole-hinterland relationships of the Twin Cities to the rural places west of it by placing a federal reserve bank there. This effort proved to be the most durable manifestation of this now-forgotten Northwest rendered by capital.[17]

The political work of creating the Ninth Federal Reserve Bank District depended entirely on measuring and demonstrating the size and scope of capital's reach across what those Minneapolis-based businessmen and financiers consistently referred to as the Northwest. Firming up the boundaries of this economically defined region, the district included Minnesota, North and South Dakota, and Montana and threw in the pine forests of northwest Wisconsin and the rich copper mines of Michigan's Upper Peninsula for good measure.[18]

Headquartered in Minneapolis, the reserve district also depended on the branch bank it opened in Helena, Montana, in 1921.[19] As the primary financial nodes in a developing web of capital relations that transformed nature and made a place, these banks embodied and sustained the economic relationships that bound together the lands and peoples between the Mississippi and the Northern Rockies. This powerful financialization of place helped secure the specific regional designation Twin Cities businessmen held tight to for their own gain.

No less a commentator than Mary Austin—best known for her famous book on the Southwest, *Land of Little Rain* (1903)—outlined her conception of the Northwest in 1920. Penned after a visit to Minnesota and North Dakota, her essay "The Culture of the Northwest,"

PRICE THIRTY-FIVE CENTS

MINNEAPOLIS

Metropolis of the Northwest

A QUARTERLY MAGAZINE PUBLISHED BY THE

Minneapolis Civic & Commerce Association

Minneapolis
The Geographic Center of North America

VOL. I   AUGUST 1927   NO. I

In This Issue

5. Cover of the August 1927 issue of the Minneapolis Civic and Commerce Association's *Minneapolis: Metropolis of the Northwest* magazine. This booster magazine identified Minneapolis as the metropole of the Northwest.

published in *The Freeman*, defined the region as Minnesota, North Dakota, South Dakota, Montana, Oregon, Idaho, and Washington. For Austin, the area produced a "forthright culture," one marked by "self respect and conscious idealism." She concluded "the great cultural achievements of the Northwest are the little country theatre and the Non-partisan League." Austin characterized the Nonpartisan League—an expression of political discontent by wheat farmers critical of corporations based in far-off Minneapolis—as "the first successful stand against economic privilege."[20]

In fact, the Nonpartisan League program called for the establishment of state-run banks. For lower-middle-class agrarians anxious to create more equity in wheat markets, economic issues stood out above all others. A system—inscribed into space by capital and recognized as a distinct place—that exploited soil and labor and then concentrated wealth in a far-off metropole drew their ire. The establishment of a state bank in North Dakota in 1919 helped moderate the worst of the disparities. That organized political opposition to concentrated capital stood out as a defining aspect of regional culture shows how thoroughly political economy defined the Northwest.[21]

The economic unfairness experienced by many in the region also sparked federal-level reforms. Farmers across the Northwest (and elsewhere) pressured the federal government to ameliorate the growing difficulties they faced finding cheap long-term credit. World War I inflated demand for American grain, and so Woodrow Wilson's administration worked quickly to secure legislation that would help increase farm productivity. The Federal Farm Loan Act of 1916 helped stabilize the agricultural economy across Minnesota, the Dakotas, and Montana, just as it did elsewhere. The reform brought some balance to a spatially uneven economy and worked independently of, but in tandem with, the Federal Reserve system to try to create stability across the region.[22]

The efforts ultimately failed. Private bankers across the Northwest resisted the reforms. In them, they rightly saw a challenge to their own businesses' profitability. Furthermore, the mitigations came too late.

During the 1920s farmers left the rural Northwest in droves, driven off the land by a collapse in land values, reduced rainfall, commodity prices, and wheat rust. Furthermore, flour millers in Minneapolis faced reduced consumer demand, growing questions about the nutritional value of their primary product, and new corporate challengers from the southern plains. Consolidation, mergers, and new wheat-based products saved the largest Minneapolis millers from ruin. But the city's slow deindustrialization indicated decline. The Great Depression fostered further turmoil in the regional economy. More farmers lost their farms to drought and crop failure. Meanwhile, the notoriously antiunion city saw weeks of violent strife during the Trucker's Strike of 1934. The Teamsters' Union prevailed, but the strike ruined more than the city's reputation. It showed the shakiness of the regional economy centered on Minneapolis.[23]

As the economic system that underpinned the Northwest faltered, so did the associated spatial constructions. Two alternative regional designations emerged to demarcate lands in the Northwest. In a series of articles in *Century* magazine in 1912, sociologist Edward Alsworth Ross included Minnesota and North and South Dakota in a region he boldly defined as the Middle West. In the 1920s, many followed up on this usage, and the association began to stick.[24] Meanwhile, commercial leaders in Portland, Oregon, began deploying the term "Pacific Northwest" as early as 1882. The descriptor seems to have not taken firm hold there, however, until the 1920s.[25]

By the late 1920s these challenges to previous understandings of the Northwest gained ground. Some followed Ross, using the term "Middle West" to refer to Minnesota and the Dakotas and parts east. Others— such as the Northern Pacific Railroad—made references to the Northwest that included not only the Upper Mississippi and Upper Missouri river basins but also Idaho, Washington, and Oregon. In the 1930s the New Deal's support of artists, writers, and intellectuals furthered this expanding range of regional expressions and understandings in the center of North America. Nonetheless, many residents and outsiders alike held on to older understandings of the Northwest.[26]

The general ferment in regionalism in the arts and humanities during the 1930s gave way to the influence of private money in the 1940s. Starting in 1942, studies of American regionalism emerged from programs launched by the Rockefeller Foundation. When World War II forced the philanthropy to scrap their plans to send American intellectuals abroad, they turned to funding the examination of differences within the United States. One Rockefeller-supported effort focused on demarcating the Great Plains—an environmentally defined spatial appellation made popular by historian Walter Prescott Webb's 1931 book of the same name.[27]

At three Rockefeller Foundation–sponsored meetings in 1942, intellectuals from across a broadly construed Great Plains sparred over what to officially include in that regional designation. The stakes were high, because the designation determined who would be eligible for Rockefeller monies. Unlike many of his colleagues, University of Minnesota historian Theodore Blegen believed that "the border states of the middle West" that "looked out toward the West"—like his own—should be closely considered for inclusion. He pointed to the "close and very real bonds" between the Twin Cities and points west.[28]

Blegen's articulation of the longstanding economic relationships between the Twin Cities and their hinterland came from an understanding of place rooted in the Northwest. Others at the meetings, however, disagreed with Blegen. They prevailed. The Great Plains would be defined by grass and annual rainfall and demarcated by the ninety-ninth meridian, following Walter Prescott Webb. The powerful economic relationships that incorporated that place into a burgeoning national economy would not be fully accounted for in the newly defined Great Plains region.[29]

At this crucial moment in the redefinition of American regions, a young Wallace Stegner emerged as a powerful new voice. The turn to embracing natural and climatic features as the primary characteristic of a region—already well underway, as Webb's work and the Rockefeller Foundation debates suggest—swept up the young writer. Stegner would follow their lead and call an environmentally defined American West into being during the postwar era.[30]

Importantly, Stegner set much of his early work in what his contemporaries often referred to as the Northwest. Iowa served as the backdrop for *Remembering Laughter* (1937) and Wisconsin for *Fire and Ice* (1941). But it is his first widely acclaimed novel—*The Big Rock Candy Mountain* (1943)—in which Stegner situated characters moving through the place that many at the time still called the Northwest. Indeed, the constant movement chronicled in the autobiographical novel marked his own emergence from a family with deep roots there.[31]

Today, given Stegner's strong identification with the American West, it is easy to forget that *The Big Rock Candy Mountain* opens in Minnesota, spends over a hundred pages in North Dakota, and includes main character Bruce Mason's law school stint in Minneapolis. Though capital proved the primary placemaker of the region—and though the character Bo Mason's never-ending search for economic success forms the arc of the novel—the Northwest remains absent.[32] Notably, Stegner largely avoided regional monikers in *The Big Rock Candy Mountain*. "Middle West," "Midwest," and "Northwest" never appear, and "West" is only used in reference to a region twice—once when describing Saltair (the tourist pavilion outside Salt Lake City) and once when Bruce Mason muses over the question of what counts as one's home.[33]

Indeed, late in *The Big Rock Candy Mountain*, Bruce Mason (based on Stegner himself) evaluates Minnesota (where he has many relatives and goes to school) as a potential home but decides that if it was really home, "I wouldn't be so glad to get out of here." Mason then turns to North Dakota but decides against it, too. Eventually, the young man decides that home "isn't where your family comes from, and it isn't where you were born. . . . Home is where you hang your hat."[34] A few pages later, Bruce Mason thinks to himself: "He was a westerner, whatever that was," going "west beyond the Dakotas toward home."[35]

Though Stegner rarely talked about the second Northwest, later in life he revealed his feelings about the area—parts of which were by then known as the Midwest. In 1975 an interviewer from the journal *Great Lakes Review* noted that Stegner had "lived both in the West and the Midwest" and asked him to compare the two regions.[36] In response, Stegner agreed that some of his first books—*Remembering Laughter* and *Fire and Ice*—were set in what was now called the Midwest, though not "self-consciously." Then he noted that while in graduate school at the University of Iowa in the 1930s, the "literary discussion was regional." Stegner, however, declared, "I'm not much of a Midwesterner." Instead, he said, "I am, by any kind of affiliation and experience, Western."[37]

The interviewer pressed again on the question of Minnesota and North Dakota and their relation to Stegner's West, noting that *The Big Rock Candy Mountain* has a good deal of it, especially in the first half of the book. Stegner replied, "Well, it's Dakota, of course, and you're on the margin there." Predictably referring to ecological differences, Stegner continued: "But I think of myself as a short grass rather than a tall grass person." Then the award-winning author said, "One of the things I discovered by going to Iowa City was that I wasn't a Midwesterner," though "I think it was the Midwest that taught me I probably was a regionalist of a certain kind." Indeed, he referred to the Northwest only in relation to his parents' early years, most notably in his 1989 essay "Finding The Place: A Migrant Childhood."[38]

Importantly, it was Lois Phillips Hudson, the author of *Reapers of the Dust* (1957) and *The Bones of Plenty* (1962) who most clearly identified Stegner's simultaneous creation and erasure of region in *The Big Rock Candy Mountain*. She was a North Dakota–centric writer whose own work garnered less attention partly because her best-known books described early twentieth-century life in the second Northwest. In an obscure essay on *The Big Rock Candy Mountain* published in 1971, Hudson pointed out Stegner's rejection of her home state (and primary subject) as "not far enough West" to count as part of the region.[39]

Just four years after publishing *The Big Rock Candy Mountain*—and seven years before he published his study of John Wesley Powell's vision of a region defined by aridity—Stegner directly articulated his vision of an environmentally defined West. In 1947 the editors of *Look* magazine published a travel guide to a part of the United States they called *The Central Northwest*. It awkwardly defined the region as North and South Dakota, Montana, Idaho, Nevada, Utah, Wyoming, Colorado, Kansas, and Nebraska. Stegner, associated with *Look* since the publication of his book *One Nation* (1945), wrote the introduction.[40]

In that introduction Stegner completely ignored this untidy invention of magazine editors.[41] Instead of calling these states the Northwest, Stegner described them as the American West. Despite its rich variety of landscapes, he argued that dryness defined the region. "The American West lies between the 98th Meridian and the crestline of the Sierra Nevada," he suggested. "Between those boundaries the rainfall averages less than twenty inches annually," he continued. Despite being "made up of three distinct belts—plains, mountains and desert—it is one region." In this travel guidebook, Stegner chose to follow the timely trend of regional definitions based on environmental features.[42]

Although this was one of the first articulations of Stegner's arid regional West, his brief introduction to *The Central Northwest* is largely forgotten. His longstanding commitment to define a regional West via aridity is not. Stegner's decision to focus on the environment involved willful forgetting as much as thoughtful creation. The capital-intensive and extractive Northwest, his parents' regional home, fell away. The arid West replaced it.

Stegner's turn to the arid West resonated widely. As one of the most visible regional voices in postwar America, Stegner's understanding of environment and place took hold in popular culture.[43] To be sure, he did not change regional monikers by himself. Internal contradictions within the Minneapolis-centered Northwest's economy came to the fore in the 1930s, hastening the region's decline. Others, like Walter Prescott Webb, made a case for aridity as the demarcation of place during that same decade. But Stegner's widely read and cited intellectual rationale for an American West fully subsumed earlier visions of region and framed the tangled relationship between identity and place for most.

As Stegner's regional West became generally accepted by the 1960s, the second Northwest moniker largely fell out of use. To be sure, the

Northern Pacific railroad adopted the slogan "Main Street of the Northwest"—referring to its connection of St. Paul to Puget Sound—in the mid-1940s. And in the region's metropole, the term took much longer to fade away. Minneapolis's WCCO-AM radio, whose powerful nightly broadcasts could be heard across the continent, called itself the "Good Neighbor to the Northwest" well into the 1970s. As late as 1982, the 10 o'clock weeknight news opening for Minneapolis's CBS-TV affiliate, WCCO-TV, made a direct reference to its Twin Cities broadcast area as the "Northwest." Even today, the Ninth Federal Reserve District embodies the mostly unrecognized region, quietly enduring in policy and financial circles.[44]

Stegner's contributions to the erasure of the Northwest continue to resonate today. For instance, long-standing debates among historians about what counts as western owe much to Stegner's environmental definitions.[45] In the 2010s the turn to region (and away from broadly construed frontiers) among western historians even gave rise to a New Midwestern History.[46] This new initiative to study a distinct region in the middle of the continent now sports an academic journal and annual conference. Yet, just like Stegner and most western historians, the New Midwestern History does violence to the ghostly Northwest. It's effort to better understand the Midwest—which includes a recent edited collection dedicated to clearly defining the boundary between the Midwest and Great Plains in the space formerly known as the Northwest—reflects the lasting power of Stegner's erasure (as well as a deep amnesia among scholars who study the Midwest).[47]

Stegner's active effort to downplay other regional constructions at the expense of an arid West helped him explode persistent myths. But it also obscured the extensive role of capital in placemaking that connected Minnesota to the Dakotas and Montana.[48] Furthermore, downplaying the role of capital in regional development made it easier for Stegner to ignore the settler colonialism that extractive industries bound up in metropole-hinterland relationships perpetuated.[49] After all, settler colonialism is not only about identities and culture and land but also the commodification of landscapes and resource bases.

Through his environmentally defined regional constructions, Stegner failed to acknowledge the structural forces that powered conquest and colonization and sustain settler colonialism today. Indeed, his emphasis on aridity as a primary factor for defining the region deflected and disguised the significance of settler capitalism in placemaking.[50]

Finally, capitalism's role in driving climate change make the consequences of Stegner's (and others) decision to ignore the history of capitalism's placemaking power in the continent's center loom large. The emergence of North Dakota and Montana as the center of America's coal industry in the 1970s and the epicenter of the Bakken oil boom of the 2000s makes the area once known as the Northwest more important than ever.[51] Home really is where you hang your hat—and after a childhood in motion, Stegner helped delineate a region where he could psychically hang his. But in so doing, he contributed to the erasure of an older region, one whose history helps us better understand some of the roots of our current climate quandary.

Notes

1. Wallace Stegner, *The American West as Living Space* (Ann Arbor: University of Michigan Press, 1987), vi, 3.
2. "The Dean of Western Letters," *Newsweek*, April 25, 1993. See also Richard H. Cracroft, "'I Have Never Recovered from the Country': The American West of Wallace Stegner," in *A Companion to the Regional Literatures of America*, ed. Charles L. Crow (Malden MA: Blackwell, 2008), 551–71.
3. Historian Katherine Morrissey defines a ghost region as "a region with layers of memory, history and meaning which continue to haunt the present." See Katherine Morrissey, *Mental Territories: Mapping the Inland Empire* (Ithaca NY: Cornell University Press, 1997), 166.
4. Donald Meinig, "Three American Northwests: Some Perspectives in Historical Geography," paper read at the annual meeting of the Association of American Geographers, April 1, 1957, Cincinnati OH, abstract in *Annals of the Association of American Geographers* 47, no. 2 (June 1957): 170–71. Thanks also to Dale Martin for pointing this out to me in a conversation in August 2018.

5. Molly Rozum, *Grasslands Grown: Creating Place on the U.S. Northern Plains and Canadian Prairies* (Lincoln: University of Nebraska Press, 2021), 304–13; John M. Findlay, "A Fishy Proposition: Regional Identity in the Pacific Northwest," in *Many Wests: Place, Culture, and Regional Identity*, ed. David M. Wrobel and Michael C. Steiner (Lawrence: University of Kansas Press, 1997), 37–70; Susan Kollin, "North and Northwest: Theorizing the Regional Literatures of Alaska and the Pacific Northwest," in Crow, *Companion to the Regional Literatures*, 412–31; John M. Findlay, "Something in the Soil: Literature and Regional Identity in the 20th-Century Pacific Northwest," *Pacific Northwest Quarterly* 97, no. 4 (Fall 2006): 179–89.

6. Donald Meinig called the Northwest during this period "an approximation of the Twin Cities nodal region." Meinig, "Three American Northwests," 171.

7. Stegner's focus on aridity obscures capital's role in the transformation of landscapes and in placemaking even in otherwise thoughtful analyses of Stegner's work. See, for example, Thomas R. Vale, "Nature and People in the American West: Guidance from Wallace Stegner's Sense of Place," in *Wallace Stegner and the Continental Vision: Essays on Literature, History, and Landscape*, ed. Curt Meine (Washington DC: Island Press, 1997), 163–79. Donald Worster consistently emphasized the role of capital in plains history. See Donald Worster, *Under Western Skies: Nature and History in the American West* (New York: Oxford University Press, 1992). For capital's role in fostering climate change, see Andreas Malm, *Fossil Capital: The Rise of Steam Power and the Roots of Global Warming* (New York: Verso, 2015).

8. Two examples of historians engaged in more thoughtful versions of regional analysis are Flannery Burke, *A Land Apart: The Southwest and the Nation in the Twentieth Century* (Tucson: University of Arizona Press, 2017); and Morrissey, *Mental Territories*.

9. Marxist, feminist, and other critical geographers have explored theories of space and place for decades. Some of the most important works include Neil Smith, *Uneven Development: Nature, Capitalism, and the Production of Space* (New York: Verso, 1984); David Harvey, *Spaces of Capital: Toward a Critical Geography* (New York: Routledge, 2001); Erik Swyngedouw, *Glocalisations* (Philadelphia: Temple University Press,

2004); Linda McDowell, *Gender, Identity and Place: Understanding Feminist Geographies* (Cambridge: Polity, 1999); Lise Nelson and Joni Seager, eds., *A Companion to Feminist Geography* (Malden MA: Blackwell, 2005).

10. Meinig, "Three American Northwests," 171.

11. Jeffrey Ostler, "The Plains," in *The Oxford Handbook of American Indian History*, ed. Frederick Hoxie (New York: Oxford University Press, 2016).

12. Walter L. Hixson, "Adaptation, Resistance, and Representation in the Modern US Settler State," in *The Routledge Handbook of the History of Settler Colonialism*, ed. Edward Cavanagh and Lorenzo Veraceni (New York: Routledge, 2017), 169–84.

13. In the late nineteenth and early twentieth centuries, the *Northwestern Miller's* status as the flour trade's most important periodical was widely recognized. See, for example, "The Northwestern Miller," *New York Times*, December 24, 1904, 6.

14. William Cronon, *Nature's Metropolis: Chicago and the Making of the Great West* (New York: W. W. Norton, 1991); Richard White, *Railroaded: The Transcontinentals and the Making of Modern America* (New York: W. W. Norton, 2011); Noam Maggor, *Brahmin Capitalism: Frontiers of Wealth and Populism in America's First Gilded Age* (Cambridge MA: Harvard University Press, 2017).

15. Neil Smith, *Uneven Development: Nature, Capitalism, and the Production of Space* (New York: Verso, 1984); Thomas Andrews, *Killing for Coal: America's Deadliest Labor War* (Cambridge MA: Harvard University Press, 2010). For Indigenous peoples and capitalism, see Brian Hosmer and Colleen O'Neill, eds., *Native Pathways: American Indian Culture and Economic Development in the Twentieth Century* (Boulder: University of Colorado Press, 2004).

16. In New York City—by then, the nation's financial center—a Minneapolis-centric vision of metropole and hinterlands defined the Northwest. See, for example, "Flour Milling in the Northwest," *New York Times*, January 5, 1902; and "Northwest Conditions Favorable," *Wall Street Journal*, June 19, 1906.

17. James Livingston, *Origins of the Federal Reserve System: Money, Class, and Corporate Capitalism, 1890–1913* (Ithaca NY: Cornell University Press, 1986); Donald R. Wells, *The Federal Reserve System: A History* (Jefferson NC: McFarland, 2004).

18. The effort to define Minneapolis as a primary financial node can be found in United States Reserve Bank Organization Committee, *Location of Reserve Districts in the United States* (Washington DC: Government Printing Office, 1914), 211–66.

19. "Our Helena Branch," Federal Reserve Bank of Minneapolis website, https://www.minneapolisfed.org/about-us/our-helena-branch.

20. Nicolas Witschi, "'The Culture of the Northwest': A Rediscovered Essay by Mary Austin," *North Dakota Quarterly* 65, no. 4 (1998): 80–90.

21. Michael J. Lansing, *Insurgent Democracy: The Nonpartisan League in North American Politics* (Chicago: University of Chicago Press, 2015).

22. Many thanks to Sara Gregg for pointing out the significance of the Federal Loan Act of 1916 in this story. Sara M. Gregg, "From Breadbasket to Dust Bowl: Rural Credit, the World War I Plow-Up, and the Transformation of American Agriculture," *Great Plains Quarterly* 35, no. 2 (Spring 2015): 129–66; Christopher W. Shaw, "'Tired of Being Exploited': The Grassroots Origin of the Federal Farm Loan of 1916," *Agricultural History* 92, no. 4 (Fall 2018): 512–40.

23. Gregg, "From Breadbasket to Dust Bowl," 156; Mary W. M. Hargreaves, *Dry Farming in the Northern Great Plains: Years of Readjustment, 1920–1990* (Lawrence: University Press of Kansas, 1993); Victor G. Pickett and Roland S. Vaile, *The Decline of Northwestern Flour Milling*, University of Minnesota Studies in Economics and Business 5 (Minneapolis: University of Minnesota Press, 1933); Michael J. Lansing, "From Wheat to Wheaties: Minneapolis, the Great Plains, and the Transformation of American Food," in *The Greater Plains: Rethinking a Region's Environmental Histories*, ed. Brian Frehner and Kathleen A. Brosnan (Lincoln: University of Nebraska Press, 2021), 230–52; Charles Runford Walker, *American City: A Rank and File History of Minneapolis* (1937; rpt., Minneapolis: University of Minnesota Press, 2005).

24. Edward Alsworth Ross, "The Middle West," *Century Magazine* 83, no. 4 (February 1912): 609–15; James R. Shortridge, *The Middle West: It's Meaning in American Culture* (Lawrence: University Press of Kansas, 1989), 25–38.

25. Google Books Ngram Viewer, "Pacific Northwest," April 11, 2019, *The Pacific Northwest: Facts Relating to the History, Topography, Climate, Soil, Agriculture, Forests, Fisheries, Mineral Resources, Commerce, Industry,*

Lands, Means of Communication, Etc., Etc., Etc., of Oregon and Washington Territory (New York: Bureau of Immigration, Portland OR, 1882), 1. Shortridge incorrectly implies a much earlier date for widespread adoption for the term "Pacific Northwest." Shortridge, *Middle West*, 20–26.

26. Lauren Coats and Nihad M. Farooq, "Regionalism in the Era of the New Deal," in Crow, *Companion to the Regional Literatures*, 74–91. Much of this 1930s regional expression connected to or articulated left-of-center politics. See Michael C. Steiner, "Introduction: Varieties of Western Regionalism," in *Regionalists on the Left: Radical Voices from the American West*, ed. Michael C. Steiner (Norman: University of Oklahoma Press, 2013), 1–20.

27. Raymond B. Fosdick, *The Story of the Rockefeller Foundation* (New York: Harper & Brothers, 1952), 256–59; Molly P. Rozum, "Grasslands Grown: A Twentieth-Century Sense of Place on North America's Prairies and Plains" (PhD diss., University of North Carolina–Chapel Hill, 2001), 296–340; Walter Prescott Webb, *The Great Plains: A Study in Institutions and Environment* (Boston: Ginn, 1931). For the significance of Webb's book on this count, see Molly P. Rozum, "The Great Plains and Middle West in 'Middle America': Historiographic Reflections," *Middle West Review* 4, no. 1 (Fall 2017): 71–84.

28. Quoted in Rozum, "Grasslands Grown," 303.

29. Rozum, "Grasslands Grown," 303. For one of the more sophisticated demarcations of the Great Plains as a region, see James R. Shortridge, "The Heart of the Prairie: Culture Areas in the Central and Northern Great Plains," *Great Plains Quarterly* 8 (Fall 1988): 206–21. The rise of the appellation "Great Plains"—nearly simultaneous with the rise of the term "Upper Midwest"—resulted in especially fuzzy boundaries between the two by the 1960s.

30. Dan Flores, "Citizen of a Larger Country: Wallace Stegner, the Environment, and the West," in *Wallace Stegner: Man and Writer*, ed. Charles Rankin (Albuquerque: University of New Mexico Press, 1996), 73–86. Hsuan L. Hsu notes that "literary works produce, reimagine, and actively restructure regional identities in the minds and hearts of their readers." See Hsuan L. Hsu, "Literature and Regional Production," *American Literary History* 17, no. 1 (Spring 2005): 36–37.

31. Wallace Stegner and Richard W. Etulain, *Stegner: Conversations on History and Literature* (Salt Lake City: University of Utah Press, 1983), 5. Rozum notes that Stegner "did not generally identify with the Northwest personally." See Rozum, *Grasslands Grown*, 308.

32. Kenneth C. Mason, "The Big Rock Candy Mountain: The Consequences of a Delusory American Dream," *Great Plains Quarterly* 6, no. 1 (Winter 1996): 34–43.

33. Wallace Stegner, *The Big Rock Candy Mountain* (New York: Duell, Sloan, and Pearce, 1943), 380.

34. Stegner, *Big Rock Candy Mountain*, 422–23.

35. Stegner, *Big Rock Candy Mountain*, 458.

36. The interviewer refers to the "Upper Midwest"—a regional designation that by the 1940s began to replace the term "Northwest" when describing Minnesota, North and South Dakota, Iowa, and Wisconsin. A Google Ngram search reveals the first printed usage of "Upper Midwest" that I could find: *Minnesota Libraries* (a quarterly publication of Minnesota's Department of Education) in 1946. James Shortridge's earliest documentation of the use of the term is 1955. Shortridge, *Middle West*, 109.

37. Wallace Stegner, "GLR/Interview," *Great Lakes Review* 2, no. 1 (Summer 1975): 1–25.

38. Stegner, "GLR/Interview," 5; Wallace Stegner, "Finding the Place: A Migrant Childhood," in *Growing Up Western*, ed. Clarus Backes (New York: Alfred Knopf, 1989).

39. Lois Phillips Hudson, "The Big Rock Candy Mountain: No Roots—and No Frontier," *South Dakota Review* 9, no. 1 (1971): 8–10. See, for example, Jennie A. Camp, "Angling for Repose: Demythologizing the American West in Wallace Stegner's *The Big Rock Candy Mountain*," *North Dakota Quarterly* 74, no. 2 (2007): 19–39.

40. Wallace Stegner, in collaboration with the editors of *Look*, *Look at America: The Central Northwest* (Boston: Houghton Mifflin, 1947). See also Rozum, *Grasslands Grown*, 308, 315.

41. *Look*'s editors may have been following Howard Odum's 1938 book *American Regionalism*, one of the most influential summations of American regionalism in its time. The book included a chapter titled "The Northwest and Its Great Plains." It defined the Northwest in exactly the same way as the travel guide. Howard W. Odum and Harry Estill Moore,

American Regionalism: A Cultural-Historical Approach to National Integration (New York: Henry Holt, 1938).

42. Stegner and the editors of *Look, Look at America*, 14.

43. Philip L. Fradkin, *Wallace Stegner and the American West* (New York: Knopf, 2008).

44. Dale Martin, *Ties, Rails, and Telegraph Wires: Railroads and Communities in Montana and the West* (Helena: Montana Historical Society Press, 2018), 14; *Good Neighbor to the Northwest: 1924–1974* (Minneapolis: WCCO-Radio, 1974); WCCO-TV, "News Opens," accessed April 10, 2019, https://www.youtube.com/watch?v=uYZuXHSJzmQ.

45. For the direct connections between Stegner and the New Western History's regional perspectives, see Stegner and Etulain, *Stegner*.

46. At the 2011 Western History Association Conference in Oakland, California, William Cronon noted the growing exclusion of the Middle West from western history: "I still regard the Western History Association as a proper home of the Middle West, but I no longer actually believe that the WHA believes that, that the Midwest is part of western history." See "Teaching Western History," roundtable discussion, C-SPAN, October 11, 2011, https://www.c-span.org/video/?302737-1/teaching-western-history. For a summary of the New Midwestern History, see Kritika Agarwal, "Midwestern History Is on the Map: Scholars Revive a Dormant Field," *Perspectives on History* 56, no. 9 (December 2018), https://www.historians.org/publications-and-directories/perspectives-on-history/december-2018/midwestern-history-is-on-the-map-scholars-revive-a-dormant-field.

47. Jon K. Lauck, ed., *The Interior Borderlands: Regional Identity in the Midwest and Great Plains* (Sioux Falls SD: Center for Western Studies, 2018).

48. Brett J. Olsen, "Wallace Stegner and the Environmental Ethic: Environmentalism as a Rejection of Western Myth," *Western American Literature* 29, no. 2 (Summer 1994): 123–42. The emergence of a Montana-centric literature stems in many ways from this unmooring from questions of capital and the separation of Montana from Minneapolis–St. Paul as an economic metropole. See Susan Kollin, "Re-envisioning the Big Sky: Regional Identity, Spatial Logics, and the Literature of Montana," in Crow, *Companion to the Regional Literatures*, 344–62. At least one scholar suggests the opposite—that by focusing on the environment, Stegner

consistently critiqued the transformations of the land driven by capital. See John L. Thomas, *A Country in the Mind: Wallace Stegner, Bernard DeVoto, History, and the American Land* (New York: Routledge, 2000).

49. For settler colonialism's relationship to capitalism, see Anthony J. Hall, *Earth into Property: Colonization, Decolonization, and Capitalism* (Montreal: McGill-Queen's University Press, 2010); and James Parisot, *How America Became Capitalist: Imperial Expansion and the Conquest of the West* (London: Pluto Press, 2019).

50. See, for instance, the critique of Stegner in Elizabeth Cook-Lynn, *Why I Can't Read Wallace Stegner and Other Essays: A Tribal Voice* (Madison: University of Wisconsin Press, 1996).

51. Ryan Driscoll Tate, "The Saudi Arabia of Coal: The Making of America's Energy Frontier, 1965–1995" (PhD diss., Rutgers University, 2019); Jason W. Moore, ed., *Anthropocene or Capitalocene: Nature, History, and the Crisis of Capitalism* (Oakland CA: PM Press, 2016); Malm, *Fossil Capital.*

4

Exploits against
the Effete

Wallace Stegner and
Bernard DeVoto,
Men of Western Letters

FLANNERY BURKE

In the summer of 1946, the writer Bernard DeVoto set off on an extensive western vacation with his family. The father of two sons and husband to the culinary editor Avis DeVoto, "Benny" had made his living
as a writer, working first as a professor of English at Northwestern
University in 1922, then as a part-time instructor at Harvard, then as
a writer and editor for *Harper's Magazine* and the *Saturday Review of
Literature*, and, ultimately, as a historian. His trilogy on the history
of the American West, *The Year of Decision: 1846*, *Across the Wide
Missouri* (winner of the Pulitzer Prize for History), and *The Course of
Empire* (winner of the National Book Award for Nonfiction), remained
classics in the field until the close of the twentieth century.[1] Of these,
only the first, *Year of Decision*, had been published in 1946 as he set
off to discover the land on which he was, presumably, an authority. As
Wallace Stegner, DeVoto's friend, fellow westerner, and fellow writer,
observed: "After almost a quarter of a century of intense writing activity,
he was identified with the Rocky Mountain West in the mind of every
reader who knew his name."[2]

Stegner, though, could not help mentioning that DeVoto did not
actually know the West, or at least, not the West with which DeVoto
had associated himself. Although DeVoto had grown up in Ogden,
Utah, "there were whole regions of the West that he did not know at

all." Stegner observed that "he had apparently never visited the Northwest, California, Nevada, Texas, or Oklahoma; and he knew southern Utah and Arizona only casually, and no part of Idaho except the southern edge. By 1946 he had lived more years in Cambridge than in Utah. Westward he walked free, like Thoreau, but he did so largely in Thoreau's fashion—in books and in imagination, from a narrow New England base."[3] Stegner's gentle gibe, one typical of his 1974 biography of DeVoto, *The Uneasy Chair*, revealed a central theme that undergirded their friendship: they were western writers. It was an identity with which the two men had, as Stegner's title for DeVoto's biography suggested, an uneasy relationship. If one was a western writer, then one was not an eastern writer. And if one was not an eastern writer, then, Stegner sometimes feared, one couldn't be a writer at all.

In his published presentation of himself and his friend, Stegner contributed to the creation of the East as a region.[4] He furthered his career as a western writer when he scorned the eastern critics who had typecast him . . . as a western writer. In a western take on the longstanding regional rivalry between Boston and New York City, he embraced New England but rejected New York, then blamed New York for rejecting him. Unlike an earlier generation of writers, mostly white women, who had cultivated the connections between New York City and the arts communities of Taos and Santa Fe, he scoffed at the city and its emissaries to the Southwest as effete and precious. He celebrated the natural world of the Rocky Mountain West, circulated among its most ardent defenders, and brought a western conservationism to the very highest levels of government. In his influential work, the East shrank to the object of Stegner's resentment, New York City, while the West shrank to his area of study, the Rocky Mountains and its watersheds.

In crafting the western writer by way of contrast, Stegner and DeVoto presented themselves and men of the National Park and National Forest Service as practical, hardworking, community-minded models of masculinity, an equally manly but superior alternative to the myth of the individualist cowboy. Their model facilitated their advocacy for public lands, but it excluded men and women with ties to the New

York literary community and the places such as northern New Mexico for which such writers advocated. They furthered representations of easterners as effeminate and westerners as masculine *and* white when they decried New York's literary establishment. Stegner and DeVoto did not only "theorize western literature according to an implicit masculine norm," as literary critic Krista Comer has shown.[5] They also theorized the West according to *their* masculine norm, which limited their support for a more diverse cast of western writers, western places, and western people.

Because Stegner played such a prominent role in defining public lands policy, western history, and western literature, the effects of his work extended well beyond his friendship with DeVoto. Stegner's efforts on behalf of western writers' inclusion led intentionally and unintentionally to exclusion—even of other western writers. The accelerating effects of climate change, the international push for racial justice, the resurgence of Indigenous activism, a reconfiguration of gender identities, and the COVID-19 pandemic have thrust North America into another recalibration of regional meaning and significance that recalls the pivotal historical moments following World War II that surface in Stegner's depiction of DeVoto. Those who call themselves westerners are redefining what it means to be local, how far they are willing to go from the places they call home, and who they consider fellow travelers. Inheritors of Stegner's legacy, western writers today stand to create both a more expansive and a more realistic vision of the future. Who and what that vision includes is up to us.[6]

In many respects Stegner and DeVoto chose opposite paths that arrived at the same destination. DeVoto steadfastly worked his way east, leaving Utah to attend Harvard University in 1915 and returning west only temporarily before teaching at Northwestern in 1922 and at Harvard beginning in 1927. Stegner presents DeVoto's ambition in *The Uneasy Chair* as fixed on a writing career in New England, headquartered at Harvard and nurtured at Vermont's annual Bread Loaf Writers' Conference. As literary critic Melody Graulich explains, "the working-class Westerner's sense of cultural inferiority to the 'privileged' East, a theme Stegner often explored in autobiographical writing, is at the heart of his portrayal of DeVoto."[7] Although DeVoto never succeeded in securing a full appointment at Harvard, he did make his home at Cambridge and wrote for eastern publications, including *Harper's Magazine*, which published his regular column "The Easy Chair" (the source of Stegner's title) beginning in 1935 and ending with his death in 1955.

The work that led DeVoto to succeed in his ambitions was his writing on the American West, particularly his historical trilogy, but it is uncertain if becoming a western regional expert was DeVoto's original goal. As Stegner speculated, "The book review editors who in 1925 had type-cast [DeVoto] as a western authority had either been extraordinarily prescient or had exerted the strongest sort of influence on his development."[8] DeVoto published novels and articles about topics other than the West, but it was his writing on Mark Twain, his editing of the Lewis and Clark journals, his trilogy on the history of the frontier, and his conservationist writing that sealed his reputation as a western writer and reinforced his identity as a western man.[9] The magazines that paid for his work actively solicited such topics from the very beginning of his career in 1920, when his Harvard professors and writing mentors encouraged him to write something "on the state of politics in the West."[10] The pattern continued. Harry Sions of *Holiday Magazine* wrote DeVoto's agent in 1953, just two years before DeVoto died, requesting an article in which DeVoto would point out "Western 'differences' . . . 'Are Western women a type?' 'Is there a greater friendliness among people?' 'Is there a scenic or environmental atmosphere which makes for these differences?' With Ben's known devotion to the cause of national parks, public lands, and Western terrain he could make a case."[11] DeVoto made his career writing about the frontier of white U.S. settlement, a topic that enhanced his reputation as a western man and a western writer. As he advised Stegner in 1937, early in their friendship, just before Stegner left the University of Utah and began working at the University of Wisconsin: "Teaching is an excellent vocation for [the young writer] if his mind is vigorous enough to resist the academic infection. The turnover is large, and if your academic standing is satisfactory you can

6. The 1938 Bread Loaf Writers' Conference. Top row: Raymond Everitt, Robeson Bailey, Herbert Agar, Herschel Brickell, Wallace Stegner, Fletcher Pratt; middle row: Gorham Munson, Bernard DeVoto, Theodore Morrison, Robert Frost, John Gassner; bottom row: Mary Stegner, Helen Everitt, Kay Morrison, Eleanor Chilton (Mrs. Herbert Agar). Courtesy the Wallace Earle Stegner Photograph Collection, J. Willard Marriott Library, University of Utah.

probably get farther east than you are." DeVoto had gone east, and he found there persuasive and powerful encouragement to write about the West. As he continued in his letter to Stegner: "These days regional and provincial cultures are extremely promising, and I think will be more important in our literary future."[12]

If DeVoto's regionalism was imposed, Stegner's was self-consciously cultivated. Twelve years DeVoto's junior, Stegner had greater freedom to choose what kind of writer he wanted to be in part because of the ground that DeVoto had cleared. Stegner, too, worked at Bread Loaf (beginning in 1938) and taught at Harvard from 1939 through

1945, but when he left Harvard for California, he made the West his home.[13] Philip L. Fradkin, in his biography of Stegner, asserts that "the acquaintances and friends that Stegner cultivated at Bread Loaf would lift him out of the boondocks of the Mountain West and the Middle West and launch him into the elevated ranks of East Coast teaching, writing, and publishing."[14] Although Stegner had taught in Wisconsin and DeVoto had taught at Northwestern, neither man saw the Midwest nor Chicago as a part of the "elevated ranks." Both men acknowledged the male writers and artists that had made Chicago a creative hub for the region in the late nineteenth and early twentieth centuries, but they considered that literary florescence a stage that had passed, a kind of western writers' frontier in reverse.[15] DeVoto looked east to what he considered deeper literary roots while Stegner's entrance to "the elevated ranks" of Bread Loaf and Harvard allowed him to choose a position in California in 1945 and to choose to write about the Mountain West for much of his career.

Stegner made it his goal to separate a regional West from a provincial West permanently ascribed to the "boondocks." In Stegner's view, regional writing identified and shared universal experiences through the material, lived experience of a particular place. In contrast, provincial literary communities, for Stegner, celebrated any writing from a place solely because it was local and regardless of its quality.[16] Stegner dedicated himself to creating the literary institutions—from public funding for the humanities to local bookstores—that would cultivate regional literature in the West. In the heady, rich days of postwar California, he became a powerful supporter of the humanities in the West from his position as a professor of writing at Stanford University. He worked as the West Coast editor of Houghton Mifflin and served on the editorial board of the *Pacific Spectator*, a journal that began with support from the Pacific Coast Committee on the Humanities and the American Council of Learned Societies.[17] Near the end of his career, and thirty-five years after DeVoto's death in 1955, Stegner celebrated in the *Los Angeles Times Book Review* what had been, in many respects, his life's work:

It is exhilarating to me, 60 years after I graduated from a Western university and 45 years after I made the decision to come back West to live and work, to see the country beyond the 100th meridian finally taking its place as a respected and self-respecting part of the literary world. I used to yearn for the day when the West would have not only writers but all the infrastructure of the literary life—a book-publishing industry, a range of literary and critical magazines, good bookstores, a reviewing corps not enslaved by foreign and eastern opinion, support organizations such as PEN, an alert reading public, and all the rest.[18]

When Stegner left Harvard in 1945, he set himself the task of building the institutions that he considered necessary for western writers and regional western writing. In 1990 he claimed success.

For Stegner, regional literary institutions guarded against provincialism, and not just in the West. The East could be guilty of its own provincialism, a trait that Stegner identified particularly in its treatment of him. In a series of oft-quoted interviews with historian Richard Etulain published in 1983 in *Stegner: Conversations on History and Literature*, Stegner complained that the *New York Times* called him the dean of western writers and got his name wrong "all in the same instant."[19] As one of Stegner's students, the writer Wendell Berry, put it: "The adjective 'western,' as all regional writers will understand, would have been dismissive even if the name had been correctly given. This is the regionalism of New York, which will use the West, indeed depend on it, but not care for it."[20] Berry articulated the resentment that Stegner felt when the eastern press used the designation "western writer," as well as the frustration that Stegner and Berry alike felt when they were unable to stir concern in the East for the western environment. Berry also marked the East as a region, something, Berry noted, that Stegner had taught him to do.

Stegner did not find all of the East and its literary institutions provincial. New England, particularly the New England of the annual Bread Loaf Writers' Conference at Middlebury College in Vermont, was altogether a different East than New York City. The conference had its roots in summer sessions at Middlebury College in the early 1920s when both Robert Frost and Willa Cather served as instructors. The formal conference at Middlebury's Bread Loaf Inn began in 1926 under the direction of John Farrar, a poet, editor of the literary monthly *The Bookman*, and later cofounder of the publishing house Farrar, Straus & Giroux. Farrar dedicated the event to nurturing writers with guidance from editors and other professionals. Instructors in the inaugural year included Farrar himself and Harriet Monroe, the founder and editor of *Poetry: A Magazine of Verse*. Frost lectured in 1927 and returned regularly thereafter.[21] Ted Morrison, a writing professor at Harvard and a former editor at *Atlantic Monthly*, became Bread Loaf's director in 1932 and hired DeVoto and Stegner both. Morrison's wife, Kay, became Frost's personal secretary in 1938. She helped nurture the connection between the poet and the conference.[22] As director, Ted Morrison managed, in DeVoto's words, "to make coherent what had been an amusing and sometimes brilliant but haphazard experiment."[23] Stegner and DeVoto both adored it. DeVoto dedicated the occasional "Easy Chair" column to the conference, and Stegner described Bread Loaf in the language of masculine athleticism as "frenziedly, manically literary. . . . It was argument, gossip, news . . . hikes . . . swims . . . square dances . . . furiously competitive tennis . . . an annual softball game down at Robert Frost's Ripton farm . . . and . . . a lot of not-uncompetitive drinking."[24]

A key figure tying Stegner, DeVoto, Morrison, and Bread Loaf together was the editor and writing instructor Edith Mirrielees. Originally from Big Timber, Montana, Mirrielees became an English professor at Stanford University, her alma mater, in 1909 and is most commonly remembered as a beloved instructor of John Steinbeck. After Mills College refused Stegner a job in 1945, Mirrielees recruited him to lead Stanford's writing program.[25] Mirrielees, along with her sister, Lucia, an assistant professor of English at the University of Montana, both worked for Bread Loaf at its inception.[26] Mirrielees and DeVoto were "improbably, the closest of friends." According to Stegner, in low moments, DeVoto turned to her. "And how could that gentle, inexperienced Victorian maiden lady ever have developed the understanding she had of the black caves of the spirit?" Stegner queried. "Yet she had, she *knew*."[27] Casting Mirrielees in the role of a maiden lady enhanced her eastern credentials. Uniting her with Morrison underscored them. The two teachers acted as mentors to both Stegner and DeVoto and allowed them to present themselves as both western men and western writers.

The camaraderie and dedication to writing that Stegner found at Bread Loaf, and, to some extent, at Harvard, led him to present Boston in more positive terms than he did New York. As he put it: "If I had gone to New York looking for an entry into the literary establishment I could not have done a quarter as well as I did in the intimate atmosphere of Bread Loaf."[28] Later in life he reflected: "Having left Harvard in 1945, I more or less withdrew from American literature. I was much more in it there, even though I didn't live in New York."[29] Stegner not only participated regularly at Bread Loaf following his departure from Harvard, but he also spent summers in the village of Greensboro, Vermont, and set his 1947 novel, *Second Growth*, there along with portions of his last novel, *Crossing to Safety*, published in 1987.[30] Greensboro functioned for Stegner somewhat as Ripton, Vermont, had for Frost. For both Frost and Stegner, New England broadly and Vermont specifically was a place and a community that nurtured their writing.

DeVoto, too, prized New England over New York City. He called himself "an apprentice New Englander." When he left Harvard briefly in 1936 to edit the *Saturday Review*, he lamented in an "Easy Chair" column, "It was a long way, in 1915, from Utah to Harvard Square, but it's a longer one, in 1936, from Harvard Square to New York." In a letter to a confidante he called Bread Loaf "the best club I've ever belonged to."[31] The DeVotos' home in Cambridge served as a headquarters for writers and literary Harvard students and professors. DeVoto memorialized their tradition of weekly cocktails in his book *The Hour*, and he cultivated students in his own image—a western man in the feminine East. "What do you do," he once asked a Harvard student upon learning that he neither drank nor smoked, "to smell like a man?"[32] DeVoto incorporated as much of the spirit of Bread Loaf into his daily life and work as he could, a spirit he found lacking in New York City.

Living in the city did not change his mind. Stegner explained that DeVoto arrived in New York intent to "never make the New Yorker's mistake of taking New York for America."[33] To that end DeVoto went to war against the city's literary left. In the pages of the *Saturday Review*, DeVoto lambasted publications such as *Seven Arts*, *The Dial*, and both the old and the new *Masses*. He decried modernist writers such as Ezra Pound and T. S. Eliot and activists such as Emma Goldman. When his biography of Mark Twain met more critical acclaim than had Van Wyck Brooks's, he drove home his triumph, a triumph that was not just his but, according to Stegner, the West's.[34] Stegner proclaimed that "[DeVoto] was not simply a red Indian dancing the scalp dance and striking the pole and boasting of his exploits against the effete. He was a sort of champion of the West, a yea sayer where there had previously been a chorus of scornful nays. . . . *Mark Twain's America* was a hymn of praise, not only a corrective report on the West and the frontier, but a celebration."[35] DeVoto's brief stint in New York City was not as the anointed western writer of the literary elite but as the self-appointed critic of the East.

In a career that otherwise closely guarded against provincialism, Stegner engaged in provincial settler colonial tropes when expressing his and DeVoto's frustrations with the East. Thus, Stegner rendered DeVoto as a "red Indian dancing the scalp dance," a cartoonish invocation of the West and westerners that dehumanized and offended Native readers and probably reinforced eastern expectations of westerners more than it satirized them.[36] Significantly, he portrayed DeVoto as "boasting of his exploits against the effete," a framing of the West as masculine and the East as feminine that Stegner employed most often when decrying eastern, specifically New York's, provincialism. Stegner, moreover, did not stop with an allusion to the effete. He made his views clear when he concluded: "All the old whipping boys, all those whose ideas and ways of thinking [DeVoto] had been resisting since he was a schoolboy, were there before him in New York, stooped over, hands grasping ankles, backsides enticingly bared."[37] Stegner presented himself and DeVoto not just as western writers but as western men and claimed regional writing for the West as an aggressive, masculine gesture against a feminized eastern literary establishment.[38]

Surprisingly, DeVoto had predicted just such opinions in his essay "Queen City of the Plains and Peaks," which he first published in the *Pacific Spectator*, a journal that Mirrielees edited beginning in 1947. DeVoto criticized westerners for a reflexive homophobia while also assuming that all writers were men. "Because writing is not male as maleness goes in the Western fantasy he [the writer] must be a homosexual," he observed. He called such sentiments a product of a western "vigilante state of mind" and concluded that a career in the East surpassed one in the West, where male writers chafed against the narrow channels of expression available to them. As DeVoto concluded: "This fixed condition of writing in the West . . . destroys some who might have had rewarding careers where I live. And in some who achieve effective functioning because they fight well I see scars I cannot like. . . . It is unhappily true that, however self-reliant the Western writer may be and however content in his decision to stay West, he is under some pressure to feel inferior simply because he is not East."[39] If DeVoto was referring to his old friend when he described those who were scarred but fought well, Stegner did not acknowledge the lesson twenty years later.

Instead, Stegner crafted a different masculine symbol in the West. In the Author's Note to *The Uneasy Chair*, Stegner described how he and DeVoto "were both Westerners by birth and upbringing, novelists by intention, teachers by necessity, and historians by the sheer compulsion of the region that shaped us. The same compulsion that made amateur historians of us made us conservationists as well: we both wrote a good deal on the subject of conservation, and we both served on the Advisory Board for National Parks, Historical Sites, Buildings, and Monuments."[40] Close alliances with Chet Olson of the Forest Service, Struthers Burt of the Dude Ranchers' Association, and fellow western writers such as A. B. Guthrie allowed DeVoto, with support from Avis, to make a strong stand against stock growers and lumber companies who advocated for a transfer of federal lands to the states in a bid to ultimately place them in private hands.[41] As Stegner put it: "They wanted to liquidate the Bureau of Land Management and *emasculate* the Forest Service and gain ownership of a princely but fragile domain that belonged to all Americans" (emphasis mine).[42] After DeVoto leaped into the political fray on behalf of public lands, Stegner followed his lead.[43] In his joint biography of the men and their environmental activism, John L. Thomas concludes: "It came down, then to a matter of values and the urgent need in a postwar age of environmental heedlessness to educate, organize, and activate national public opinion. This task, Stegner agreed with DeVoto, now fell to a new agent, the enlightened and energized public intellectual: novelist, short story writer, biographer but also environmental spokesman."[44] This new agent was the figure that Stegner and DeVoto chose as the West's masculine symbol.

That it included themselves was no accident. As he suggested in "Queen City of the Plains and Peaks," DeVoto regularly met criticism for his residence and employment in the East. He countered, not just by citing his boyhood in Ogden but with his superior mastery of the West's ecology. When the editor of the *Denver Post*, himself a newcomer to the Rocky Mountain West, took DeVoto to task for what the editor saw as eastern condescension in his opposition to Echo Dam, DeVoto mocked the editor's own regional background when he addressed his rejoinder to the "native Westerner from Roseville, Illinois," and insisted that "repulsive émigré that I am, I understand that necessity [to conserve water] better than, apparently, the *Post* does."[45] Stegner did not endure the same accusations of regional betrayal, but he deplored the myth of the individualist cowboy possibly even more virulently than DeVoto did. In his 1990 celebration of western literary institutions, Stegner recalled, "Nothing could convince them in New York or Massachusetts that there was anything of literary interest in the West except cowboys," and of the mythic cowboy himself he said that he was "a culture hero, given . . . by the novelist Owen Wister, an Eastern snob who saw in the common cowherd the lineaments of Lancelot."[46] It was not just eastern industry that had exploited the West but also myths created largely by eastern writers. For Stegner and DeVoto, to be a western writer was to be a defender of western lands, and that identity put both men at odds with the East and the mythology of masculinity that it had imposed upon its plundered province.[47]

One positive outcome of their defense was the rising importance of the environment in American humanist inquiry. The opening issue of the *Pacific Spectator*, for which Stegner and Mirrielees served as editors, read: "Edited and published in the West, *The Pacific Spectator* could not—even if it would—avoid the influence of its environment, but it will not be confined to Western topics. The sponsors propose that it shall serve as a spokesman for humanistic interests in the West and for similar interests everywhere."[48] As the voice of western humanities, the *Pacific Spectator* undergirded some of Stegner's efforts to make the West a literary center and to provide humanist interpretations of the natural world. He furthered such endeavors when, in 1961, Secretary of the Interior Stewart Udall invited him to be a writer-in-residence at the Interior Department. Stegner, among other duties, helped deepen the connection between Udall and Frost, who, at Udall's invitation, recited at John Kennedy's inauguration. Stegner also advised Udall in the writing of his first book, *The Quiet Crisis*, and supported Udall when considering the establishment of a National Arts Foundation. "I would think the formation of such a committee a step in the right direction," Stegner wrote Udall, "and I would hope that it would carry on the sort of thing that you started with your Night with Robert Frost and Night with Carl Sandburg."[49] Stegner highlighted those cultural events that encouraged exploration of the natural world and American regionalism. For Stegner, support for culture meant support for nature. In this respect, he believed that western writers could lead the way. Years later, Berry said as much in a letter to Stegner following the memorial service for environmental activist Edward Abbey: "I left Utah thinking again what I have thought often before: that if we ever do develop a culture capable of taking care of the world, it will grow eastward out of the west, and that you and your work and example will be right at the center of it."[50]

Distinguishing between an effete East and a rugged West, however, did not serve all parts of the western literary community equally. In distancing themselves from New York, Stegner and DeVoto also occluded the influence of those western writers, mostly women, with New York connections. When speaking of the western literary tradition, Stegner rarely mentioned Mary Austin, Alice Corbin, or Mabel Dodge Luhan, all white women of the Santa Fe and Taos arts communities, and all connected to the magazines that DeVoto had chosen as his targets during his time in New York. Stegner praised Willa Cather's novels about Nebraska but gave little or no attention to *Death Comes for the Archbishop* and *The Professor's House*, both set in the Southwest. He probably overemphasized Frost's role in Bread Loaf's conception and never mentioned Cather's. It is surprising that he did not include Corbin among western writers, especially because she was from Chicago and had partnered with Monroe to edit *Poetry*. *The Quiet Crisis*, which Udall wrote with Stegner's guidance, contains an epigraph at the beginning of each chapter. Robert Frost, Mark Twain, Aldo Leopold, DeVoto, and Stegner himself are all quoted. The only non-American quoted in an epigraph is D. H. Lawrence, describing Taos in a chapter about American Indians. No women, no Indigenous people, and no people of color are quoted at all.[51] The slight may have been unintentional on Stegner's and Udall's part, but it had the effect of excising from environmental advocacy much of the Southwest's land, people, and writers.

Stegner's and DeVoto's dismissal of the Southwest was often glancing and temporary, but it could also be intentional. DeVoto's correspondence with Mirrielees suggests as much. Of the community with the tightest ties to New York City, Taos, Mirrielees did not speak favorably. DeVoto visited Taos in 1940 while on a cross-country trip with Arthur Schlesinger Jr. when Mirrielees was teaching at the Indian School in Albuquerque. She wrote him in mock frustration when they failed to cross paths. "Oh dear, oh dear, oh dear!" she wrote. "A human being of intelligence—of supposed intelligence—and he comes to see the

West and goes to Santa Fe and to Taos. . . . And he chooses to go to Taos, where once I saw a man, a full grown man, leading a lamb by a blue ribbon down the street in full daylight. Probably he even called on Mabel Luhan, but he does have the grace to conceal that."[52] That Taos and Santa Fe were precious and a little ridiculous seems to have been a running joke between them. Moreover, it was a joke expressed in gendered terms. Not just women of the arts community but men who did not follow traditional gender norms came in for their scorn.

DeVoto and Mirrielees had never been amenable to the aesthetics and politics of northern New Mexico's Anglo arts community. DeVoto wrote a scathing condemnation of Mary Austin's *American Rhythm* in "How to Not Write History," an essay for *Harper's*, in which he took her to task for her "literary" approach to the past and her romanticized view of American Indians.[53] He mocked regional (Stegner would have said "provincial") literature as a "coterie manifesto," and in reference to the artists and writers surrounding Mabel Dodge Luhan, such as D. H. Lawrence, he asserted that "fiction that wears a squash blossom in its hair or talks about the plumed serpent is just silly."[54] Mirrielees appears to have echoed his opinions of Austin, Luhan, and Lawrence. As a Montanan, perhaps she agreed with Stegner's and DeVoto's opinions regarding the eastern literary elite and their connections to the Southwest. As a writer who frequently edited both men's prose, she may have shared their literary opinions of work such as Lawrence's *The Plumed Serpent*. As an employee of the Indian Service, she may also have disagreed with the style of patronage that Austin extended to Native people, or perhaps she took issue with Luhan's marriage to a member of Taos of Pueblo, Tony Lujan. Historians have observed that the Anglo arts community practiced a romantic primitivism, and Mirrielees may have been an early observer of its flaws.[55] Or maybe Mirrielees shared Stegner's and DeVoto's animosity to effeminate western writers. Her own gender, in Stegner's eyes, reinforced her literary credentials by aligning her with the East. Perhaps she did not want to weaken her own standing.

Whatever her criticisms of Taos and its artists, Mirrielees remained a sympathetic audience for DeVoto in 1947, just one year after the trip that had transformed him into a conservationist. He wrote Mirrielees that year about a correspondent from Santa Fe who had asked for DeVoto's attention to Native water rights along the Rio Grande. The letter came in the midst of the widespread criticism that DeVoto endured following his advocacy for protection of Forest Service lands and watersheds. "It is being borne in on me that I'm being hanged and shot in many Western areas," began DeVoto as he introduced the letter that he had recently received.

> The enclosure comes under this general heading, and I wish you'd read it and tell me if you think I'm right in thinking that she is to be classed as a Santa Fe mind and disregarded. What she's talking about here comes under the Rio Grande project and it *is* full of inequities and injustices, and God knows I know how many assaults the Indians in general are getting these days. But I have quite a few things to do and, as I told her when I answered her first, only-three-page letter, I won't write about things I don't know about. Now this deep throb. She's Owen Wister's daughter.[56]

DeVoto made clear that he would write only about that which he had knowledge, which did not include management of the Rio Grande River. Further, while sympathetic to the water rights of American Indians, he would not extend his conservation activism to them unless fully versed in their particular conflict in New Mexico. That Marina Wister, the wife of artist Andrew Dasburg, also of Mabel Dodge's circle, had written to solicit his support mattered little to DeVoto. Wister lived in Taos, but she was "to be classed as a Santa Fe mind and disregarded." Literally and figuratively, Wister was a daughter of the mythic cowboy, the East's most pernicious symbol, and was married to the "coterie manifesto." She was the cowboy's progeny "with a squash blossom in her hair" come to life.

DeVoto's snub is nonetheless surprising given how much he prided himself on his research and pursuit of facts. If any member of the 1947 white, eastern literary establishment was capable of a thorough investigation of Indian rights and the Rio Grande watershed in the Spanish borderlands, it was he. His settler colonial outlook and steadfast prejudice against the Southwest's Spanish and Mexican past, however, prevented him from taking on the project.[57] He continued to build his extensive knowledge of Anglos' westward settlement rather than deeply engage Indigenous communities or the West's Spanish and Mexican past. The effect of his and Mirrielees's shared scorn for the New Mexico arts communities was similar to the effect of Stegner's literary criticism: a diminishment of both white southwestern women writers and the nonwhite communities for which such writers had advocated.

Writing in 1975, twenty years after DeVoto's death, Stegner lamented that his friend had not lived to see the successful defeat of a proposed dam at Dinosaur National Monument or to "hail the Wilderness Act or any of the major conservation legislation of the Kennedy and Johnson administrations under the leadership of Secretary of the Interior Stewart Udall."[58] In later years Stegner might also have lamented that DeVoto did not live to witness other transformations too. DeVoto did not live to see his friend, ally, and fellow western writer revise his own views of the West and western writing. He did not live to see Stegner acknowledge southwestern Indian writers N. Scott Momaday or Leslie Marmon Silko for demonstrating that "literature comes out of deeply lived-in places, out of a long shared tradition," or to argue that such writers along with "James Welch . . . Louise Erdrich and other Western Indians speak from the present, from the very battlefields of cultures."[59] He did not live to read Stegner condemn the "hoodlums who come to San Francisco to beat up gays" as "vigilantes, enforcing their prejudices with violence, just as surely as were the miners who used to hunt down Indians and hang Chinese in the mother lode."[60] He did not live to hear Stegner call Maxine Hong Kingston's character Wittman Ah Sing "as American as Huck Finn" or to hear her reflect, following a lecture that she delivered "back East," that she shared his view that "there is a Western mind and reality—just by writing about the land and people we know, we are taking literature into a far out avant garde."[61] Stegner never praised Mexican American authors in the same tone; he never seems to have gotten over his impression of New Mexico's villages as precious and "overrun by tourists," and he never articulated a theory of Indigenous sovereignty.[62] What he did do was come to see his role in creating a western literature that "inevitably reflect(s) a different . . . orientation: a different history, a different emphasis and expectation, a different ethnic mix, a different culture."[63] In establishing himself as a western writer, Stegner had helped readers acquire a new orientation, one that looked to the East from a literary base in the West.

Soon after his death, DeVoto's wife, Avis, wrote Stegner regarding DeVoto's last book in progress. She had decided not to ask Stegner to finish it because she thought it needed another draft from DeVoto himself. "Of course I hate having an unfinished book that would have meant so damn much to us all," she confided, "but if he had lived to be 90 there would still have been an unfinished book."[64] There will always be work of the kind Stegner and DeVoto did and did not do. Those of us who read and write about the West can recall the battles they won and lost. We can dissect the consequences of their attacks on the effete and the East as they remade western literature in their own idealized white settler, masculine image. We can lament the loss of the postwar columns and political campaigns that may have acknowledged Indigenous sovereignty, centered Spanish and Mexican history, included women's writing and advocacy, and championed water conservation along the Rio Grande. We can mourn what they were never able to write, and then we can write it ourselves.

Notes

1. Bernard DeVoto, *The Year of Decision: 1846* (Boston: Little, Brown, 1943); DeVoto, *Across the Wide Missouri* (Boston: Houghton Mifflin, 1947); DeVoto, *The Course of Empire* (Boston: Houghton Mifflin, 1952).
2. Wallace Stegner, *The Uneasy Chair* (New York: Doubleday, 1974), 287.
3. Stegner, *Uneasy Chair*, 288.
4. I am not interested in defining the East and West as specific regions with unchanging boundaries. Rather, I am interested in how Stegner employed regional definitions in the course of his career. For discussions of regionalism, see Robert Dorman, *Revolt of the Provinces: The Region-*

alist Movement in America, 1920–1945 (Chapel Hill: University of North Carolina Press, 1993); and Edward L. Ayers, Patricia Nelson Limerick, Stephen Nissenbaum, and Peter Onuf, eds., *All Over the Map: Rethinking American Regions* (Baltimore: Johns Hopkins University Press, 1996). David M. Wrobel and Michael C. Steiner, eds., *Many Wests: Place, Culture, and Regional Identity* (Lawrence: University Press of Kansas, 1997).

5. Krista Comer, "Feminism, Women Writers and the New Western Regionalism: Revising Critical Paradigms," in *Updating the Literary West*, ed. Thomas J. Lyon (Fort Worth: Texas Christian University Press, 1997), 21.

6. In using "us" and "we," I intend to invoke the collective "we" described in conversation between Priscilla Solis Ybarra and Cherríe Moraga as enabling human and nonhuman healing. As Moraga concludes, "We need to see the 'we' in it," to transcend individualist and ego-centered approaches to nature. See Priscilla Solis Ybarra, "'The Body Knows and the Land Has Memory': An Interview with Cherríe Moraga," in *Latinx Environmentalisms: Place, Justice and the Decolonial*, ed. Sarah D. Wald, David J. Vásquez, Priscilla Solis Ybarra, and Sarah Jaquette Ray (Philadelphia: Temple University Press, 2019), 284–85.

7. Melody Graulich, "Cultural Criticism, circa 1947," *American Literary History* 16, no. 3 (Autumn 2004): 538.

8. Stegner, *Uneasy Chair*, 287.

9. Bernard DeVoto, *Mark Twain's America* (New York: Little, Brown, 1932); DeVoto, "The West: A Plundered Province," *Harper's*, August 1934, 355–64; DeVoto, "The West against Itself," *Harper's*, January 1947, 1–13; Meriwether Lewis and William Clark, *The Journals of Lewis and Clark*, ed. Bernard DeVoto (Boston: Houghton Mifflin, 1953).

10. Bernard DeVoto to Melville Smith, Ogden, Utah, July 8, 1920, box 5, Bernard Augustine DeVoto Papers, M0242, Dept. of Special Collections, Stanford University Libraries, Stanford, California (collection cited hereafter as DeVoto Papers).

11. Harry Sions to Carl Brandt, June 17, 1953, box 2, DeVoto Papers.

12. Bernard DeVoto to Wallace Stegner, April 12, 1937, box 5, DeVoto Papers.

13. Ted Morrison to Wallace Stegner, November 8, [1945], Ms 676, box 18, Wallace Earle Stegner Papers, Special Collections and Archives, J. Willard Marriott Library, University of Utah, Salt Lake City (collection cited hereafter as Stegner Papers).

14. Philip L. Fradkin, *Wallace Stegner and the American West* (New York: Alfred A. Knopf, 2008), 87.

15. Wallace Stegner, "Regionalism in Art," *Delphian Quarterly* 22, no. 1 (Winter 1939): 3. Also see Liesl Olson, *Literature and Art in the Midwest Metropolis* (New Haven CT: Yale University Press, 2017).

16. Wallace Stegner, "The Writer's Sense of Place," *South Dakota Review* 13, no. 3 (Autumn 1975): 49–52.

17. Wallace Stegner, "The West Coast: A Region with a View," *Saturday Review of Literature*, May 2, 1959, 15–17, 47; *Pacific Spectator: A Journal of Interpretation*, 1947–56.

18. Wallace Stegner, "Out Where the Sense of Place Is a Sense of Motion," *Los Angeles Times Book Review*, June 3, 1990, 15. See also Stegner, "Publishing in the Provinces," *Delphian Quarterly* 22, no. 3 (Summer 1939): 2–7; Wallace Stegner, address to the Western Literature Association, 9th annual meeting, box 166, Stegner Papers.

19. Wallace Stegner and Richard Etulain, *Stegner: Conversations on History and Literature*, rev. ed. (Salt Lake City: University of Utah Press, 1990), 14.

20. Wendell Berry, *What Are People For? Essays by Wendell Berry* (San Francisco: North Point Press, 1990), 56–57.

21. David Haward Bain, *Whose Woods These Are: A History of the Bread Loaf Writers' Conference, 1926–1992*, ed. David Haward Bain and Mary Smyth Duffy (Hopewell NJ: Ecco Press, 1993), 13.

22. Theodore Morrison, *Bread Loaf Writers' Conference: The First Thirty Years (1926–1955)* (Middlebury VT: Middlebury College Press, 1976), 98–99; David Haward Bain, "Bread Loaf at Sixty: From 'Haphazard Experiment' to the Granddaddy of Writers' Conferences," *Middlebury College Magazine* 59, no. 2 (Spring 1985): 22–27.

23. Bain, *Whose Woods These Are*, 13.

24. Stegner, *Uneasy Chair*, 122.

25. Edith Mirrielees to Wallace Stegner, November 24, [1944?], box 18, Stegner Papers.

26. Katherine H. Adams, *A Group of Their Own: College Writing Courses and American Women Writers* (Albany NY: State University of New York Press, 2001), 132; "Lucia Mirrielees Finishes School Composition Text," *Montana Kaiman*, October 2, 1931, 1; "Middlebury College Catalogue,

1926 Supplement," accessed September 1, 2019, https://archive.org/stream
/middleburyCourseCatalogs_a10-3_1926s/a10-3_1926s_djvu.txt.

27. Stegner, *Uneasy Chair*, 125, 194; Edith R. Mirrielees, "The Writer," in
Four Portraits and One Subject: Bernard DeVoto, by Catherine Drinker
Bowen, Edith R. Mirrielees, Arthur M. Schlesinger Jr., and Wallace Steg-
ner (Boston: Houghton Mifflin, 1963), 30.

28. Fradkin, *Wallace Stegner*, 86.

29. Stegner and Etulain, *Stegner*, 98.

30. Wallace Stegner, *Second Growth* (Boston: Houghton Mifflin, 1947); Stegner, *Crossing to Safety* (New York: Random House, 1987).

31. Stegner, *Uneasy Chair*, 194.

32. George C. Homans, *Coming to My Senses: The Autobiography of a Sociologist* (Piscataway NJ: Transactions, 1984), 86.

33. Stegner, *Uneasy Chair*, 175.

34. DeVoto, *Mark Twain's America*; Van Wyck Brooks, *The Ordeal of Mark
Twain* (New York: E. P. Dutton, 1920).

35. Stegner, *Uneasy Chair*, 115.

36. Elizabeth Cook-Lynn notes Stegner's similar treatment of the term "savage" in her *Why I Can't Read Wallace Stegner and Other Essays: A Tribal
Voice* (Madison: University of Wisconsin Press, 1996), 32, 34–35.

37. Stegner, *Uneasy Chair*, 176.

38. Stegner's interviews and nonfiction writing contrast with some of his
fictional explorations of gender and regionalism, particularly in *Angle
of Repose*, in which the character of Susan, an eastern white woman
who goes west, creates and represents a western literary tradition, one
actually created and represented by the character's historical model,
Mary Hallock Foote. See Melody Graulich, "Book Learning: *Angle of
Repose* as Literary History," in Radkin, *Wallace Stegner*, 231–53. Paired,
Stegner's fiction and nonfiction suggest that he did envision women as
western writers, but his vision did not include the writers of northern
New Mexico's Anglo art colonies.

39. Bernard DeVoto, "Queen City of the Plains and Peaks," in *Spectator
Sampler*, ed. Robert C. North and Edith R. Mirrielees (Stanford CA:
Stanford University Press, 1955), 38.

40. Stegner, *Uneasy Chair*, ix.

41. Nate Schweber, *This America of Ours: Bernard and Avis DeVoto and the Forgotten Fight to Save the Wild* (Boston: Mariner Books, 2022).

42. Stegner, *Uneasy Chair*, 302.

43. Stegner and Etulain, *Stegner*, 168; John L. Thomas, *A Country in the Mind: Wallace Stegner, Bernard DeVoto, History, and the American Land* (New York: Routledge, 2000), 111–13.

44. Thomas, *A Country in the Mind*, 125.

45. Thomas, *A Country in the Mind*, 137.

46. Wallace Stegner, "Out Where the Sense of Place Is a Sense of Motion," *Los Angeles Times*, June 3, 1990, 15; Stegner, "Who Are the Westerners?" *American Heritage*, December 1987, 38.

47. Bernard DeVoto, "The Plundered Province," in *The Western Paradox: A Conservation Reader*, ed. Douglas Brinkly and Patricia Nelson Limerick (New Haven CT: Yale University Press, 2000), 3–21.

48. Editorial Statement, *The Pacific Spectator* 1, no. 1 (Winter 1947): 1.

49. Wallace Stegner to Stewart Udall, November 7, 1961, box 190, folder 21, Stewart L. Udall Papers, AZ 372, Special Collections, University of Arizona Libraries.

50. Wendell Berry to Wallace Stegner, May 23, 1989, box 12, Stegner Papers.

51. L. Boyd Finch, *Legacies of Camelot: Stewart and Lee Udall, American Culture, and the Arts* (Norman: University of Oklahoma Press, 2007), 73.

52. Edith Mirrielees to Bernard DeVoto, 1940, box 16, Bernard Augustine DeVoto Papers, M001, Dept. of Special Collections, Stanford University Libraries, Stanford, California.

53. Bernard DeVoto, "How Not to Write History," *Harper's*, January 1934, 199–208.

54. Bernard DeVoto, "Regionalism or the Coterie Manifesto," *Saturday Review of Literature* 15 (November 28, 1936): 8.

55. Flannery Burke, *From Greenwich Village to Taos: Primitivism and Place at Mabel Dodge Luhan's* (Lawrence: University Press of Kansas, 2008); Margaret Jacobs, *Engendered Encounters: Feminism and Pueblo Cultures, 1879–1934* (Lincoln: University of Nebraska Press, 1999); Molly Mullin, *Culture in the Marketplace: Gender, Art, and Value in the American Southwest* (Durham NC: Duke University Press, 2001). Most recently Krista Comer has observed how whiteness influences discussions of western feminism in women who have followed in the tradition of those of the

Taos and Santa Fe art communities. See Comer, "Staying with the White Trouble of Recent Feminist Westerns," *Western American Literature* 56, no. 2 (Summer 2021): 101–23.

56. Bernard DeVoto to Edith Mirrielees, May 20, 1947, box 1, Edith R. Mirrielees Papers, SC1028, Dept. of Special Collections, Stanford University Libraries, Stanford, California.

57. See Mark Harvey, "Bernard DeVoto and the Environmental History of the West," *Weber: The Contemporary West*, Fall 2021, 68. Priscilla Ybarra notes similarly that Stegner's elevation of Aldo Leopold was at the expense of Mexican women's contributions to environmental understanding despite the fact that Leopold was married to a Mexican American woman and developed aspects of his land ethic in New Mexico and Arizona. See Ybarra, *Writing the Good Life: Mexican American Literature and the Environment* (Tucson: University of Arizona Press, 2016), 348.

58. Stegner, *Uneasy Chair*, 321.

59. Wallace Stegner, "The Geography of Hope," lecture delivered at University of Colorado at Boulder, October 19, 1988, 14; Stegner, "Out Where the Sense of Place," 15.

60. Stegner, "Who Are the Westerners?," 39.

61. Maxine Hong Kingston to Wallace Stegner, August 24, 1990, box 17, Stegner Papers.

62. Wallace Stegner to Eliot Porter, March 7, 1978, box 19, Stegner Papers.

63. Stegner, "Out Where the Sense of Place," 15.

64. Avis DeVoto to Wallace Stegner as cited by Mark DeVoto in Brinkley and Limerick, *Western Paradox*, 469. Stegner describes their 1956 decision to forego publication in Stegner and Etulain, *Stegner*, 146. *The Western Paradox* includes the unfinished manuscript along with many of DeVoto's most significant *Harper's* articles.

5

Returning to the
Best Idea We Ever Had   MICHAEL CHILDERS

"Let me bear my testimony, as the Mormons say, and acknowledge the debt I owe to a federal bureau for more than sixty years of physical and spiritual refreshment, and for the reassurance it gives me that despite all its faults, democracy is still the worst form of government except all the others."[1]

So opens Wallace Stegner's 1983 essay "The Best Idea We Ever Had: An Overview." Published in the Wilderness Society's monthly magazine *Wilderness*, it remains one of the most quoted—and misread—treatises on the power of the national parks. And while he later attributed the phrase to Lord James Bryce, Stegner's assertion that "America's Best Idea" offers a cure for our deeply held cultural cynicism and a respite from the competitive materialism we call the American Way continues to resonate with millions of visitors who flock to our national parks every year.[2]

Countless tourists, journalists, and historians (myself included) have cribbed Stegner's title in an attempt to capture the national parks' power. The most recognized? Documentarian Ken Burns in his 2009 series *The National Parks: America's Best Idea*. The twelve-hour series opens with narrator Peter Coyote proclaiming the national parks "as uniquely American as the Declaration of Independence, and just as radical," as images of stunning scenery flash across the screen. Burns builds upon that romance throughout the series in a naked attempt to mirror Stegner's argument from nearly a quarter century before.[3]

But if we read "America's Best Idea" more closely, we see that Stegner was less concerned in extolling the national parks as symbols of

American exceptionalism than bludgeoning the Reagan administration's efforts to reverse decades of environmental gains. Stegner specifically targets Reagan's secretary of the interior, James Watt, a point few contemporary readers note. Thus they understand the essay as a celebration of the national parks rather than one of Stegner's most pointed political statements.

Honestly, for many years I had never read much beyond Stegner's now famous line calling national parks "absolutely American, absolutely democratic, they reflect us at our best rather than at our worse. Without them, millions of American lives, including mine, would have been poorer." It is a nifty bit of prose. Which is likely why many have appropriated it over the past several decades. Yet, returning to the essay's specific context and history is worth our while. If we read beyond Stegner's opening stanza, we stand to gain a deeper insight into the writer's personal politics and perhaps even a little perspective on current conversations over the state of our national parks.

In the opening of "America's Best Idea," Stegner confesses to never being a great admirer of the American people. Especially when it came to issues concerning public lands. Too often he watched voters make almost criminally irresponsible choices electing politicians who pushed legislation that placed private (read corporate) interests above their own. It was enough to make anyone deeply pessimistic about the country's future. "But ever since I was old enough to be cynical, I have been visiting the national parks and they are a cure for cynicism," he optimistically declared, "an exhilarating rest from the competitive avarice we call the American way." Stegner often needed that rest to cure his deep skepticism over his fellow Americans willingness to place corporate interests above their own when it came to managing their public lands. That trend remains as true today as it did then.[4]

It would have been easy to become cynical watching the Reagan administration race to erase the environmental achievements of the previous three decades—achievements in which Stegner himself had a hand. Referred to as a reluctant conservationist by one of his biographers, Stegner had become an environmentalist through his deep love

7. Page, Mary, and Wallace Stegner resting on a Yosemite National Park hiking trail, Yosemite National Park, California, probably in the 1950s. Courtesy Special Collections, J. Willard Marriott Library, University of Utah.

8. Wallace and Mary Stegner at Grand Canyon National Park in Arizona, probably in the late 1930s or 1940s. Courtesy Special Collections, J. Willard Marriott Library, University of Utah.

of the American West. Driven by his father's restlessness, he had spent his childhood migrating from one western boomtown to another. The family's constant migration shaped the young Wallace's view of the region, both as a place of eternal hope and spiritual rebirth—themes he spent most of his writing life grappling with. However, it was Stegner's interest in John Wesley Powell that transformed him into a true conservationist.

Stegner's legacy as a conservationist lay in his writings—possibly none more so than *Beyond the Hundredth Meridian: John Wesley Powell and the Second Opening of the West*. Published in 1953, the biography remains one of Stegner's most beloved books. In it he traced Powell's explorations of the Colorado River Basin and subsequent warnings of the West's finite resources. The book was more than a biography. It was a stirring piece of political writing that sought to warn its readers of the region's limits and the need for stronger government management. In the book's final chapter, Stegner noted that Powell would have undoubtedly argued, "there are values too critical and resources too perishable to be entrusted entirely to private exploitation." That restraint was necessary to ensure the conservation of the West not only for the present generation but for future generations to come. Reading these words, it is easy to see that thirty years later Stegner watched with alarm the Reagan administration's promotion of private interests over environmental concerns.[5]

Stegner's biography of Powell struck a chord with many concerned with the West's environmental future, including David Brower. The Sierra Club director recruited Stegner after reading the biography to edit *This Is Dinosaur: Echo Park Country and Its Magic Rivers* as a part of the club's campaign to halt the Bureau of Reclamation's damming of the Green River within Dinosaur National Monument. Soon afterward, Secretary of the Interior Stewart Udall recruited Stegner to work within Interior as an adviser, a stint that lasted for all of four months but helped yield Udall's *The Quiet Crisis*. Stegner would go on to hold positions on the National Parks Advisory Board, as well as the governing boards of the Sierra Club and the Wilderness Society. But he often found himself ill-suited for such work, later confessing to wanting to spend his time writing books rather than advocating for legislation.[6]

His writing issued a clarion call for environmental action. In 1960 Stegner published his "Wilderness Letter." Composed over a month in collaboration with Brower and David Pesonen, a forester in Berkeley's Wildland Research Center, the letter captured Stegner's deeply held sentiments toward the nation's wild places. Pesonen had reached out to Stegner for help after being tasked to consider recreation's place within wilderness for the Outdoor Recreation Commission. Stegner agreed and set to work on one of his most popular pieces of writing. Addressed to Pesonen, the letter argues that wilderness has as much to do with recreation as churches. He concluded: "We simply need that wild country available to us, even if we never do more than drive to its edge and look in. For it can be a means of reassuring ourselves of our sanity as creatures, a part of the geography of hope." Stegner would spend the rest of his life attempting to define the meaning of that hope.[7]

Which gets us back to "The Best Idea We Ever Had." In it Stegner confessed to becoming a national park addict when his family first visited Yellowstone National Park in 1920. A few short years later, they visited Zion, Grand Canyon, Bryce, and Capitol Reef. And by the time he sat down to write "America's Best Idea," Stegner reckoned he had toured more than a hundred units within the national park system, rejoicing in the sheer wonder the parks represented.

Like Stegner, I too am a park addict. Having grown up in the shadow of Colorado's Rocky Mountain National Park, I have spent years visiting national parks. I have watched the sunset from the Point Reyes Light House, stood atop Half Dome, watched wolves frolic in Yellowstone's Lamar Valley, smelled the cherry blossoms along the Washington Mall, and stood in contemplation of the burial mounds at Effigy Mounds National Monument. And yet, I too find it too easy to become cynical about the future of our national parks.

I have watched powerlessly as friends and family who work for the National Park Service (NPS) struggle to simply do their job while being buffeted by changing administrations, anemic budgets, and unrelenting crises. Morale within the NPS plummeted under the Trump administration as it slashed park budgets, undercut all efforts to confront climate change, and dramatically reduced the size of Bears Ears and Escalante National Monuments. While the Biden administration seeks to address some of the national park system's nearly $12 billion backlog in deferred maintenance, it has been silent on the severe labor shortage that has crippled the agency for decades. All the while, growing numbers of visitors inundate the most popular parks, wreaking havoc on the natural and built environments.

Such worries underline that the national parks are more than simply sublime landscapes and historical monuments. They are an idea, one that has captivated generations for its promise of both respite and beauty, with the possibility that we all can share in our country's most striking places. Landscape architect Frederick Law Olmstead first framed this ideal in 1865, arguing that the Yosemite Valley should be set aside for "the occasional contemplation of natural scenes of an impressive character," to provide visitors a needed respite from daily life. That idea, of nature's aspirational power, laid the foundation for the establishment of the National Park Service in 1916, with the mandate to conserve the parks in a manner that they would be enjoyed not just for this generation but for all future generations.[8]

What this meant was often open to debate. The NPS's first director, Stephen Mather, sought to secure the public's embrace of the national parks by promoting the parks' recreational and scenic values to the American public. And the public responded, buying into the ideal that the national parks were theirs to enjoy. But by the middle part of the century, growing numbers criticized this interpretation of the NPS's mandate, arguing instead that the Organic Act required the park service to prioritize the preservation, not the conservation, of each park's natural resources above all else and to allow all visitors to enjoy the contemplation of nature's sublime beauty, and in doing so find the same respite Stegner found within the parks.

There were, of course, problems with both of these interpretations. First, the Organic Act's authors saw the national parks through a very distinctive class and racial lens. It would have been impossible for Mather or others of his generation to foresee the numbers of Americans who would join the middle class and embrace his consumeristic view of the national parks. Even by 1916 few had the means to travel to the few national parks scattered largely across the American West—particularly people of color, who remained largely excluded from the social wealth needed for such ventures. Worse was the NPS's long history of excluding Native peoples. Many of the early parks had in fact been vehicles of imperialism that removed all Native peoples from within their borders. This removal of Indigenous people became synonymous with the view of the national parks as natural, a core value that remained a part of the environmental movement of the mid-twentieth century.[9]

After sharing his connections with the national parks in "The Best Idea We Ever Had," Stegner turned to telling their history. The national parks were inevitable as soon as Americans learned to confront the wild, not with fear but with delight and wonder, he wrote. The idea spread from explorer and artist George Catlin to the nature philosophers of the Concord School, to the cession of the Yosemite Valley and Mariposa Grove in the final days of the Civil War. Nearly a decade later, President Ulysses Grant signed the Yellowstone National Protection Act into law, creating the nation's first truly national park.[10]

More parks followed, including Sequoia, Yosemite, Rocky Mountain, and Lassen. The passage of the Organic Act in 1916 established the National Park Service and charged the new agency with protecting the natural and historic treasures within each park for the public's enjoyment, leaving them unimpaired for future generations. The addition of the national monuments, battlefields, and historic sites in 1933 expanded the national park system even further. Congress continued to add new national parks, expanding the number of national parks to forty-eight by 1982. Visitation also grew. Stegner pointed out that while the nation's population had grown an astounding 50 percent since the end of World War II, visitor numbers to the nation's parks grew by a jaw dropping 800 percent, underscoring Americans' embrace of the national park idea.[11]

The essay then takes an interesting turn, becoming overtly political. Stegner points to a series of laws that have helped preserve the parks, starting with the General Authorities Act, the Antiquities Act, the Wilderness Act, and finally the Land and Water Conservation Act. Each piece of legislation helped "the steady advance of a splendid idea through more than a century and throughout the world." None was more important than the Land and Water Conservation Fund, or LWCF. Established by Congress in 1965, the LWCF sought to "preserve, develop, and ensure access to outdoor recreation facilities to strengthen the health of U.S. citizens."[12]

Stegner had politics in mind when he emphasized the LWCF. First suggested by the Outdoor Recreation Resource Review Commission some seven years prior, the idea behind the LCWF was simple. The federal government would create a pot of money collected from user fees, the sale of surplus lands, and a tax on motorboat fuel to pay for the management and acquisition of federal lands while also providing grants to state and local governments for recreational planning and building recreational projects both large and small. The LWCF quickly became so successful that within three years Congress amended its funding sources to include a share of oil and gas receipts from drilling on the Outer Continental Shelf. Later, the entirety of the fund would come from royalties taken from offshore drilling. Cities large and small built new parks and facilities. Birmingham, Alabama, built nine new swimming pools in 1967. Reno, Nevada, purchased land along the Truckee River as open space. And Montpelier, Vermont, used LWCF funds to build facilities in the Dog River Recreation Area.[13]

Stegner knew that the federal program was a win-win for legislators looking to both prove their conservationist credentials and send some money home for popular projects such as city and state parks, roads and trails, and golf courses and reservoirs. All were for the American public's recreational use. But it was the funds used by the National Park Service where the LWCF fell into controversy. The agency used the funds in two ways. One was the acquisition of inholdings within national parks that the NPS felt threatened their ability to manage those parks. Testifying before Congress in 1968, NPS director George B. Hartzog Jr. argued inholdings posed "a serious and growing threat to the integrity of our National Park System." For this reason, Hartzog directed superintendents to remove all inholdings from within the parks. Inholders across the country erupted in opposition, helping spark the property rights movement of the 1980s. Stegner knew that, too.[14]

The second use of the LWCF involved purchasing land for the creation of new national park units. Following World War II, growing national affluence, corresponding leisure time, and a new interstate highway system drew millions of Americans to their national parks. Seeking to meet this growing demand, Congress established new national recreation areas, national seashores, national lakeshores, and national rivers. Second-generation parks such as Point Reyes National Seashore, Golden Gate National Recreation Area, and the Apostle Islands National Lakeshore marked an important expansion of the national park idea. Many of the new units lay either in or near the country's growing metropolitan population centers. And like the LWCF, such new national park units were political winners for both sides of the political aisle. The public loved the national parks, local communities loved the revenues the national park arrowhead brought, conservationists loved the preservation of more open space, and so Congress continued to add more and more units to the system.[15]

Not everyone agreed that the continued expansion of the national parks was a good thing, however. Fiscal conservatives such as Watt argued that the costs of adding new park units meant there was less money to maintain existing parks. Others viewed the NPS's attempts to purchase inholdings as federal overreach. And many critics contended that many of the new park units of the past two decades failed to meet the standard of holding national historical importance or stunning scenery equal to that of existing parks. Watt asserted that newer urban parks such as San Francisco's Golden Gate National Park were little more than "city playgrounds," and federal dollars would be much better spent in maintaining existing park units.[16]

Immediately after taking office, Watt halted the acquisition of new lands for the addition of national parks—the first secretary of the interior to do so within living memory. Testifying before the House of Representatives Subcommittee on Public Lands and National Parks, he noted, "It is perfectly obvious that the national park system has grown in the past several years far beyond its capacity to manage what Congress has forced it to acquire." This "park-a-month program" had led to the degradation of the entire system. And according to the General Accounting Office (GAO), the national parks were in deplorable condition. "The park visitor and employee may be subjugating himself or herself to conditions which do not meet Federal or State health and safety standards," Watt told the subcommittee, noting the GAO reported a needed $1.6 billion to bring the park system's infrastructure up to the needed health and safety standards.[17]

Conservationists rejected Watt's claims, believing them as little more than smoke screen to gut the National Park Service. "The national parks have never been as threatened as they are today," executive director of the National Parks Conservation Association Paul Pritchard wrote, attacking Watt's emphasis on infrastructure over natural resources. Additionally, the Wilderness Society countered that in the face of overcrowding within the national parks, it was wrong to stop the purchase of more parklands. Most of the threats to the conditions of the parks presented in the GAO report were external, and the $1.9 billion backlog was little more than a "wish list" of possible future construction projects by concessioners.[18]

On its face, the fight between the Interior Department and conservationists was a continuation of the decade's long struggle over the national parks' fundamental purpose. Should it be for the enjoyment of visitors or the preservation of each park's natural and historic wonders? But what made Watt's actions so divisive was that for a little more than two decades conservationists had largely had their way when it came to the national parks. Watt embodied the wholesale rejection of those efforts, if not an outright reversal, making him enemy number one to environmental groups such as the Wilderness Society.

The casting of James Watt as an unremorseful enemy of the environment is a narrative so accepted that few of us ever question its validity. He admittedly enjoyed them as much as Stegner. Tales of his driving his advisers bonkers by quickly naming Grand Teton as his favorite park were well known during his tenure as secretary. So why did he target the national parks? This question haunted me as I reread "America's Best Idea." Seeking an answer, I traveled to the American Heritage Center archives on the University of Wyoming's campus. There, within the center's archives, I began digging through the James G. Watt Papers for an answer. Consisting mostly of materials related to his twenty-one-year governmental career, the collection includes some fifty-two boxes of letters, media coverage, speeches, and photographs. But one box was of particular interest, and the reason I had driven north to Laramie: Box 17 and its copy of the Wilderness Society's "Watt Book."

Published in 1981, the Watt Book was the Wilderness Society's opening salvo in its efforts to remove the secretary from office. In a letter commenting on an early draft of the book to its authors Rebecca Leet, Meg Maguire, and Chuck Clausen, the Wilderness Society's councilor Gaylord Nelson noted, "The dismissal of Watt as Secretary is, without question our principal present objective." To meet this goal, he argued, the book's evidence must be overwhelming. The four spent nearly a year culling through newspapers, speech transcripts, the *Congressional Record*, and correspondence in laying out the case against Watt. Finally satisfied, the Wilderness Society mailed hundreds of copies of the Watt Book to reporters, activists, and politicians.[19]

Actually composed of two large red binders, the Watt Book details Watt's pro-development policies and questions the legality of the secretary's actions in managing the nation's public lands. I am greeted with the words "Watt's Wrongs" written in bold letters across the first page of volume 1. Quickly scanning the two brief opening paragraphs I pause on the sentence, "Mr. Watt is systematically failing to implement, or proposing to alter radically, some of the most significant conservation legislation of the past two decades, including the BLM Organic Act of 1976 (FLMPA), the Alaska National Interest Lands Conservation Act of 1980 (ANILCA), the Surface Mining Act of 1977, and the Land and Conservation Act of 1965 (LWCF)." A list of Watt's failings, at least in the Wilderness Society's eyes, then followed.[20]

It is an extended litany of wrongs, including the secretary's moratorium on the acquisition of additional national parklands—a decision that promised to lead to further development within existing national parks, increased overcrowding, and ensuring higher costs when Congress did approve the purchase of new lands for the national parks. Furthermore, the authors warned that the secretary was proposing to give popular national parks in metropolitan areas to state and local governments, placing those parks at risk and burdening state and local agencies with the financial costs of operating those parks. Sitting back in thought, I realize I have read this argument before. It is the very same case Stegner used against Watt in "America's Best Idea."[21]

I spent the next several hours reading through the two binders, paying particular interest to the sections on the national parks. The Watt Book covers a wide array of issues, from the moratorium on new parks to the current state of park facilities to the role of concessioners within the national parks. On the moratorium, the book's authors note both the LWCF's popularity as well as the need for more parks to meet the public's growing demand. They question Secretary Watt's assertion that the federal government should halt adding new parklands until the NPS can effectively manage the units it currently holds. The authors counter, "In the face of overwhelming popularity and overcrowding in some parks, it is wrong to stop the purchase of more parkland, including thousands of acres already approved by Congress." Once again, it was an argument Stegner wrote nearly word for word two years later, concluding the only solution to the secretary's intransigence was the hope Congress would soon intervene or replace Watt with "someone friendly to the laws he is sworn to uphold."[22]

Watt took a dim view on the Wilderness Society's efforts to remove him, refusing to even sit down with members of several conservationist organizations he believed were out to get him. "These groups are after my hide," Watt told reporters in November 1981. "They have

9. Secretary of the Interior James Watt with Yosemite National Park superintendent Robert Binnewies in the Yosemite Valley, October 31, 1981. Courtesy the American Heritage Center, University of Wyoming.

the assumption that we cannot combine environmental protection and development of our resources. They are wrong." Believing that conservation groups such as the Wilderness Society, Friends of the Earth, and the Sierra Club were conspiring against him, which they were, the secretary saw little use in engaging in any conversation with them. Philosophically, Watt differed greatly from conservationists on what role the Department of the Interior played in the management of public lands, especially national parks. National parks were to be enjoyed, not set aside as nature preserves, he argued. While members of the Wilderness Society, like Stegner, were aghast at such views coming from the secretary's office, Watt did have a valid point.[23]

The millions visiting the national parks every summer expected that they would be able to find adequate parking, camping, and concessions. These expectations came from generations believing the promise that their enjoyment was the fundamental purpose of all national parks. Such expectations had led to the NPS's ambitious Mission 66 program thirty years before. Focusing on the construction of visitor centers, roads, parking lots, and other infrastructure, the program did help modernize visitor facilities throughout the parks.

But to conservationists, such modernization came at an unacceptable cost to the ecological health of the national parks. Believing the parks should be managed as "vignettes of primitive America," environmentalists railed against the commercialization of the national parks. Most pointed to the Organic Act, which directed the park service to conserve the natural scenery while providing for visitors' enjoyment. Environmentalists tended to focus on the act's conservation mandate, framing any development or commercial use within the national parks as antithetical to their purpose.[24]

Watt emphatically disagreed with this interpretation. Believing rather the purpose of the national parks was to provide recreational opportunities, a viewpoint garnered from his three-year stint as director of the Outdoor Recreation Commission. This combined with his conservative politics that valued public lands for their economic potential and use, and his fundamentalist religious beliefs, shaped Watt's environmental ethos. While he intensely disagreed with preservationists over the fundamental purpose of the national parks, Watt certainly embraced the belief that our national parks were indeed America's best idea. He just had a much different view of what that idea was.

Watt lamented that the agency had failed to meet its mandate to serve visitors in recent years. "No agency in Government has a clearer mandate," he wrote to his newly appointed National Park Service director, Russell Dickenson, setting his agenda for the national parks as secretary of the interior. Stating that he believed the system was largely rounded out, he ordered newly appointed Director Dickenson to emphasize bringing old-line parks up to a standard rather than look to add any new park units to the system.[25]

Watt often cited a 1980 General Accounting Office report in supporting his argument that the system needed to focus more on maintaining existing units than adding more. The report noted conditions within many parks failed to meet federal and state health and safety standards, requiring $1.6 billion in repairs. In testifying before the House Subcommittee on Public Lands, he argued, "The GAO report documents a park system that is quite literally falling apart because past administrations and past Congresses have been so intent on grabbing more land that proper concern for stewardship has been neglected." Likewise, he saw little use for the federal government to manage park units in and near the country's urban areas. Such parks were "wonderful parks . . . good playgrounds" but should not be sustained "at the expense of the federal government." Conservationists noted that Watt's use of the GAO report was little more than a gambit to shift policy within the national parks away from natural resource protection toward a more visitor-friendly model. In fact, within a year of the GAO's report, most of the problems mentioned within the report had been addressed.[26]

By 1983 the public's opinion had soured against the secretary. Political cartoons lampooned Watt as willing to go out of his way to stomp on wildflowers, strip-mine Mount Rushmore, and use Smokey the Bear as a rug. Journalists attacked Watt's policies, pointing out the court's continued rejection of the Interior Department's attempts to circumnavigate environmental legislation. Watt's tendency toward offensive public remarks did not help. While his allies chuckled at statements such as, "I never use the words Democrats and Republicans. It's liberals and Americans," most voters did not. This reality was not lost on President Reagan, who finally asked Watt to resign after the secretary's comment, "I have a black, a woman, two Jews, and a cripple. And we have talent," to the U.S. Chamber of Commerce on the department's embrace of affirmative action became public.[27]

Yet by the time Stegner sat down to write "America's Best Idea," it appeared Watt would remain in office. Armed with the Watt Book, Stegner had all the ammunition he needed to take on the increasingly unpopular secretary of the interior. From slicing budgets to ending the policy of purchasing new lands for parks, Stegner provided a litany of the secretary's wrongs. Among them was the backing of concessioners in further commercializing the parks, the promotion of motorized boats within the Grand Canyon, and the allowance of snowmobiles within Mount Lasson and Grand Teton National Parks. Watt was failing the best idea, Stegner argued, and in doing so was failing the American people.

The West is still haunted by Watt's tenure as secretary of the interior. Nostalgia for Reagan-era policies continues to shape federal policy. Conflicts over the designation of parks and monuments remain as heated, if not more so, as they were nearly four decades ago. Rural communities historically reliant on ranching and mining continue to rage against what they believe to be the federal government's callous disregard of their opinion on the establishment of national parks and monuments in their backyards. Environmental groups remain ever vigilant against what they deem as inappropriate development within the parks, often viewing national parks as wilderness preserves rather than recreational spaces. Fears over the country's insatiable appetite for energy endures, driving a bonanza of oil and natural gas development across the region, and threatening national park units such as North Dakota's Theodore Roosevelt National Park and Colorado and Utah's Dinosaur National Monument. All the while, record numbers of visitors continue to flood the national parks, monuments, recreational areas, seashores, and historic sites, causing alarm that we are loving our parks to death.

Furthermore, the same arguments over the expansion of the NPS remain. In 1994 former director of the National Park Service James Ridenour published *The National Parks Compromised: Pork Barrel Politics and America's Treasures*, in which he argued Congress's continued addition of new park units were taking away from the agency's ability to maintain the hundreds of units they were already responsible for managing. Nearly two decades later, Senator Tom Coburn of Oklahoma employed the same argument in his 208-page report condemning the continued addition of park units, writing, "With each new park and program diluting limited resources, Congress has been effectively sequestering our national parks for decades. As a result, the NPS is now being asked to do more with less." More recently, the free market environmental think tank the Property and Environment Research Center (PERC) has put forth a similar argument that decades of neglect and misplaced priorities have contributed to the ever-growing backlog of deferred maintenance throughout the national park system.[28]

Solutions to these issues feel elusive, as ideological debates over the federal government's role have only intensified. In 2020 President Donald Trump signed into law the Great American Outdoors Act. Fully and permanently funding the LWCF and providing $9.5 billion to address the backlog of deferred maintenance, it was largely acclaimed as the most significant piece of conservation legislation of the last half century. However, within months, Secretary of the Interior David Bernhardt announced that state and local governments would veto any land acquisition made through the LWCF, making a similar argument as Secretary Watt's forty years prior. President Joseph Biden's rescission of the decision felt like little more than a temporary reprieve in the political tug-of-war over national parks.

It is easy to be cynical about the future of the national parks. They are all too often overcrowded and underfunded, and yet we still adore them. This is why we need to return to Stegner's "America's Best Idea"—

not just its opening paragraphs but Stegner's strident defense of the national parks. "America's Best Idea" was not just a celebration of the national parks. It was a call to arms. While we may not agree with Stegner that the national parks are an occupied country, we do need to remain vigilant that their ideal remains in place. This vigilance will no doubt continue to fuel debate over how best to manage the parks, but that is the point. Like our nation, the national parks are meant to be a conversation. And it is in that discussion over their fundamental purpose that will keep them both relevant and protected for future generations to come. We will always not agree, but we all must remain engaged.[29]

Notes

1. Wallace Stegner, "The Best Idea We Ever Had: An Overview," *Wilderness* 46 (Spring 1983): 4.
2. Alan MacEachern, "Canada's Best Idea? The Canadian and American National Park Services in the 1910s," in *National Parks Beyond the Nation: Global Perspectives on "America's Best Idea,"* ed. Adrian Howkins, Jared Orsi, and Mark Fiege (Norman: University of Oklahoma Press, 2016), 51–53.
3. Ken Burns, dir., *The National Parks: America's Best Idea, Episode One* (Arlington: PBS Home Video, 2009).
4. Stegner, "Best Idea We Ever Had," 4.
5. Brett Olsen, "Wallace Stegner and Environmental Ethic: Environmentalism as a Rejection of the Western Myth," *Western American Literature* 29, no. 2 (Summer 1994): 130; Wallace Stegner, *Beyond the Hundredth Meridian: John Wesley Powell and the Second Opening of the West* (New York: Penguin Books, 1992), 362.
6. Wallace Stegner, *This Is Dinosaur: Echo Park Country and Its Magic Rivers* (New York: Knopf, 1955).
7. Wallace Stegner, "Coda: Wilderness Letter," in *The Sound of Mountain Water: The Changing American West* (New York: Penguin Books, 1996), 156; Stegner, "A Geography of Hope," in *A Society to Match the Scenery: Personal Visions of the Future of the American West*, ed. Gary H. Holthaus (Boulder: University of Colorado Press, 1991), 218–29.

8. Frederick Law Olmsted Sr., "Yosemite and the Mariposa Grove: A Preliminary Report with an Introductory Note by Laura Wood Roper," *Landscape Architecture* 43, no. 1 (October 1952): 13; National Park Service Organic Act, 39 Stat. 535, August 25, 1916.

9. Mark David Spence, *Dispossessing the Wilderness: Indian Removal and the Making of the National Parks* (New York: Oxford University Press, 1999); Marguerite S. Shaffer, "Performing Bears and Packaged Wilderness: Reframing the History of National Parks," in *Cities and Nature in the American West*, ed. Char Miller (Reno: University of Nevada Press, 2010), 138–51; Dina Gilio-Whitaker, *As Long as Grass Grows: The Indigenous Fight for Environmental Justice, from Colonization to Standing Rock* (Boston: Beacon Press, 2019), 91–110.

10. Alfred Runte, *National Parks: The American Experience* (Lincoln: University of Nebraska Press, 1979), 33–46; Richard Sellar, *Preserving Nature in the National Parks: A History* (New Haven CT: Yale University Press, 1997), 7–27; Mark David Spence, *Dispossessing the Wilderness: Indian Removal and the Making of the National Parks* (New York: Oxford University Press, 1999), 55–70; Karl Jacoby, *Crimes against Nature: Squatters, Poachers, and Thieves, and the Hidden History of American Conservation* (Berkeley: University of California Press, 2001), 81–148; Dennis Drabelle, *The Power of Scenery: Frederick Law Olmsted and the Origin of the National Parks* (Lincoln: University of Nebraska Press, 2021), 151–64.

11. Stegner, "Best Idea We Ever Had," 4.

12. Stegner, "Best Idea We Ever Had," 8; Land and Water Conservation Fund Act of 1965, 16 U.S.C. § 4601–4.

13. Jason Alcorn, "Public Parks for Sale: The List of Grants," *Investigatewest*, http://www.invw.org/2012/06/11/lwcf-grants-database-1283/.

14. "Briefing by George B. Hartzog, Jr., Director, National Park Service, Department of the Interior, on Matters Relating to the National Park Service," House of Representatives, Subcommittee on National Parks and Recreation of the Committee on Interior and Insular Affairs, January 18, 1968.

15. Hal Rothman, *The New Urban Park: Golden Gate National Recreation Area and Civic Environmentalism* (Lawrence: University of Kansas Press, 2004); James Feldman, *A Storied Wilderness: Rewilding the Apostle Islands* (Seattle: University of Washington Press, 2011); Laura Alice Watt, *The*

Paradox of Preservation: Wilderness and Working Landscapes at Point Reyes National Seashore (Berkeley: University of California Press, 2016).

16. Stegner, "Best Idea We Ever Had," 4.

17. "Secretary of the Department of the Interior James G. Watt Testimony, House of Representatives, Subcommittee on Public Lands and National Parks, Committee on Interior and Insular Affairs. Thursday, May 14, 1981," James G. Watt Papers, accession #7667, box 17, American Heritage Center.

18. Quote in Ron Wolf, "Crisis in the National Parks," *Rocky Mountain Magazine*, November 1981, 7; The Wilderness Society, "National Parks & Recreation," in *The Watt Book*, vol. 1 (Washington DC: The Wilderness Society, 1981), James G. Watt Papers, accession #7667, box 17, American Heritage Center.

19. Gaylord Nelson to Rebecca Leet, Meg Maguire, and Chuck Clausen, June 29, 1981, Wilderness Society Papers, Denver Public Library Conservation Collection, CONS 130, series 5, box 35, FF 20.

20. The Wilderness Society, "Watt's Wrongs," in *The Watt Book*, vol. 1 (Washington DC: The Wilderness Society, 1981), James G. Watt Papers, accession #7667, box 17, American Heritage Center; James Morton Turner, *The Promise of Wilderness: American Environmental Politics since 1964* (Seattle: University of Washington Press, 2012), 236.

21. The Wilderness Society, "Watt's Wrongs," in *The Watt Book*, vol. 1.

22. Stegner, "Best Idea We Ever Had," 13.

23. United Press International (UPI), November 11, 1981, Wilderness Society Papers, Denver Public Library Conservation Collection, CONS 130, series 5, box 35, FF 20.

24. A. S. Leopold, S. A. Cain, C. M. Cottam, I. N. Gabrielson, and T. L. Kimball, "Wildlife Management in the National Parks" (Washington DC: U.S. Department of the Interior, National Park Service, 1969), 3; Richard West Sellers, *Preserving Nature in the National Parks: A History* (New Haven CT: Yale University Press, 1997), 214–16; Robin Winks, "The National Park Service Organic Act of 1916: A Contradictory Mandate?" *Denver University Law Review* 74, no. 3 (1997): 573–623.

25. Memorandum: Secretary of the Interior to Director, National Park Service, Re: Management of the National Parks System, July 6, 1981.

26. U.S. Congress, House of Representatives, Subcommittee on Public Lands, "Testimony of Secretary of the Interior James Watt," 97th Cong., 1st sess., 1981, 8; "Watt: Interior Shouldn't Keep 'Playground' Parks," *Rocky Mountain News*, April 16, 1981, 13; Ronald Taylor, KM Chrysler, and Harold Kennedy, "The Interior's James Watt: Hero or Villain," *U.S. News and World Report*, June 6, 1983, 51.

27. Dale Russkoff, "Watt's Off-the-Cuff Remark Sparks Storm of Criticism," *Washington Post*, September 22, 1983.

28. James Ridenour, *The National Parks Compromised: Pork Barrel Politics and America's Treasures* (Merrillville IN: ICS Books, 1994); Sen. Tom Coburn, *Parked! How Congress' Misplace Priorities Are Trashing Our National Treasures* (self-published, 2013), 7; Shawn Regan, "Deferred Maintenance and Operational Needs in the National Park Service," PERC, April 17, 2018, https://www.perc.org/2018/04/17/deferred-maintenance -and-operational-needs-of-the-national-park-service/.

29. Stegner, "Best Idea We Ever Had," 13.

Realism

Hope in the West is so entangled with fantasy
that it's hard to talk about it without knocking it.

—Wallace Stegner to Patty Limerick, 1988

6

The Legacies of Wallace Stegner and the Stegner Fellowships in a Changing American West

NANCY S. COOK

Most of the published work on Wallace Stegner focuses on his novels, his conservation work, and his representations of the American West. Stegner's biographers reveal an expanded sphere of influence, considering not only his publishing career, but his role as both the founder of the creative writing program at Stanford University and his teaching career. I locate in their accounts both much left unsaid as well as significant distortion of these roles in the narratives they create from Stegner's career. Here I argue that both Jackson J. Benson, author of *Wallace Stegner: His Life and Work*, and Philip L. Fradkin, in *Wallace Stegner and the American West*, among others, address these roles in ways that, regardless of their design, build upon the idea of Stegner as the "dean of western American letters," an idea that limits our view of both Stegner and his legacies. Less dean than facilitator, agent, or conduit, Stegner had a profound impact on western letters and environmental writing beyond his career as an author.

I argue that much of Stegner's most influential work has been overlooked in published accounts. As interviews and materials from the Stanford archive establish, Stegner's work as a teacher, mentor, and academic administrator proved important in shifting literary and market power away from the East Coast.[1] Less patriarch than coach, Stegner strove to decenter New York as a literary mecca, even as he worked assiduously to use his connections there to promote writers working in the American West, and at Stanford in particular. His work in these areas fostered and supported a cadre of activist writers, conservationists, and place-based advocates for a diverse, urban, western, and outback America. Together they shifted literary, social, and environmental conversations, giving the West a voice in national and global discourse.

My essay examines the *institutional* Wallace Stegner, through his roles as teacher, mentor, and academic administrator. Regardless of changes in his reputation as writer and critic, Stegner's legacy through his institutional roles carries his influence well into the twenty-first century. To be sure, Stegner's influence was national, but I focus on the ways he fostered lively, diverse, and expansive literary cultures and communities within the U.S. West. Before Stegner and the creative writing program at Stanford, western writers often were treated by the literary establishment as second-rate producers of literary romance or as native informants.[2] Wallace Stegner helped writers become less dependent upon New York, as he further uncoupled "making it" as a writer from the New York literary scene. Stegner Fellows and Stanford students established presses and journals.[3] They became teachers and editors, and they created satellite writing communities. They promoted workshops and programs, particularly important to developing and sustaining literary cultures throughout the West. And, in turn, such developments proved essential to the diversification of western American writing.

Stegner arrived at Stanford in 1945, after teaching at several colleges and universities, including Harvard. With an endorsement from his mentor and fellow westerner, Edith Mirrielees, who was retiring from Stanford, Stegner, then thirty-six, found himself back in the American West. Stanford offered a position with the rank of full professor, tenure after the first year, and half-time teaching. The money wasn't bad either. Although Mirrielees had been teaching creative writing classes, Stanford wanted to develop this area and put Stegner in charge.[4] His qualifications—from the University of Iowa, the writing program at

Harvard, and the Bread Loaf Writers' Conference—made him ideal for the position. In demand as the author of *One Nation*, his 1945 photo essay collaboration with the editors of *Look* magazine that examined prejudice in America, Stegner continued his work on race relations once he was in Palo Alto. Among other things, he joined the board of the local ACLU, and he worked to make the Stanford writing program diverse.[5] By 1946, with the encouragement of department chair Richard F. Jones, Stegner had a plan for a master's degree in creative writing as well as fellowships to support the writers and money to bring in visiting writers. Soon he realized that with the help of his benefactor, E. H. Jones, the wealthy brother of the department chair, there was an opportunity at Stanford to create something unlike the program at Iowa or anywhere else. Jones's brother made money in the oil business and, admiring both Stegner and his plan, bankrolled both the program and fellowships. Stegner tried and then rejected on-campus writing prizes as divisive, so instead he chose a structure with multiple named fellowships and lectureships to create a cohort of peer writers.

In addition to writing courses for undergraduates and advanced courses for graduate students, Stegner developed a separate fellowship program to give talented writers on the cusp of success time to write and fostered a community of talented writers with whom to share work. Moreover, they need not be regularly matriculated students or candidates for degrees.[6] This made a difference, and it made the fellowships singular: not a degree program, not a short-term residency, the fellowships offered a year, and later two years, primarily to write and to engage with a community of serious writers. The fellows were not students but peers, albeit not as advanced in the profession as Stegner himself. They were offered a modest stipend on which they might live frugally and were required to participate in a weekly advanced writing seminar. Beyond that, they were to write. Neither students nor teachers, they constituted a community of writers to critique each other, with visiting writers adding variety and a creative writing faculty to offer written critiques of their work. Moreover, they had the resources of a major university at their fingertips.

Stegner eagerly sought mature students, based on his success with military veterans returning to school after the war. The early advanced writing classes included students seeking degrees, some writers from Australia, and a handful of these newly minted Stegner Fellows. From the beginning, Stegner recruited women and persons of color and included westerners of various stripes. By 1947 Richard Scowcroft, a Utah native with a PhD from Harvard and a recently published novel, joined Stegner, and together they ran the creative writing program until Stegner's departure in 1971.

The fellowship program, along with frequent visiting writers, did for Stegner's cohort of writers what Bread Loaf had done for him—they gave "the young and unaffiliated" a community, as good as New York.[7] By 1947 the program was fully up and running. As colleague and codirector of the creative writing program, Richard Scowcroft explained, the Stanford program was a booming success:

> For years almost every prominent writer applied for a Stegner fellowship. Stanford was the place where you could be paid to starve to death for a year with no responsibilities. My guess is that fewer than half the fellows got degrees. [But] you had to attend the writing class; you had to be part of the writing group. And of course, that is what made it a workable and successful plan—that it was more like a congregation of talented young people than an academic situation.
>
> Having these three or four Fellows who were almost professional was a great help in raising the standard of a class. It was rare—almost unheard of—when you didn't have a high standard of expectation and achievement. Students wouldn't do less than their best because they were being judged by people whose talents and judgments they respected.[8]

From the beginning, the Stanford writing program benefited from a sense of community—first Edith Mirrielees, Stegner's mentor from the Bread Loaf summer program for writers and a Montanan, urged Stanford to hire Stegner as her replacement. Then, with the help of

English department chair R. F. Jones and his brother E. H. Jones, Stegner designed a unique program. And very soon after that, he hired Richard Scowcroft to share in the development and administration of the new program.

The program grew, and Stegner developed a protocol for his advanced classes. In weekly workshops he read a piece aloud and then guided the conversation, with critique from all participants. Several fellows commented on the sound of Stegner's voice and the ways in which the ear caught aspects of the prose the eye might overlook. Attentive to the craft of writing, Stegner collaborated with the workshop participants on honing their skills. And he treated them as colleagues, occasionally asking to workshop his own prose.

Unlike arts colony residencies or national awards such as the Guggenheim, the duration, structured by the rhythm of academic quarters, and the university setting made for the possibility of a community of writers. The fellowships gave these writers time to write, something Stegner felt he didn't have. Beyond their cohort, the fellows had access to other communities—ones formed with visiting writers and the faculty, as well as with former fellows and fellow travelers in inclination, mission, and place.

Stegner, leading by example, focused on the writing and the work of writing. He had no harem, he saved his drinking until evening, and he guided, rather than proclaimed, in the workshop.[9] He did not promote acolytes, but he did encourage westerners. He mentored and sponsored the fellows. For example, early on Stegner took undergraduate army veteran Eugene Burdick to Bread Loaf and supported him for a Rhodes Scholarship, as well as other fellowships and prizes. The Stegners even sent Burdick care packages while he was at Oxford. Burdick was the first among many apprentice writers Stegner supported. Biographer Jackson Benson writes: "Stegner was extremely generous to all his students not only in time and support while they were enrolled, but after they had gone out on their own. He was constantly reading manuscripts of ex-students who had requested his help even long after he had quit teaching, making suggestions, helping to find publishers, and writing blurbs."[10] My interviews with writers and my examination of letters in the Stanford archive, along with the volume of collected correspondence, edited by Page Stegner, reflect longstanding, highly supportive relationships he had with students, fellows, and younger writers, whether they had successful writing careers or not.[11]

With the tasks he took upon himself, it is a wonder he published at all. Yet he kept publishing. For some years, the pace kept him from regularly producing novels, but from his arrival at Stanford in 1945 to his departure in 1971, he published twelve books, edited several more, including two collections of scholarly articles on American literature, and also published short stories, articles, and essays. He arranged his teaching schedule so he had time away from campus each year, and he traveled, often productive when away from home. Among his many self-appointed tasks, he found writers on the cusp of success and gave them the push to make it happen. He taught the craft of writing, and he modeled a successful writing career. He found and raised money to keep the program going, and he guided it, including its ethics, ideals, and mission. He selected his teaching and visiting cohort of writers, he worked to keep creative writing out of the hands of the English department, and he led by example in decorum, behavior, and work habits. An adept political academic—protecting turf and fundraising—Stegner was an exemplary, if cranky, academic citizen.

Correspondence shows him to be adroit at negotiations with the university president, provost, deans, and department chairs. When he wanted something, an adjustment to his schedule or supplementary funds while away on fellowship, or to receive his salary in advance, Wallace Steger calmly, logically, and clearly made his case. His budgets were detailed down to the penny. Even from abroad, as when he held a residency at the American Academy in Rome, Stegner had a precise sense of the creative writing program's budget. For example, while in Italy in the fall of 1959, Stegner wrote to his codirector Scowcroft, detailing from memory the creative writing budgets for two academic years. He knew where they were short, and he had ideas about where to raise more funds. After listing the itemized budget, he added: "As you can see, it's close enough. We can cut the budget, or put the finger on R. E. Fowle, or do something else to make things break about even." In this letter Stegner went on to discuss scheduling at length, departmental politics, a death, and possible companions for recently divorced Carvel Collins. Although mostly about business, the letter managed to be by turns sober, playful, and gossipy.[12] Other letters reveal that without much of a support staff, Stegner and Scowcroft saw to the smallest details involving the program. In a newsy letter to Scowcroft from the Stegners' summer cabin in Vermont, he wrote: "One damned little detail I didn't get around to before we left—the venetian blinds for the Jones Room. Would it be a big strain for you to call some blind company and have them measure and give you the price, and then have them install the things?" He then explained where the key to the Jones Room could be found, what color the blinds should be, what material, and when they should be installed. He mentioned chair repairs for the same room, then moved on to discuss Scowcroft's and his own book projects.[13] Elsewhere Stegner offered Scowcroft humorous advice about negotiating university politics: "Keep a stiff (buttoned) upper lip in those Senate meetings. Let Rebholtz [sic] do the talking, and always vote no."[14]

According to biographers, the Stegner era came to a very unhappy end. He left in 1971, frustrated by distractions of a chaotic campus, students' bad manners, and the wandering, as he saw it, from the mission. The Merry Pranksters who hijacked the center of the writing community and whose work ethic he found sorely wanting helped drive him away from the program, as did colleagues such as H. Bruce Franklin, at the front lines of protests and spearheading, as Stegner saw it, the wanton destruction of bricks and mortar as well as civil engagement. Stegner's biographers detail his period of discontent, beginning with the arrival of Ken Kesey, while they also link Stegner's unhappiness at work with the cantankerous characters who appear in *Angle of Repose* and *All the Little Live Things*. Repeatedly Wallace Stegner advised those who wrote about him not to read his fiction through the lens of his biography. In an exchange of letters first with Forrest Robinson and then with biographer Jackson Benson, Stegner cautioned them, repeatedly, about making too direct a connection between the life and the work. He warned Benson that his adult life had little drama; he was a private person, and seeing his personal life "becoming the major character in a psychodrama—would give me nothing but a pain in the tail."[15]

In 1971, at age sixty-two, he was worn down by the demands of his administrative and teaching duties, particularly his undergraduate students, as he felt a greater urgency to publish more books. The biographers aren't wrong, exactly, but I think they exaggerate the conflicts to create greater drama in their biographical narratives. Mary Stegner cautioned Jackson Benson on a number of issues, including the desire of interviewers and journalists "to make a big deal" about one or two controversies from Stegner's career at Stanford. "You'd think that was the whole thing that ever happened in the writing program," she groused.[16] Stegner, too, changed his description of these years. Sometimes he claimed that he resigned from Stanford, sometimes he said he retired. And at least once he put it in the terms that any business-minded author might. Noting that he already was the highest paid person in the English department, and that was a modest "$22,000 or something like that," Stegner negotiated a contract with Doubleday that would replace his salary and allow him to write full-time. Doubleday "paid me something like $22,000 a year for five or six years . . . then we all ended up in the black and happy with one another."[17] The contract with Doubleday sounds like a much better deal, where everyone ends with money and "happy with one another," than his appointment at Stanford.

And yet, just because Stegner quit teaching in 1971, that was by no means the end of his relationship with former students, Stegner Fellows, or Stanford University. This was a famous writer whose phone number was listed in the phonebook. Until his death in 1993, he received letters, manuscripts, galleys, books, as well as requests for letters of recommendation, blurbs, and critiques from a large number of people with whom he had crossed paths. He answered every letter, promptly, and it appears he read every manuscript and every set of galleys. He continued to write blurbs long after he said he would no longer do so, and Nancy Packer joked that he "must appear on the back of more books than anybody else in the world."[18] After examining the letters in the Stanford archive, I believe Stegner might also hold a record for the number of letters of support written to the Guggenheim Foundation.[19] Moreover, Stanford continued to ask him to write, to appear, and to aid in fundraising and in alumni events. For the most part he agreed to do this work. Sometimes he was paid, sometimes not.

In examining his role as a teacher, most writers—biographers and journalists alike—list a handful of his most famous male students, and sometimes they include one woman.[20] My examination of his career seeks to get at something else. Beyond the usual suspects, Stegner Fellows, and, up to 1971, those who worked directly with Stegner, there included a significant number of working-class writers, women, writers of color, and westerners. While the writers who gained national prizes helped the Stegner Fellowship program and Stanford gain attention, as well as burnished Wallace Stegner's reputation, it is those who became teachers, editors, publishers, western writers, environmental writers, and writers of place who gave Stegner hope.

It is these literary people, with Stegner's support, who gave the West an intellectual community and a body of serious literature. Through their astute writing about places, often those under threat, they continued a tradition of writer-activists arguing for the preservation, conservation, and care for western places and the people who inhabit them. Less overtly competitive than the Iowa Writers' Workshop, the program at Stanford often achieved Stegner's goal of community creation. Alums collaborated, hired each other, edited each other, published each other, and supported each other in myriad ways. And while he was alive, Stegner continued to help connect a cadre of writers who cared about place, about the West, and about environmental activism. The list of *these* writers is a lot longer, and arguably more important than the short list of the boisterous men who have come to stand in for the legacies of Wallace Stegner and the Stegner Fellowship. The fellows who became editors and publishers are important, too, and are too often overlooked, for they played a key role in decoupling literary arts, especially, but also conservation activism from the East Coast.[21]

If we recalibrate common ideas about Stegner and the writing program at Stanford, we pull a different but no less important Stegner into view. Eschewing, or resituating, anyway, the "manly men" of fellowship fame, I offer a partial, alternative list of important Stegner Fellows: Hannah Green; Evan Connell (1947–48); John Ferrone (1950–51); Leonard Casper (1951–52); Miriam Merritt (1952–53); Robin White (1956–57); Donald Moser; Philip Levine (1957–58); Ernest Gaines (1958–59); Nancy Packer (1959–60); N. Scott Momaday (poetry and PhD in American literature, 1960); Peter Beagle; Gurney Norman (1960–61); Merrill Joan Gerber (1962–63); Frank Bergon; Zeese Papanikolas (1965–66); James D. Houston; Al Young (1966–67); Blanche Boyd; William Hjortsberg (1967–68); Max Crawford (1968–69); Judith Rascoe (1969–70); a few fellows from the 1970s: Katherine Haake, Joanne Meschery, Ron Hansen, Greg Sarris; from the 1980s: Neil McMahon, John Daniel, Fred Haefle; and a few fellows of later generations such as Kevin Young, Marilyn Chin, Sterling HolyWhiteMountain, Eric Puchner, Laurie Kutchins, Caroline Patterson, Jesmyn Ward, and Maggie Shipstead. Nearly everyone who has written about Wallace Stegner and the Stegner Fellowships offers a list, and as Mary Stegner remarked to Jackson Benson, they were never the list Wallace Stegner might have made (see note 16). My list begins to suggest the diversity of writers in genre, success, gender, race, class, and location that the common list of the usual suspects obscures.

These fellows, whether as authors or editors, connect place and region to nation and globe and have taken up contemporary issues from firmly grounded places; through them Stegner's legacy continues even in the absence of explicit ties to his life and work. One point I wish to make here is that arguably few or none of the writers named above is a household name, yet each has made contributions that should be seen as part of Stegner's legacy. And each deserves our attention. These fellows wrote prize-winning novels, poetry, and important works on place. They edited anthologies that challenged orthodoxies about

California and the West, they published literary journals, they edited major American writers and published work from other fellows. For example, James D. Houston, with Al Young, Maxine Hong Kingston, and Jack Hicks, edited an important anthology of California writing.[22] Frank Bergon and Zeese Papanikolas edited the anthology *Looking Far West: The Search for the American West in History, Myth, and Literature*. Don Moser, an editor, first at *Life*, then at *Smithsonian Magazine*, published several pieces by Edward Abbey. John Ferrone edited Alice Walker and Anaïs Nin, among others. Were scholars and other readers to pursue the work of these *other* Stegner Fellows, we might have very different and very diverse literary histories of twentieth- and twenty-first-century western American and American letters.

Crucial to the ongoing success of the Stegner Fellowships, Stegner also created teachers. Although fellows were free from obligations other than workshop participation, Stegner encouraged creative writing teachers and academics. After their funding expired, fellows could apply for a Jones Teaching Fellowship, offering two years of Stanford teaching. After serving an apprenticeship of sorts at Stanford, many went on to teach at community colleges and other public institutions, to liberal arts colleges, and to the Ivies. And they, in turn, fostered other writers and teachers. Some of these teachers encouraged their best students to apply for Stegner Fellowships. Among the many Stegner Fellows who had teaching careers, many cultivated their own students who wrote about the contemporary West. Philip Levine nurtured a number of working-class poets, including Gary Soto and Greg Pape, from his position at California State University, Fresno, and William Kittredge legitimized writing about the New West from his job at the University of Montana, while also encouraging strong students to apply for Stegner Fellowships.[23] Indeed, Neil McMahon, Fred Haefle, and Caroline Patterson had studied at UM before taking up fellowships at Stanford. Long after Kittredge retired from the University of Montana, the legacy of Stegner Fellows continued. In 2021–22 poets Katje Kuipers and Sean Hill, both Stegner Fellows, taught creative writing at Montana.

Whether former fellows took on temporary academic positions to make ends meet or to break the isolation of their work, or whether they became career teachers, they carried some of Stegner's and Scowcroft's sensibilities and methods into their own classrooms.[24] And they taught across the United States, at all kinds of institutions—a high school in the Los Angeles Basin, Ivy League schools, elite private colleges, state universities, community colleges, and prep schools. Several mentees appreciated Stegner's willingness to discuss the business of writing, something rare in the first decades of creative writing programs. By now the generation of fellows taught by Stegner have passed those methods and sensibilities to their students, who, in many cases, have passed them on to younger generations of students. If Wallace Stegner's work on American literature isn't read as much as it once was, and if his fiction has been identified with settler colonialist ideologies, and therefore no longer part of every course in western American literature, or in courses on the short story, nevertheless Stegner's legacy seems assured. Much of that legacy persists because of the teachers he trained.

Also forgotten, but essential, Stegner's skills as an academic administrator assured the ongoing success of the creative writing program at Stanford and the continued prestige of the Stegner Fellowships. Letters and interviews testify to his skilled negotiation of academic landscapes and his sense of just what kind of performance would yield donations to Stanford. On a few occasions Stegner scored a true fundraising coup, as when he single-handedly raised the funds to buy the Bernard DeVoto papers. Here he managed a "twofer," securing the materials for two books as he helped DeVoto's widow, Avis, secure her financial future.[25]

Stegner's legacies as a writer, teacher, and mentor also seem assured within environmental writing and green politics. Stegner Fellows, often themselves teachers, continue to nourish writers who make region and environment central in their work. This list of Stegner Fellows might include poets such as Philip Levine, Scott Momaday, and Robert Hass, and fiction fellows such as Wendell Berry, Donald Moser, Zeese Papanikolas, Frank Bergon, James Houston, William Kittredge, John Daniel, Katherine Haake, Greg Sarris, C. L. Rawlins, Alison Hawthorne

Deming, David Vann, Eric Puchner, and Ruchika Tomar. In addition, Stegner supported other writers in this vein such as Barry Lopez, Terry Tempest Williams, and Ivan Doig.

Perhaps some of these names are recognizable. My point here is that if we shift the ground, even slightly, we can come up with a lineage of writers on topics of crucial importance to the West and the planet, and that lineage leads directly to Wallace Stegner. Not only do Stegner's own works remain relevant, but the work he supported remains crucial. Whether directly as a mentor, or indirectly through the creative writing program at Stanford, or through the many teachers and professors he trained, Wallace Stegner's legacy endures. All of the above-named writers merit rediscovery or re-situation, and each, I contend, would benefit from placement in a conversation that includes Stegner and the writing program.

In addition to the scholarly and archival research for this essay, I wanted to get a sense of Stegner's legacy firsthand, so I conducted a few interviews with fellows. The Stegner Fellows I interviewed have taught at universities after their fellowships. Frank Bergon spent 1965 as a Stegner Fellow. Straight out of college, he was more than a little intimidated. "Stegner's method," he says, "was one of natural selection—to let us fling whatever we wanted into the seminar room without direction on his part," and yet his "elegantly written responses to my stories were typed on 6x9 sheets of paper, an industrious and respectful gesture toward student work that I recalled with guilt as I scribbled comments on student papers in later years." Bergon says he was "slow to infer from these responses that what merited Stegner's approval were my attempts to write about the West and my Western experiences in a realistic mode." "Failing was part of the process, and nothing to fear," Bergon adds. "What mattered was to get the work done: to just do it." Bergon corresponded with Stegner over the years. At one point he sent Stegner a copy of a syllabus from an American studies course at Vassar, remarking that the West features promi-nently. He asked to include something by Stegner in an anthology he and Zeese Papanikolas were editing. Stegner complied. Nearly all of

Bergon's published writing works to reimagine the West, in resistance to its prevailing myths.[26] Bergon is not alone here. Stegner's support of writers such as Terry Tempest Williams, Rick Bass, or Ivan Doig helped assure them readers, and his advocacy of a complex American West, diverse in cultures, fragile in its environments, influenced many Stegner Fellows as they lobbied for an ethic of care for both people and place.

Zeese Papanikolas was in that 1965 class, too. Both Scowcroft and Stegner knew his mother, Helen Papanikolas, a well-respected Utah writer. Zeese Papanikolas came to Palo Alto with a wife and children and immediately figured out that he could not live on the stipend. Stegner found him more money. Papanikolas noticed that Stegner went out of his way to be helpful to everyone and inclusive. Later, Stegner wrote the introduction to one of Zeese's books. But by 1965 everyone could see, Papanikolas said, that Stegner was fed up with rude students who took education for granted. Stegner had worked very hard for his place at Stanford, and he valued a strong work ethic.[27]

William Kittredge had earned an MFA from Iowa and was teaching creative writing at the University of Montana when he was awarded a Stegner Fellowship for 1973. He took a leave from Montana, and former Stegner Fellow Ed McClanahan filled in. Kittredge arrived at Stanford just after Stegner left. Kittredge's era has been well documented, even mythologized in biographies of Raymond Carver and a roman à clef by Chuck Kinder. While Kittredge felt out of place at Stanford—claiming he and Max Crawford might have been mistaken for gardeners on the manicured campus—nevertheless, the friendships made at Stanford continued in Missoula, Montana, and extended to other former fellows who for years maintained connections, communities, and legends. While Kittredge did not meet Stegner until much later, he was on Stegner's radar, and Stegner repeatedly singled out Kittredge's work: first as a teacher who could be trusted in a Stanford classroom, then for his writing on the West, its working cultures, and the environment. Much of what Kittredge told me was prefaced with "don't write this down," but suffice it to say that the communities formed in the early 1970s were complex and further complicated by a dizzying number of romantic relationships and rivalries. Many of the Stegner Fellows of this era also had strong ties to the Iowa creative writing program, so the web of influence, and sometimes intrigue, is very tangled. For Kittredge, the time in Palo Alto created communities that lasted a lifetime.[28]

Neil McMahon went to Stanford after an MFA in Missoula, where he had studied with Bill Kittredge. In 1982 Stegner Fellows were still not paid a living wage, but McMahon had studied psychology as an undergraduate at Stanford, had connections there, and found cheap housing. He house-sat for the Stegners, and as a trained carpenter, he worked for Stegner, too. Although in the 1980s few fellows met Stegner, especially in 1982, the year he asked to have his name removed from the fellowships, he made time for McMahon, a westerner and a student of Kittredge's. McMahon, with a recent story published in *The Atlantic*, found himself in the company of writers at the top of their game. In addition to the fellows, other writers, Harriet Doerr and Denis Johnson among them, sat in on workshops, and visiting writers such as Donald Bartheleme expanded the stylistic possibilities. McMahon made lasting friendships there, and he and his cohort made more than one road trip to connect with former teachers and fellows.[29]

Caroline Patterson arrived in Palo Alto with her partner, Fred Haefle, a Stegner Fellow. She applied to numerous MFA programs, and as a long shot, she applied for the Stegner. She held a two-year fellowship, beginning in 1990. She found that without an MFA she was at a disadvantage, being new to the dynamics of the workshop. She found the atmosphere extremely competitive and unconducive to forming friendships. By 1991, although completely disconnected from the creative writing program, Stegner could be coaxed to a dinner with fellows at Nancy Packer's home, and as a Missoula native and avid reader of Stegner, Patterson found him an amiable conversation partner. But the other students, perhaps too intimidated, avoided Stegner. At a time when the campus writing communities seemed to disdain her interest in her western homeland, Patterson was heartened by Stegner's conversation and support of western writers.

Each of these fellows was given the opportunity to move from "promising" to accomplished; they found a place where they had the time to hone their craft and engage with writers of uniformly high caliber, where they made professionally useful contacts, and where they made friends and community. The time at Stanford, Patterson said, "calmed everyone down. We learned to see writing not as a competition for awards and recognition, but as a life's work."[30]

Writing as "a life's work," rather than fame and recognition, endured as a valued sensibility two decades after Stegner left Stanford. Wallace Stegner, administrator, teacher, writer, and mentor, managed to make something remarkable in the U.S. West. He helped create communities of writers, communities that cohere in spite of distances or the pull of academic work, and he nurtured them. Stegner developed networks so that fellows had contacts—agents, editors, publishers. They published each other, hired each other, and read each other. Sometimes they reviewed each other's work (not always kindly). They corresponded, they traveled to give readings at each other's universities, they made road trips. They talked. That western mobility. Diane Smith's book in progress covers the Missoula gang in the 1970s, a coterie as cohesive as the Algonquin Round Table or Paris in the 1920s. At times they challenged an entrenched publishing business in New York. Former Stegner Fellows clustered in outback places such as Livingston or Missoula, Montana, Los Angeles, and around the Bay Area. The academic writers sometimes sent their students off to Stanford as fellows, and now *their* students send students off to Stanford. And sometimes those students write about the West.

Responsibility, Bill Kittredge labeled it. In a tribute to Stegner, "Taking Our Turn, or Responsibilities," Kittredge links Stegner's values to his own mother's, thereby to the outback West: "My mother and Wallace Stegner," he writes, "both believed we are defined by, and responsible for, the things we do . . . they taught me that I could, while trying to be an artist, also be useful."[31] In the twenty-first century, it is useful to resituate Wallace Stegner, to honor his legacies that endure, even as they have been overlooked. Let's not duplicate the standards of evaluation that discounted Stegner's work in his lifetime. Neither his Pulitzer Prize-winning novel nor his National Book Award novel was reviewed in the *New York Times*, and we do him a similar injustice if we recall only a handful of nationally recognized fellows and students. Likewise, his least favorite students and colleagues tend to lead the narrative of Stegner's academic life, rather than sit among the others, where they belong. We have a responsibility to read his fiction as *fiction* and to read his life as that of a writer who sat at a typewriter for a good bit of it rather than creating juicy bits for his biographers. As scholars of western American literature have argued, critics, for too long, have seen writers from the West as faithful recorders, documentarians rather than imaginers.[32] Wallace Stegner wasn't able to change that view, but many of the writers he communed with have unsettled the limitations that have come with representing the American West.

A reappraisal of Wallace Stegner's legacies, then, has much to offer in the twenty-first century. We can examine the work to create what Arthur Schlesinger Jr. called "an infrastructure for literary life in the West—publishing houses, critical magazines, bookstores, a reviewing corps independent of eastern and international opinion, an alert reading public." While I quibble with Schlesinger's worry about an eastern or international reviewing corps—a lot *has* changed since the 1970s. I value the literary infrastructure, largely due to Stegner's influence, that has been developed in the western United States.[33] Literary historians have begun this work, but there is much to do. We might shift our focus from the authors associated with national literary prizes to those whose names are less familiar. One might put the "big names" from Stanford's creative writing program into conversation with their colleagues in the seminar room, as Merrill Joan Gerber did in her essay of remembrance.[34] One might read the Vietnam War reporting of Don Moser alongside the Vietnam War novels of Tom Mayer and Robert Stone. One might add the books on 1960s counterculture by Ed McClanahan, Gwen Davis, Gurney Norman, and Robin White to Tom Wolfe's *The Electric Kool-aid Acid Test*. One might look at the women writers who juggled careers with family responsibilities, especially in conversation with the wild men so often named. One might add the western fiction of Miriam Merritt to that of Joanne Meschery, Caroline Patterson, and Ruchika Tomar, tracing a different arc of women and the contemporary West. My point here is that in an attempt to canonize Wallace Stegner, critics have ignored much of his legacy. They have cast him and his legacy in bronze, a Lyman Ward–like rigid relic, so that no shifting or re-situation can occur. With the wealth of alternative literary and cultural histories waiting, with reclamation, recalibration, and re-centering possible, let's work on ways to be useful, while we allow Wallace Stegner to continue to be useful through the legacies of his teaching, his mentorship, and his administrative acumen that insured the institutional longevity of the Stegner Fellowships. It is the people Stegner trained and supported and the program he built that created an evolving infrastructure for vibrant literary cultures in the American West.

Notes

1. Jackson J. Benson, *Wallace Stegner: His Life and Work* (New York: Viking Press, 1996); Philip L. Fradkin, *Wallace Stegner and the American West* (New York: Alfred A. Knopf, 2008). While I disagree with many of Benson's choices as a biographer, I thank him for depositing his extensive research materials at Stanford University. They help make the archive there a rich one for scholars. Russell Martin is to blame for popularizing, if not coining, "the dean of western American letters" moniker in his essay "Writers of the Purple Sage: Voice in Western American Literature," *New York Times Magazine*, December 27, 1981. In that survey of contemporary western writers, he manages to get a few facts wrong (Scott Momaday earned his PhD from Stanford), and a hapless caption writer mislabeled a photo, now infamously, as that of "William Stegner."

2. The literature on the perceived animosity of indifference to the literary production of western writers is extensive. Many of the literary critics involved in the creation of the Western Literature Association railed against both the East Coast literary establishment and the Modern Language Association. Hints of this rancor can be detected in Max Westbrook's preface to *A Literary History of the American West* (Fort Worth:

Texas Christian University Press, 1987), xv–xx. A reading of the disdain for Steinbeck's Nobel Prize with a focus on the response in California appears in Krista Comer's *Landscapes of the New West: Gender and Geography in Contemporary Women's Writing* (Chapel Hill: University of North Carolina Press, 1999), 20–25. For a survey of some developments in western American studies, from the founding of the Western Literature Association in 1965 to 2020, see Nancy S. Cook, "Trends in Western American Studies," in *The New American West in Literature and the Arts: A Journey across Boundaries*, ed. Amaia Ibarraran-Bigalondo (New York: Routledge, 2020), 10–20.

3. A discussion of the singular Stegner Fellowship program follows. Stanford University describes the program: "Unique among writing programs, Stanford University offers 10 two-year fellowships each year, 5 in fiction and 5 in poetry. All the fellows in each genre convene weekly in a 3-hour workshop with faculty. Stegner Fellows are regarded as working artists, intent upon practicing and perfecting their craft. The only requirements are writing and workshop attendance. The fellowship offers no degree. We view it as more of an artist-in-residence opportunity for promising writers to spend two years developing their writing in the company of peers and under the guidance of Stanford faculty." "Wallace Stegner Fellowship," Stanford Creative Writing Program, Stanford University, https://creativewriting.stanford.edu/stegner-fellowship/wallace -stegner-fellowship.

4. Benson, *Wallace Stegner*, 152.

5. Benson, *Wallace Stegner*, 152.

6. Benson, *Wallace Stegner*, 166.

7. Benson, *Wallace Stegner*, 165.

8. Richard Scowcroft, quoted in Benson, *Wallace Stegner*, 165.

9. Mark McGurl's *The Program Era* (Cambridge MA: Harvard University Press, 2009) features Wallace Stegner and his relationship to both the Iowa Writers' Workshop and the creative writing program he developed at Stanford. Although the book is thoroughly researched and well argued, I find that McGurl, too, follows the standard mythologies about Stegner as a teacher and makes his relationship with Ken Kesey a cornerstone of his argument. I agree with McGurl that the programs at Iowa first and then Stanford worked to make a space in American

letters and the publishing industry that decentered Boston and New York. McGurl's analysis of Stegner's desire to create a small community of writers as essential to nurturing careers matches my interest in the creation of community at Stanford, but in evaluating the effects of the writing program on writers and their work, we part ways. In this essay I am uninterested in the stylistic influences. From my conversations with writers and from correspondence, I think McGurl overstates the limitations of Stegner's critiques of style. Eric Bennett also takes up the significance of the Iowa and Stanford creative writing programs, but Bennett engages Stegner the writer more than he does Stegner the program administrator in his *Workshops of Empire: Stegner, Engle, and American Creative Writing during the Cold War* (Iowa City: University of Iowa Press, 2015).

10. Benson, *Wallace Stegner*, 163.

11. Page Stegner, *The Selected Letters of Wallace Stegner* (Emeryville CA: Shoemaker & Hoard, 2007); Benson, *Wallace Stegner*, 114, 128; Philip L. Fradkin, *Wallace Stegner and the American West* (New York: Alfred A. Knopf, 2008), 145. I will say more on the archival record later. It is also noteworthy that Shoemaker & Hoard, now subsumed into the Perseus Books Group, was the imprint of Jack Shoemaker. First as a bookseller, then as a publisher, Shoemaker has done a great deal for California writers and for poets, and he has published several Stegner Fellows, including Wendell Berry, Evan Connell, and Robert Hass. The Stegner path might lead to multiple alternative histories of western American letters. Jack Shoemaker's influence is but one.

12. Wallace Stegner to Richard Scowcroft, November 20, 1959, Richard Scowcroft Papers, SC 585, box 1, folder 28, Stanford University Archives. R.F. is English department chair R. F. Jones, R. E. Fowle, possibly Ruth Eleanor Cranston Fowle Cameron (1909–2008), avid writer, student of Wallace Stegner, advocate for preservation of Palo Alto and Los Altos green space, biographer, and sister of Senator Alan Cranston of California. The Fowles were close friends of the Stegners, and they had money.

13. Wallace Stegner to Richard Scowcroft, July 14, 1962, Richard Scowcroft Papers, SC 585, box 1, folder 28. The Jones Room, for many years in the library, was the room where the advanced creative writing seminars were held. It had a large oval table rather than student desks.

14. Wallace Stegner to Richard Scowcroft, October 4, 1972, Richard Scowcroft Papers, SC 585, box 1, folder 29. Ron Rebholz (1932–2013) was hired in the English department at Stanford in 1961 as a Renaissance scholar who taught very popular Shakespeare courses.

15. Wallace Stegner to Forrest Robinson, October 16, 1981, and Wallace Stegner to Jackson J. Benson, January 14, 1986, in P. Stegner, *Selected Letters of Wallace Stegner*, 59–60, 75–76. Forrest and Margaret Robinson wrote the first book-length study of Stegner, *Wallace Stegner* (Boston: Twayne, 1977). Forrest Robinson continued to publish criticism of Stegner's work, as this letter suggests. While both Fradkin and Benson create a story of betrayal out of Stegner's departure from Stanford in 1971, the situation was both less dramatic and more complex. As Nancy Packer recalled, in an interview with Jackson Benson, Stanford had begun to offer incentives for early retirement. Although Stegner was by no means the "dead wood" they encouraged to retire, he took advantage of the deal. See Nancy Packer, interview with Jackson J. Benson, June 3, 1987, Benson files, Stanford University Archives. I cannot imagine any English professor surviving a career in an English department without expressing frustration or without forming some antipathies to a colleague or two. It comes with the territory.

16. Mary Stegner, interview with Jackson J. Benson, January 19, 1988, Benson files. In a later interview, Mary Stegner noted the limited number of Stegner Fellows always listed in articles and remarked, "I wish they would just lay off. . . . But, always to attach a name, to attach the same list, which is not the list Wally would give." In fact, Wallace Stegner addressed the list from time to time, as in the introduction to *Twenty Years of Stanford Short Stories*, ed. Wallace Stegner and Richard Scowcroft with Nancy Packer (Stanford CA: Stanford University Press, 1966), xv–xix.

17. Wallace Stegner, interview with Jackson J. Benson, November 4, 1987, Benson files.

18. Wallace Stegner, interview with Jackson J. Benson, June 3, 1987, Benson files.

19. Perhaps due to Stegner's modesty, Jackson J. Benson mentions only the Guggenheim award that Stegner won in 1959. According to the Guggenheim Foundation website, it was his third (1949, 1952, and 1959), putting him in rarified company. He wrote dozens of letters and often

updated letters for repeated applications. At least a dozen Stegner Fellows from Stegner's era have won Guggenheims, and I suspect the number is significantly higher, but as of this writing I was repeatedly locked out of the Guggenheim site after too many queries.

20. That list almost invariably names Edward Abbey, Wendell Berry, Ken Kesey, Thomas McGuane, Larry McMurtry, and Robert Stone. When the list includes a woman, Tillie Olsen is named. There is some variation, with Ernest Gaines making some lists, N. Scott Momaday others, and in reaching for well-known writers, some writers who arrived after Wallace Stegner quit teaching are named. Raymond Carver comes to mind.

21. Useful treatments of the roles that publishers and editors at small presses and little magazines played in the development of a diverse and just American West include Krista Comer's *Landscapes of the New West: Gender and Geography in Contemporary Women's Writing* (Chapel Hill: University of North Carolina Press, 1999); and Gioia Woods's *Left in the West: Literature, Culture, and Progressive Politics in the American West* (Reno: University of Nevada Press, 2015).

22. This is a landmark collection: Al Young, Jack Hicks, James D. Houston, and Maxine Hong Kingston, eds., *The Literature of California*, vol. 1, *Native American Beginnings to 1945* (Berkeley: University of California Press, 2000).

23. The lists are fraught in many ways. In addition to the tendency to list the same small group, repeatedly, Stanford also practiced inconsistent record keeping. Over the years, several efforts were made at list making. In 2019 the website of the creative writing program lists Philip Levine as a Stegner Fellow, although he is listed as a Jones Fellow in most biographical sketches of him. Further clouding the issue, some Stegner Fellows also earned advanced degrees at Stanford. A degree, whether an MA or PhD, helped them in the academic job market.

24. The archives at Stanford contain dozens, if not hundreds, of letters from former students and fellows. While few admit to adopting any of Stegner's seminar strategies, dozens recall, with gratitude, what the time at Stanford helped them accomplish. They credit Stegner's equanimity, particularly in critiquing their work. Often they thank Stegner for his repeated acts of support and kindness. Many of the authors interviewed by Jackson Benson recall Stegner's extraordinary acts of kindness, usually

done quietly. See, for example Benson's interviews with Ernest Gaines, Al Young, Kay House, Boris Ilyn, Wendell Berry, and Ed McClanahan in the Stanford archives. Merrill Joan Gerber's remembrance addresses the quality of Stegner's mentorship. See her "A Recollection of Wallace Stegner and the Stanford Writing Workshop," *Sewanee Review* 103, no. 1 (Winter 1995): 128–35.

25. The anecdote Stegner tells about acquiring the DeVoto papers for Stanford can be found in Jackson Benson's interview transcripts. Stegner interview with Benson, November 4, 1987.

26. From unpublished essay, "My Year in the Stanford Writing Seminar," by Frank Bergon, and brief interview by the author with Bergon, March 14, 2019, Reno NV.

27. Interview by the author with Zeese Papanikolas, March 14, 2019, Reno NV.

28. Interview by the author with William Kittredge, April 25, 2019, Missoula MT.

29. Interview by the author with Neil McMahon and Kim Anderson, May 7, 2019, Missoula MT.

30. Interview by the author with Caroline Patterson, May 6, 2019, Missoula MT. Patterson subsequently earned an MFA at the University of Montana. She has published a collection of short stories and a novel, set in Montana, and edited *Montana Women Writers: A Geography of the Heart* (Helena MT: Farcountry Press, 2006).

31. In Wallace Stegner, *The Geography of Hope: A Tribute to Wallace Stegner*, ed. Page Stegner and Mary Stegner (San Francisco: Sierra Club Books, 1996), 112.

32. I'm thinking of Nathaniel Lewis's *Unsettling the Literary West: Authenticity and Authorship* (Lincoln: University of Nebraska Press, 2003).

33. Arthur Schlesinger Jr., "No Agenda but the Truth," in P. Stegner and M. Stegner, *Geography of Hope*, 19.

34. Merrill Joan Gerber, "A Recollection of Wallace Stegner and the Stanford Writing Workshop," *Sewanee Review* 103, no. 1 (Winter 1995): 128–35. Any list of periodicals, publishers, book stores, and literary festivals will be long and varied, but I think of City Lights in San Francisco, the *Los Angeles Review of Books*, Heyday Books, and university presses as examples.

7

Sludge in the Cup

Wallace Stegner's
Philosophical Legacy
and the Hard
Job Ahead

MICHAEL A. BROWN

In the 1990s we discovered that Wallace Stegner was perhaps not a staid western American who did little more than dress up and peddle stereotypes. Melody Graulich suggested he was instead an "eccentric man of learning" who subtly brought fresh ideas to his writing, a suggestion impacting how his work might be read and its significance for western American literature and culture. The wealth of literary history running through *Angle of Repose*, for example, encourages the idea that "we *must* understand" the intellectual life of the American West "more broadly," by recognizing "points of intersection, and borrowings between different disciplines," primarily, literature, history, and literary or cultural criticism.[1]

Graulich's suggestion has often been followed, in examining Stegner's environmental ethic, for example, but those efforts don't go far enough.[2] Each of the noted disciplines "intersects with" and "borrows from" philosophy. Yet critics who have turned their attention to Stegner have either assumed that "philosophy" just is what they have uncritically taken it to be, or that Stegner's own borrowings from and intersections with "philosophy" are largely irrelevant to his work. To date, even among those inspired by Graulich's suggestion, there has been no investigation of what Stegner hoped would be his philosophical legacy—at least none in terms he would have recognized as "philosophical."

After comparing assumptions about "philosophy" typically made by critics who have followed Graulich's suggestion with Stegner's own assumptions, I sketch a reading of the framing structure of *Angle of Repose* informed by his assumptions, not theirs. This reading emphasizes the book's opening reference to "Heraclitus" and Stegner's desire to express truths, especially moral truths, in his writing. His reference to "Heraclitus" expresses a "philosophical" truth at odds with both recent postwestern criticism and the spirit of the radical 1960s. The moral truth Stegner expresses, or "refracts through the lens" of the novel at the end, is that magnanimity is the ideal moral capstone of a life well lived. Then I sketch a new reading of *Angle of Repose*, based on a philosophical idea eccentric to both Stegner and to postwestern assumptions about philosophy.

Under this new reading, *Angle of Repose* and the "Wilderness Letter" of 1960 are two chapters of one book. In the "Wilderness Letter" Stegner picks up a theme introduced at the end of *Angle of Repose*, the relation between "civilized" neoclassical economy and its "wild" or "natural" counterparts. At a crucial juncture in the way Stegner addresses this theme, the argument he says he is "urging" involves little more than mockery. I conclude with an "urging" of my own that skips the mockery and is designed to fill certain philosophical gaps in Stegner's thinking about wilderness, neoclassical economy, and impending catastrophe for our species.

Stegner said that if there were anything lasting in what he had written, it would be a "philosophical residue," the "sludge," as he put it, in the bottom of the coffee cup.[3] After an apology for the seeming pretentiousness, he compares what he hopes he will have left his readers to what he thought Aristotle left his. No comparisons with any more recent postmodern philosopher (of the kind typically invoked by the postwestern literary and cultural critics who since the 1990s have considered Stegner's work). Stegner only offers the evocative reference to Aristotle and the style of "philosophy" that Aristotle represents.

If the sludge in the bottom of Stegner's cup is to be reconstituted and used to revive attention to our ongoing environmental and economic predicament, then Aristotle must be taken more seriously as a philosopher than postwestern literary and cultural critics have taken him. Postmodern philosophies oppose both "philosophy" as Aristotle understood it and Aristotle's core philosophical principles. In postmodernism and its "postwestern" offshoots, meaning and everything else derive not from something stable or unchanging, as they do for Aristotle, but from the interminable play across time of absence and presence. If Aristotle is right that existence requires complete presence at a time, then the postmodern and postwestern idea of "play" entails that ordinary physical things "really" don't exist. For Aristotle ordinary things "really" do exist since they are fully present across some but not all intervals of time.

Aristotle, like Plato, distinguished a sense of "philosophy" in which it means the persistent exercise of curiosity, along lines of "theory" or observation, from their own more technical sense, in which *being*, the most general or abstract principle, is the proper topic.[4] In the other, earlier sense of "philosophy," which has existed from before Plato and Aristotle until today, literary or cultural critics often do "philosophy." But in the later sense they don't, since even if they are somehow concerned with being, they don't treat it in the abstract terms required in Aristotle's sense of "philosophy." Instead, they treat it with more vivid, less abstract terms expected in their respective disciplines.

The contrast between the postmodern approach and Aristotle's approach can be illustrated by a pair of contrasting images. Say that ordinary physical things are bounded along the four dimensions of space-time. At this moment your paper copy of *Angle of Repose* is 5.2 by 7.92 inches and is 1.1 inches thick. It can't at the same time also be larger or smaller. Later, it might be smaller; earlier it might have been larger. Maybe later you will reduce the font size as you copy it at a copy machine, to be less bulky when you carry it around, and then destroy the original. Yesterday it might have been larger—if you had copied the whole book, enlarged the font, and then destroyed the original. Those are possibilities, whereas being larger or smaller than it is at a time, or during one interval of time, is impossible.

Your copy of *Angle of Repose* completely fills all the space by which it is bounded, or so Aristotle would claim. It is fully "present," or really exists, whenever it completely fills that bounded volume. If that volume were not completely filled, then the book would not exist. If, for example, the first three chapters of your copy filled only a third of that 5.2 by 7.92 by 1.1 inch area, at or during a given time, then no copy of *Angle of Repose* would be "present" or exist there. The idea that it could still be present involves a contradiction, for Aristotle, and there can be no true contradictions, no existing beings that embody a contradiction. While for present purposes this is a serviceable illustration of certain key features of Aristotle's account of being, from his "philosophical" point of view it should ideally be refined and expressed in more abstract terms to make it less misleading.

By contrast, postmodernists assume every volume of space "occupied" by an ordinary physical thing is only partially filled by that thing. Part of it is always "absent," or fails to fill part of that volume. In the final analysis, the apparent contradiction of "one" thing being both present and "absent" is avoided or rendered irrelevant by appealing to the "play" of language, which is grounded in the idea that "philosophy" should be modeled after poetry or some other art.[5] Postmodern philosophy insists that Aristotle's account of *being* misses the mark and is instead only a distorting account of abstract *beings*. Ordinary beings or things are understood through more practical categories, such as being available for use by us, categories that can't be understood as abstractly as Aristotle intended. Being itself can be approached only poetically or in terms of art.

The postmodern approach has been borrowed by postwestern literary and cultural critics from the likes of Jacques Derrida and, before him, Martin Heidegger. Since postwestern critics assume that the dispute about what "philosophy" is has been settled, the "intersection with" philosophy in their criticism is typically a practical application of postmodern assumptions, with special emphasis on ethical or political issues. They neglect the more theoretical issue of whether the postmodern understanding of being, or its alternative in Aristotle, should be preferred.

Consider an influential example of postwestern literary or cultural criticism directed Stegner's way. Since he identified with the American West as a region, and derived an ethics and a politics from that identification, postwestern critic Krista Comer suggests that as a writer Stegner was philosophically disoriented, or "didn't really know where he was." She claims that Stegner was "lost" in his writing and thus equally "lost" in his regionally derived ethics and politics—since the American West as a region is never fully present at a place or in a literary or historical work.[6] This matters greatly when considering the originality of *Angle of Repose*. Was Stegner "lost" in his own "western ethic," since in *Angle of Repose* he acknowledges so little his "borrowing" from the work of Mary Hallock Foote?

As Comer admits, the answer depends on the standard of attribution appropriate to fiction. For the "popular reader," and for Stegner biographer Philip Fradkin, since fiction always involves "borrowings" from various sources, expecting more attribution than what Stegner provided "would undermine fiction as a genre." Comer counters that "literary critics" aren't "likely to be so easily persuaded," unless, she says, they are the kind of critic who thinks the American West as a region can be fully present. She then supposes there are two, and apparently only two, relevant options. One is the postwestern, in which, like everything else, region and genre are subject to the postmodern assumptions about being. The other is the "popular" or uncritical "regionalist," which by default, and without knowing it, is undergirded by Aristotle's alternative. Since within the discipline of philosophy there are in fact other options, and since Comer doesn't argue directly against Aristotle's account of being, her criticism of Stegner and *Angle of Repose* is a clear case of the relatively narrow philosophical orientation that has informed the postwestern literary and cultural criticism so far directed Stegner's way. If philosophical sludge in the bottom of Stegner's cup is to be reconstituted, we must pay attention to the difference between

Aristotle and his view of philosophy, on the one hand, and the way in which postmodern literary and historical criticism rejects that view, on the other.

Really being lost, for Stegner, is not knowing the truth about your location. He says he always tries to express how things really are, not how we want or merely imagine them to be.[7] Moral truths and their expression prove especially important to Stegner. But he also thinks that the style of expression must fit the genre of writing through which the expression occurs. Stegner claims, for example, that his own views are "refracted through the lens" of his novels, meaning they are decomposed and distributed, like light passing through a prism. During the writing process they take on vivid colorations they didn't originally have.

Stegner's claim maps nicely onto one of Aristotle's core philosophical principles: no way of expressing truth is fully reducible to any other.[8] Nonphilosophical writing can express obliquely a theoretical truth that philosophy expresses more clearly (but also more abstractly). For example, Aristotle thinks that when a nonphilosopher, say, a historian or an author of literary fiction, writes that a specific historical or fictional person *lived until he was eighty-four*, they are saying something more vivid, and potentially no less true, than when Aristotle says, as a philosopher, and at a completely general or abstract level, that *form guarantees diachronic persistence of individual substance*. What makes Aristotle's statement true is the most general or abstract structure of reality, or being, and what makes the historical or fictional statement true, if it is true, is some fact about history or the fictional person in question. If it is true, then the historical or fictional statement expresses obliquely Aristotle's statement about *form* and *diachronic persistence*; it expresses the truth of his statement as applied to a specific historical or fictional person. The historical or fictional person is the *individual substance* that *persists* as one individual across an interval of eighty-four years. It can do so, because there is something about it, what Aristotle calls its *form*, that guarantees it can survive across the changes that invariably occur as time moves forward.

Stegner recognized that his concern with expressing moral truth put *Angle of Repose* at odds with the radical 1960s. Stegner's sense of "morality," however, is nothing as definite as what we find in either 1960s radicals or the preachers of Establishment morality to which they were reacting. His moral ideal is simply being responsible to anything "higher" or "larger" than momentary pleasure or narrow self-interest. Stegner describes his morality in various ways, but it always involves more than "present-tense life," which has no awareness of, or continuity with, the past and assumes no responsibility for the future.

Angle of Repose opens with the protagonist Lyman Ward wondering about his son Rodman, the novel's official spokesman for the intellectual orientation of the radical 1960s, which has also been assumed by Ellen, Ward's estranged wife. How could his son be so radically different? It's not that they differ in the usual ways children differ from their parents. As Ward in effect puts it, the difference between them is nothing less than "philosophical."

Like his grandparents, Ward "believes in Time," and "the life chronological" rather than "the life existential."[9] The latter phrase represents Stegner's own idea of "present-tense life." Ward thinks of his grandparents, and himself, as termini of a process of historical accumulation, events in time moving ahead, building upon one another—"the life chronological." Rodman, by contrast, champions "the life existential," or a life lived only now, one moment to the next, with no accumulation of meaning across time, and thus no sense of the continuous flow of history.

Graulich recognizes that Stegner's novel "originates in literary history." But readers who don't think philosophically about what a novel really is, at the abstract level of being, could think they are free to pick any thread of that literary history and use it as a master clue to reading the novel. This approach is codified in postmodern reading and criticism, which assumes that since "philosophy" ends with recognition of the interminable play of presence and absence, it is a form of art. No artist, including the postmodern critic, feels he or she has an obligation to "correctly" understand either the whole structure of a literary work or the intention of the author in writing it. As Hans-Georg Gadamer, an influential follower of Heidegger, puts it, "to understand is to understand differently."[10]

If we take a novel or any work of art to be what Aristotle took it to be—a concrete, formally organized whole—then reading and understanding what is read are quite different. The work to be read is somehow "framed," typically at beginning and end, by a structure that supports or informs the work as a whole. Readers are not simply free to pick any detail from the text being read and use it as a master clue for reading that text. If they miss or fail to understand the framing structure, they will misread and thus misunderstand what the author intends. To date, postwestern critics who have turned their attention to *Angle of Repose* have missed the specifically "philosophical" framing of the novel, in Aristotle's sense of "philosophy," the sense that Stegner apparently had in mind when he hoped his legacy would be somehow comparable to Aristotle's. These critics have chosen to look elsewhere, and differently.

Ward wonders during the beginning frame of *Angle of Repose* why his son Rodman "doesn't believe in time." How can he not, since everyone presumably knows that time "flows" into the future? Ward clarifies his concern through reference to a certain "Heraclitus," thereby suggesting the philosophical concern being introduced into the beginning frame of the novel, nothing less than a concern with being and time. This "Heraclitus" is a fictional version of the historical Heraclitus—or what we know of the historical figure by that name. Ward declares he is a theoretical ally of this "Heraclitus," and Rodman, an antagonist. "Before I can say I am, I was," according to Ward. "Heraclitus and I, prophets of flux, know that the flux is composed of parts that imitate and repeat each other."[11]

Stegner is alluding to the "river" or "flux" passages of the philosopher Heraclitus. While these passages are consistent with the idea that everything, in every respect, and every time, is in flux, or changing, they don't entail that idea. That idea is known in the philosophical literature as *the extreme doctrine of flux*.[12] It is often attributed to the historical Heraclitus but should be attributed only to Cratylus, a later student of Heraclitus's work. Given the sketchy historical record, at most we can say that Cratylus interpreted the historical Heraclitus, so that Heraclitus endorsed the extreme doctrine of flux. Heraclitus's "flux" passages are also consistent with, but don't imply, *the weak doctrine of flux*, according to which everything in nature, at some times but not others, and not in every respect, is changing. Since things are exempt at some times and in some respects from change, at those times no change occurs, and they are fully present.

To illustrate the difference between those two accounts of flux, consider the passage from Heraclitus standardly interpreted as follows: *you can't step into the same river twice.* You're standing on the bank of a river, you thrust your foot into the water and shortly thereafter remove it back to dry land. Then you repeat the action a second or two later. The river in this example represents the flow or change of things forward in time. The shore of the river represents the stable perspective from which you are observing the river flow by. You conclude that you didn't step into the same river twice but into a different river the second time, since the first river had by then flowed on and was gone.

While no doubt suggestive, the example is misleading. If *everything* is in flux, or changing as it moves forward in time, then both you and the bank of the river must also be changing. It might seem then that to make the example less misleading, as an expression of the extreme doctrine of flux, you must be placed in the river, not on the bank from which you observe or step into the river.

Say then that you are out in the river, up to your knees, holding your own against the current by bracing yourself against some rocks on the bottom with a long, sturdy branch. You raise your leg until your foot is out of the river, and then put it back in a second or two later. You still conclude, for the same reason as you did before, that when your foot reenters the water, it isn't reentering "the same river" as the river from which you removed it when the process began. This second example might seem like a better example of what Hercalitus had in mind when he is interpreted to have said that *you can't step into*

10. The "same river" twice. George Ostertag / Alamy Stock Photo.

the same river twice, since now you are in the river, part of its flow. By being in the river, you "flow" to some degree yourself, since you now feel less stable than you did when you were on solid land. Your legs waver and slip in a way they didn't in the first example.

You can see where this is going. The second example is still misleading, if *everything* is changing at or during *every* time, and in *every* respect. The bodily parts of you, such as your foot, are also things, and so are the rocks and the branch. So, to be less misleading, none of those things could be "in" the river as relatively stable reference points. They would have to "*be* the river," or "dissolve" into it, as it were. All the things you are, all the parts of you, in other words, would have to "dissolve" away into the river. You wouldn't even have to worry about drowning, as you "dissolve" away. Since dissolution is a process that takes some time, and since under the extreme doctrine of flux *every-thing*, at or during *every* time, is changing in *every* respect, there could be no "you" to dissolve away in the first place; no rocks or branches, no stable perspective, or anything else. There's only the "the flow of the river," whatever that might mean.

Aristotle thinks he has a solution to the "philosophical" problem just rehearsed. He argues that not being able to *step into the same river twice* doesn't imply the doctrine of extreme flux. Change requires that there be some point at which change doesn't occur. Rocks, branches, you and your foot, and the other midsized furniture of nature all have enough stability somehow built into them that they endure for a time, despite the changes occurring during that time. Whether Aristotle succeeds, in what he calls his "first" or most fundamental philosophy of being, he thinks he spells out the theoretical details whereby the moderate doctrine of flux is rendered coherent and intelligible, in a way that its extreme counterpart isn't. To step into a river even once, or to exist in the first place, for Aristotle, something must remain unchanging.

The doctrine of extreme flux is a historical precursor to the way postmodernisms understand existence. Both entail, from Aristotle's perspective, that nothing ever really exists or is fully present at or during a time. Moderate flux, as he abstractly develops the idea, is consistent with our commonsense idea that some things really do exist and are fully present at some but not all times.

Those two different doctrines of "flux" structure *Angle of Repose* from beginning to end. Which understanding of flux do Ward and his fictional Heraclitus endorse? It turns out that what Ward says on the topic implies that they endorse the weak doctrine. So, it must be the weak doctrine that Stegner has refracted and distributed through-out the novel, especially in Ward's engagement with the contrasting intellectual approaches embodied by radicals of the 1960s. Given the contrast between the extreme and weak doctrines of flux, both of which have been attributed to the historical Heraclitus, Stegner's use of his fictional "Heraclitus" serves as a literary Trojan Horse against the extreme doctrine.

To underscore Ward's belief in weak flux, and to set the stage for the accumulation of philosophical meaning as the novel proceeds, Ward declares not only that he exists then and there, as the novel opens, "Zodiac Cottage, Grass Valley, California, April 12, 1970," but also that, in his words, Ward is "cumulative." He is "everything" he "ever was." He is also much of what his parents and his grandparents were, especially their "moralities, and moral errors."[13]

Ward then constructs from the lives of his grandparents a story by which he hopes to understand what he may yet become. This illustrates just how he differs from those like Rodman and Ellen, who live only in the "present-tense." Toward the novel's end, there is no direct encounter between Ward and Rodman or Ellen, but there is an encounter with Shelly, Ward's young assistant, who has been helping him research the lives of his grandparents. Shelly is a surrogate for Rodman and Ellen, before they committed to "present-tense" life, and thus to the extreme doctrine of flux.

Should Shelly take her own decisive moral step toward the trends of the radical 1960s? Since the two of them have become friendly, Shelly wonders whether Ward might not be able to help answer that question. Should she join the commune in North San Juan, which she has recently visited? "We believe," the commune declares, that "he is the wealthiest who owns nothing and needs nothing," and that "children are natural creatures close to the earth," who should grow up as part of "the wildlife."[14] Ward responds by addressing the core issue separating "realists" like himself from the "utopian idealists" at the commune. Not unlike those idealists, he wants a society that will encourage and protect "wildlife." He believes that they aren't completely wrong; it's just that they fail to achieve the needed balance between wild and civilized life.

Seeking balance between extremes is a hallmark of Aristotle's moral theory. If in roughly Aristotle's terms being "civilized" or being "wild" are moral virtues, then they are dispositions to have positive feelings about the meaning of "being civilized" and "being wild," whatever those meanings happen to be. The proper balance between too much and too little, of either virtue, won't be determined by any universal rule, for Aristotle, but requires expertise and attention to circumstance, analogous to what is found among experts of any craft.

Ward makes his point about the needed balance indirectly. "Natural-credit economies" fail when they encounter a "high-powered, ruthless economy such as ours." In contrast, he points to Henry David Thoreau, off and alone in his cabin "in the woods," supposedly a champion of the wild, who nonetheless winds up "a surveyor of Concord house lots."[15] Thoreau's experiment in the woods ends with a return to the dominant economic practices of the day, which were a precursor to our own "high-powered, ruthless economy," based as it is, on private ownership of land—and made possible in part by the surveyor laying out his grid. Ward notes that Thoreau tried to achieve a pure, natural economy while "alone in the woods" but failed to strike the needed balance between being civilized and being wild. Ward is suggesting that Thoreau may have come closer to realizing this balance, if when as a surveyor Thoreau had given up, to a degree Ward doesn't specify, Thoreau's extreme, idealistic conception of "wildlife."

After the conversation between Ward and Shelly ends, the novel builds to a philosophical culmination. Ward comes to grips with the most important event in his story of his grandparent's lives, their "catastrophe." Their young daughter drowns, apparently due to the neglect of her mother, who at the crucial moment was distracted by the attentions of a potential lover. This catastrophe mirrors Ward's own catastrophe. He has recently become an invalid, and his wife, Ellen, has left him at his time of greatest need. Why she left him is left unclear, though the suggestion is that it had something to do with the radical colorations of the 1960s she has taken on.

Ward at this point has an imagined encounter with Ellen, presumably a rehearsal for a later encounter with the flesh-and-blood Ellen. Ellen's "ghost" asks Ward whether he will be able to gain, with her, and for himself, any better accommodation or "angle of repose" than his grandparents achieved with one another. Will it be anything better than the "living death" they shared for decades after their catastrophe? No answer is given in the novel. Stegner seems to leave the reader hanging, morally and philosophically. If he is using the novel to express a moral truth about seeking balance between being "civilized" and being "wild" in the wake of personal catastrophe, then he is apparently not telling it like it is. He seems to be violating a key tenet of his own western American ethic.

At the end, as at the beginning of the novel, Ward is alone and wondering. He worries about the "moralities and moral errors" inherited from his grandparents, which he presumably understands better than he did at the beginning. Is he now better prepared for his eventual encounter with flesh-and-blood Ellen, and her radical 1960s assumptions, than he was before constructing the story of his grandparents' lives? In the time left to him, will he, as he puts it, be "man enough to be a bigger man than his grandfather"?[16] If Ward is refracting through the lens of the novel Stegner's culminating thought about his own "borrowing from" or "intersection with" philosophy, then in Ward's reference to being a "bigger man" Stegner is expressing in literary terms a culminating moral truth, a truth more vivid than its abstract counterpart in Aristotle. Without considering this purported truth, the reader will be in no position to reconstitute the philosophical sludge in Stegner's cup.

No doubt "being a big man" resonates with the toxic or overweening masculinity found in so much western American history and literature. Noting only that resonance, however, disguises other levels of accumulated meaning in the novel. Especially what Ward (and Stegner) take to be moral and philosophical truth, built on the foundation set forth in the early reference to Heraclitus and the present imitating the past. Without the foundation of moderate flux, attributed by Ward to "Heraclitus," there can be no such thing as the moral culmination to a life. Culmination of any kind is impossible without some stable imitation of one thing by another, which implies moderate, not extreme, flux.

In Aristotle's moral theory, we find both the ideal of becoming "big" or magnanimous and the recognition that achieving it to any degree is impossible without first acquiring the wealth required to meet basic needs and to secure the corresponding minimum of psychological satisfaction. Magnanimity is, for Aristotle, not a separate virtue but more like the climactic, organizing virtue of an entire life.[17] For Ward, and presumably for Stegner, handling personal catastrophe well requires balance between a "wild" and a "civilized" response to that catastrophe, all set against the effort to be more rather than less magnanimous. For Aristotle, one can be magnanimous in the face of catastrophe without being "happy" in the sense of maximal psychological satisfaction dominant in the 1960s.

One reason the novel doesn't include exactly what Ward will do if he ever meets flesh-and-blood Ellen again is that throughout the book the tone has been contemplative. This begins with Ward's contemplation of the figure of Heraclitus and the role Heraclitus plays in understanding his "philosophical" difference with Rodman, Ellen, and the radical 1960s. Ward is portrayed as constructing the story of his grandparents' lives, alone in his wheelchair, and then observing it pass before his mind's eye. For Aristotle, theoretical contemplation, rather than more practical activity, is the capstone of moral and "philosophical" life. Without some magnanimity, such contemplation can't get off the ground.

Say that Ward by the end has acquired greater moral expertise than he had at the start. Since for Aristotle there would be no universal rule for achieving balance between the extremes of being "wild" and being "civilized," and since the circumstances of flesh-and-blood Ellen appearing in the future are unknown, the moral truth being expressed at the end of the novel is just that the ideal of magnanimity is the capstone of a life well lived. It is the capstone apart from how much of it is in fact achieved, or whether any "happiness" or psychological satisfaction beyond the obvious minimum we all need is ever achieved.

If Stegner was indeed an "eccentric man of learning," who used the eccentric idea of moderate flux to frame philosophically *Angle of Repose*, then perhaps he is suggesting through the novel that to understand the American West "more broadly," we could all do with more critical eccentricity. Consider for example the idea of *unrestricted composition* for physical things, as it is called in the philosophical literature, bearing in mind that the idea is eccentric at the level of what it is to be, or to exist, a level familiar to Aristotle and postmodern philosophers but presumably not to the conventional reader of western American literature, history, and criticism.[18]

Unrestricted composition is the view that for any collection of material objects *whatsoever*, there is an additional object that they compose. Put differently, a little less abstractly, but also unfortunately less accurately, it is the view that the whole is always greater than the sum of its parts, in the sense that such a whole is a thing in addition to the things that are its parts, and that there is no restriction on how things, or parts, are summed. Though there will be a strong inclination to miss the point, among those who think less abstractly, unrestricted composition is not a view about how we "interpret" or understand what a material object is but a view of what a material object is—what it really is.

If the idea of unrestricted composition is true, then any set of things constitutes another, numerically distinct thing. Factors such as proximity of parts, or actual contact between things or their parts, or having forces binding them together are not required. An atom is a single, numerically distinct but "scattered" thing, for example, despite its subatomic parts being spatially removed from one another. Your brain, the tallest tree in the grove where Stegner's ashes were scattered, and the Skywalk over the Grand Canyon—name this tripartite thing "Eccentric"—is an even more eccentric example than an atom. Being a set of filled regions of space-time, no matter how far removed from one another these regions are, is sufficient for being a single, existing thing.

Our recognizing a particular thing with scattered parts is not necessary for being that thing, under unrestricted composition, any more than being a set, atom, tree, or the Skywalk requires that it be recognized by us. The tree does not depend on our perceiving or thinking about it for its existence, though when falling in the forest it would make no sound heard by us, unless we were within earshot when it fell. Each thing, even Eccentric, would continue to exist even if there were no humans or anything else that could recognize it. However, having some appropriate interest in its possible significance for us is necessary for a thing to be recognized by us, as when a moment ago you presumably started having some interest in how the idea of unrestricted composition might have some significance for further understanding of Stegner as an "eccentric man of learning."

Since books and other writings are material things, under unrestricted composition there are whole texts of Stegner's so far hidden in plain view, not in some dusty attic or university archive. They have been "hidden," in the sense that readers of Stegner have not read his work assuming unrestricted composition. In some of these previously "hidden" writings he tries to overcome an apparent shortcoming in the moral attitude he conveys through *Angle of Repose*. Recall that the culminating, moral thrust of the novel is toward a personal decision Ward must make. But there is much more to the moral life than personal decision, as Stegner recognizes. He thought that we have the obligation to be concerned for the entire species, for the "larger" thing outside ourselves, an idea not buried not too deeply in most of the books he wrote. The ideal of magnanimity always exceeds in scope the ideal of maximizing individual, psychological satisfaction.

What is missing in *Angle of Repose* is the question of moral responsibility to future generations. How should we act if we want to achieve moral balance yet magnanimity, as a species, facing into the future our own likely catastrophe? How, if the focus is the relation between "ruthless, high-powered economy," as Ward puts it, and some more "natural" economy of the kind he mentions in his harangue against Thoreau? During a 1987 interview, Stegner said that if there were anything that might "help the species survive," and thus answer such questions, we must quit thinking of the American "as simply an animated economic opportunity," opposed to any "notion of the public good."[19]

Assume unrestricted composition, and consider against that backdrop *Out West*, a so far unrecognized book of Stegner's, baptized with that title just now, since evidently he never got around to naming it himself. He never named it, in part because like the conventional reader of western American literature and history, Stegner assumed some conventional view of what a material object is, not the eccentric view of unrestricted composition. *Out West* exists, or really is a book, though it has never been published, as the one unified book it is.

Out West has three chapters, consisting of *Angle of Repose* as the long main chapter and framed at the beginning by "Overture: The Sound of Mountain Water" and at the end by the "Wilderness Letter" of 1960. Under unrestricted composition, a "scattered" material thing such as *Out West* will go unnoticed unless we have an interest in whatever it takes to first recognize it. *Out West* is there to be noticed, but only if we are sufficiently interested in both the future welfare of the species and wary of elevating any author—Aristotle, Heidegger, Stegner, or any other—to the status of an oracle. It is there to be noticed, if under unrestricted composition we realize that a human life is a whole, material thing in addition to the moments of time by which it is constituted, and that magnanimity as the culminating virtue of a life would be impossible, unless that life is such a whole. If the philosophical sludge in the bottom of Stegner's cup is to be reconstituted, reading *Out West* is a required ingredient. Unrestricted composition is the mixing tool and new source of heat.

As *Out West* opens, it's 1920, and the adolescent Stegner has just emerged from the high, dry plains of southern Saskatchewan and northern Montana. He is standing on the banks of a mountain river for the first time, the Henry's Fork of the Snake. Not unlike Heraclitus millennia before, he is posed before the flux, or "river" of things. He is fascinated by how the river "runs," and runs on continually—without ever running entirely away and then disappearing, as a "running" horse or human would. "By such a river," he announces, "it is impossible to believe that one will ever be tired or old."[20] If the philosophical preoccupation of Ward in *Angle of Repose* is any indication, philosophical fascination with Heraclitus was a constant theme of Stegner's, youth to old age.

But by the second chapter of *Out West*, Ward knows only too well what it is to be tired and old. His earlier, youthful romanticism, or infatuation with the sublime without terror, is by then the wrong mix of civilization and the wild. It makes no reference to magnanimity, the culminating virtue of an entire life, but only to the music young Stegner hears on the Henry's Fork, a "secret symphony" that focuses his attention on the magnificence of the here and now. The sublime, or the higher or deeper dimension of things, can focus attention in just that way, or it can focus attention on the terror that accompanies the magnificent. A mountain river or, better yet, the river ocean voices a music that makes us feel puny, Ward recognizes.[21] The refrain to the song is a reminder of mortality and death.

The third, concluding chapter of *Out West* adds a social and a global dimension to Stegner's moral ideals of balancing civilization and the wild and of being magnanimous. It would be hard to overestimate how influential Stegner's "Wilderness Letter" has been, and by no means just in the United States. "Altogether, this letter, the labor of an afternoon, has gone farther around the world," Stegner remarks, "than other writings on which I have spent years." In his estimation, the "Wilderness Letter" struck this chord not because of its literary merit but because it expresses, "an earnest, world-wide belief." "There are millions of people on every continent," Stegner writes, "who feel the need for a bigness outside ourselves," for something to drain away the shrillness and infighting to which we are increasingly disposed.[22]

Think of young or able-bodied people actively spending time in wilderness, and simple acknowledgment by the aged or the infirm that wilderness continues to exist. These provide appropriate experience, Stegner thinks, of both the magnificent and the terrible sublime, of the "bigness outside ourselves," not simply of one, to the exclusion of the other. Without enough of this complex experience of magnificence and terror, he thinks we tend to act as if either we are immortal or we have no responsibility to anything very "large," such as the future of the species.

Of the several arguments Stegner says he is rhetorically "urging" in the "Wilderness Letter," one does all the heavy lifting. He thinks that in the United States, our moral character should retain the same essential features it has had throughout our past. He mentions the first generation of European colonists who left Europe out of longing for "the wildlife" no longer found there. But his point can and should be extended to Indigenous nations the world over, whose own sense of "the wildlife" was undermined by European colonialists and their descendants. Stegner suggests that we all should preserve what wilderness remains, Indigenous nations and descendants of colonialists alike, or increase it—but without naively thinking we can or should return all the land to wilderness, or all the going economy to some purely "natural" state.

In the various arguments he urges, Stegner doesn't go beyond mockery when responding to those who he predicts will resist on economic grounds. Mockery not too unlike Aristotle's, when Aristotle announces, using the odd style of "argument" or narrative he devises for just this purpose, that the extreme Heraclitans are "no better than vegetables."[23] Stegner mocks "the bulldozer types" who he predicts will not be moved by the "spiritual" aspect of his letter, dismissing it as so much impractical romanticism. The "bulldozer types" are for Stegner tone deaf, when it comes to the "romantic poets and philosophers" by whom he acknowledges he has been moved, not only in his youth but throughout his life.[24]

Stegner misses something important when he responds to the bulldozer types. Had he been more charitable, when not only responding to but also anticipating their objections, Stegner would have first reconstructed what was even then, in 1960, a perfectly cogent economic objection on their part. This is an objection that articulates the legitimate interests of working people, or people who when they work do more than manipulate a computer keyboard. Do the required science, or so this obvious objection would go, and we will discover that Stegner's key assumption has been undercut. This is the assumption that preserving enough continuity with the past for the health of the species requires imitation of our prior, more rustic encounters with "the wildlife," rather than imitation of later, more "civilized" encounters with it. When one thing "imitates" or is continuous with another across time, a huge number of factors are involved. The continuity doesn't require that any particular factor be preserved across that time, only that enough of the others are preserved. Today you are continuous with your yesterday self, for example, but that doesn't require that today you have every memory you had yesterday. Enough of what you were yesterday has to be preserved, including enough of your memories, but that doesn't mean any particular memory must be preserved.

On the assumptions that if land is preserved as "wild," it must be removed from the store of land available for economic use, and that a healthy economy requires continual growth, we will discover, this more obvious objection continues, that when it comes to the health of both human individuals and the species, the majority of Americans would just as much prefer a walk along the canyons of an American city, or a manicured garden in the suburbs, as a walk in the Utah canyonlands or the northern Rockies.

Why suppose then, as Stegner does, that our health requires an experience of wild nature, rather than the different kind of "wildlife" found in a city or suburb? The lines of a skyscraper, or fields stretching out from the edge of a suburb, can induce an aesthetic feel for the magnificent sublime no less than the lines of a rock canyon or the prominence of the Tetons. The chance of death by mugging gone wrong, by unseen pollution, or by a drunken driver on a freeway can be no less a reminder of the terrible sublime than the chance of slipping off a precarious mountain trail or being eaten by a grizzly.

In the last chapter of *Out West*, Stegner gives his answer, to the degree he has any beyond mockery, by referring to the case of already established cattle grazing rights in or near official wilderness. Without saying why, he concedes that, other things being equal, these rights should be permitted to continue, but only if doing so doesn't render the wilderness less wild by overgrazing.

Are economic factors ever so equal as Stegner supposes? Consider ranchers in "the West" with their range cattle, or owner-operators of Nebraska feedlots, or farmers, miners, loggers, and migrant workers. Or anyone else who works relatively close to the earth, compared to urbanite and suburbanite, with their greater investment in the information economy. All those closer to the earth already exist at the economic margins. In our "high-powered, ruthless" economy, it would spell widespread, even global economic disaster if too many more migrated to those margins, by virtue of removing too much land from the store of land available for economic development. Or so the noted objection would go, and end.

Despite the arguments Stegner rhetorically "urges" in the "Wilderness Letter," there is in that concluding chapter, or anywhere else in *Out West*, no philosophically adequate answer to the entirely reasonable question of why we should think at present that more officially designated wilderness is a version of "the wildlife" necessary for our animal health. What would it mean for us to follow Ward's lead, in *Angle of Repose*, having already concluded with him, and with many philosophers not represented in postmodernism, that the moderate understanding of flux should be preferred over the extreme understanding? What would it mean for us to be magnanimous as a species, given our felt need to balance "wildlife" and the going "ruthless, high-powered economy"?

History teaches that the philosophical transition from classical economic theory to its neoclassical counterpart, and thus eventually to our "ruthless, high-powered economy," was largely the result of accepting the principles of marginal utility and diminishing marginal utility. Both assume that while there is a threshold beyond which there is no additional psychological satisfaction from additional consumption of a good, there is also no moral threshold beyond which having more is having too much. It follows that there is no specifically moral limit to economic growth, or to the number and kinds of goods that should be available for consumption, even if there are limits of other kinds. Having or privately wanting "too much," as an individual, a moral vice for Aristotle, is morally neutral according to neoclassical economics. For Aristotle, by contrast, wanting "too much" is the motivating vice for every other kind of moral failing, a creeping moral disease that assumes falsely there is only one source of value rather than many sui generis sources.[25]

Neoclassical economics recognizes the fundamental importance of capital and labor but misses the fundamental importance of land as a limit to the availability of goods. To think there is no limit to growth and the availability of goods on a finite land mass is equivalent to thinking a steady state economy can exist on a perpetually diminishing area of land. It follows that the farm or the ranch could shrink in size and still grow without limit in productivity. It also follows that the global economy could be concentrated into a single continent, nation, city, neighborhood, ranch, or farm. And since our "ruthless, high-powered economy" is an information economy, it also follows that it could be concentrated "into your iPad, leaving the rest of the planet as a designated wilderness."[26] Rain will always follow the plow, if only we pay homage to some fancy version of *Campbell's Soil Culture Manual.* Those who know the American West and its history have heard such nonsense before.

Let me tell it like it is. History gives clues to the type of collective magnanimity needed to face the hard job ahead, the job of handling impending catastrophe. Public ownership of the land—all the land—modeled to some degree after the relation of Indigenous nations to the land before European intrusion. Recognition that Epicurus was right, morally: nothing is enough for those who think enough is too little. And to go with it, a zero-growth economy that recognizes, as good farmers and ranchers do, that the land is no less important than labor and capital.[27] We need an economy that reflects both that truth from Epicurus and the scientific truth that for economic purposes the earth is a closed system always moving toward depletion of energy and resources, even if locally it seems otherwise.[28] These are the philosophical ingredients here being "urged," for reconstituting the sludge in Stegner's cup, without either mocking the "bulldozer types" or marginalizing those who live and work closer to the earth than to the flow of information and capital. In the future both paths, already well worn, lead to our downfall. Neither the path of radical environmentalism, beholden to the overwrought romanticism of the 1960s, nor the unthinking faith of the bulldozer types will suffice over the long

11. The hard job ahead. David Winger / Alamy Stock Photo.

run for ensuring that we continue to flourish, or even survive. Instead, we must venture onto the rough ground between them. The hard job ahead requires the creation of a new path.

Any less penetrating response to our situation will be more advertisement for "the life existential" and a denigration of "the life chronological." At the philosophical level it will likely represent another failure to understand the abstract conflict between the doctrines of extreme and moderate flux found in Heraclitus—a conflict Stegner articulated vividly, in literary terms, in *Angle of Repose* and through his argumentative "urgings" in the last chapter of *Out West*.

Notes

1. Melody Graulich, "Book Learning: *Angle of Repose* as Literary History," in *Wallace Stegner: Man and Writer*, ed. Charles E. Rankin (Albuquerque: University of New Mexico Press, 1996), 250.

2. Brett J. Olson, "Wallace Stegner and the Environmental Ethic: Environmentalism as a Rejection of Western Myth," *Western American Literature* (Summer 1994): 123–42.

3. Wallace Stegner and Richard W. Etulain, *Stegner: Conversations on History and Literature* (Las Vegas: University of Nevada Press, 1990), 196.

4. Andrea Wilson Nightingale, *Genres in Dialogue: Plato and the Construct of Philosophy* (New York: Cambridge University Press, 1999). See also Justin H. Smith, *The Philosopher: A History in Six Types* (Princeton NJ: Princeton University Press, 2016).

5. Gilles Deleuze and Felix Guattari, *What Is Philosophy?*, trans. Hugh Tomlinson and Graham Burchell (New York: Columbia University Press, 1994). Deleuze has had a decisive influence on much recent, postwestern literary and cultural criticism. See Neil Campbell, *The Rhizomatic West: Representing the American West in a Transnational, Global, Media Age* (Lincoln: University of Nebraska Press, 2008), 9.

6. Krista Comer, "Exceptionalism, Other Wests, Critical Regionalism," *American Literary History* 23, no. 1 (Spring 2011): 167.

7. Jackson J. Benson, *Down by the Lemonade Springs: Essays on Wallace Stegner* (Reno: University of Nevada Press, 2001), 9.

8. This is a matter of scholarly controversy, among philosophers and historians of philosophy. For the perspective assumed herein, see Martha Husain, *Ontology and the Art of Tragedy: An Approach to Aristotle's Poetics* (Albany: State University of New York Press, 2002).

9. Wallace Stegner, *Angle of Repose* (New York: Doubleday, 1971), 18.

10. Hans-Georg Gadamer, *Truth and Method*, trans. G. Barden and J. Cumming (New York: Bloomsbury Academic, 1975), 264.

11. Stegner, *Angle of Repose*, 15.

12. Jonathan Barnes, *The Presocratic Philosophers* (London: Routledge, 2000), 65–75.

13. Stegner, *Angle of Repose*, 15.

14. Stegner, *Angle of Repose*, 514.

15. Stegner, *Angle of Repose*, 514.

16. Stegner, *Angle of Repose*, 569.

17. Aristotle, *Ethics*, 1123a 34–1125a 35. See also W. F. R. Hardie, "'Magnanimity' in Aristotle's 'Ethics,'" *Phronesis* 23, no. 1 (1978).

18. Peter van Inwagen, *Material Beings* (Ithaca NY: Cornell University Press, 1990).

19. James Hepworth, *Stealing Glances: Three Interviews with Wallace Stegner* (Albuquerque: University of New Mexico Press, 1998), 108.

20. Wallace Stegner, *The Sound of Mountain Water* (Lincoln: University of Nebraska Press, 1980), 42.

21. Longinus, *On the Sublime*, sec. 35.

22. Wallace Stegner, "The Geography of Hope: Introduction to the Wilderness Letter," *Eco-Speak*, https://web.stanford.edu/~cbross/Ecospeak /wildernessletterintro.html.

23. Aristotle, *Metaphysics*, 1005b25. See also Jonathan Lear, *Aristotle and Logical Theory* (New York: Cambridge University Press, 1980), 98–114.

24. Wallace Stegner, *Wolf Willow: A History, a Story, and a Memory of the Last Plains Frontier* (New York: Penguin, 1990), 292.

25. Scott Meikle, *Aristotle's Economic Thought* (Oxford: Oxford University Press, 1995).

26. Brian Czech, *Supply Shock: Economic Growth at the Crossroads and the Steady State Solution* (Gabriola Island BC: New Society Publishers, 2013), 178.

27. Regarding the economic importance of land, there is no better place to begin the historical reorientation of economic thought in the American West than by reading an eccentric classic, largely suppressed by the forces supporting neoclassical economics: Henry George, *Progress and Poverty* (New York: Robert Schalkenbach Foundation, 2008). See also Edward T. O'Donnell, *Henry George and the Crisis of Inequality* (New York: Columbia University Press, 2015).

28. Dan O'Neill, "The Economics of Enough," TEDX Talks, June 13, 2014, https://www.youtube.com/watch?v=WIG33QtLRyA.

8

Hope in Public Lands   A Conversation

LEISL CARR CHILDERS

AND ADAM M. SOWARDS

Authors' note on method: We wrote this, as a conversation, over five months preceding the Wallace Stegner symposium held in May 2019 and then revised it in the months afterward relying on new insights gained from other presentations and subsequent conversations. One of us wrote a section, shared it with the other, who then responded and extended the thoughts and ideas. Although we considered revising the conversation into a traditional essay, we elected to maintain the back-and-forth element, in part because we believe Stegner valued the give-and-take of ideas and in part because its vitality is more evident in this form. The richness of our discussion took us down unforeseen paths, and the conversation is as revealing as our conclusions.

AMS (January 3, 2019)

In the early twenty-first century, hope can be hard to come by, and the history of the U.S. West easily can turn to a litany of disasters: extinctions of cultures and species, expropriation of property and sovereignty, exploitation of labor and land. Yet historians are storytellers, among other things, and so we can frame our past with hope—or despair.[1] Whatever our choice entails, we might recognize this power and realize, as Wallace Stegner did, that historians connect past to present to shape the future. Despite all the chatter about the future belonging to the STEM (science, technology, engineering, math) fields, the humanities and arts are not only important but central and relevant to solving problems and changing the world, by telling stories of injury and hope.

Perhaps today's deepest thinker and most eloquent writer about hope is Rebecca Solnit. Her wide-ranging body of work frequently circles hope and history. A collection of her essays on the topic, *Hope in the Dark*, appeared first in 2004 in the lead-up to the Iraq War and was updated and reissued in 2016 in anticipation of a historic election. To counter hopelessness, Solnit maintains that we must change the stories we tell. "Making an injury visible and public is often the first step in remedying it, and political change often follows culture, as what was long tolerated is seen to be intolerable, or what was overlooked becomes obvious," Solnit observes, "which means that every conflict is in part a battle over the story we tell, or who tells and who is heard."[2] Historians are storytellers, and so we are—like it or not—in the fray. Armed with the right stories, the culture and then our politics can shift.

Stegner understood this, too. He knew the cultural role historians could and, in his view, needed to play. In 1967 Stegner concluded his essay "History, Myth, and the Western Writer" with a folksy anecdote paired with a serious call for action. "In the old days," he explained, "in blizzardy weather, we used to tie a string of lariats from house to barn so as to make it from shelter to responsibility and back again. With personal, family, and cultural chores to do, I think we had better rig up such a line between past and present."[3] Writing during a moment of building unrest and uncertainty, akin to our own, Stegner asked intellectuals and artists of the West, writers and historians both, to do cultural work, to ground a culture, a society, a nation with a history, a story of who we have been, who we are, and who we might be.

Stegner had begun such work earlier. Just as the stagnant 1950s cracked into the turbulent 1960s, he deployed his sterling reputation as a writer and historian. Already the author of more than a dozen books, including the immediate classic western biography when it was published in 1953, *Beyond the Hundredth Meridian: John Wesley Powell and the Second Opening of the West*, Stegner conveyed an authority and authenticity about the American West that only a habitué could, so people sought him out and listened when he spoke. His study of Powell raised the nineteenth-century explorer and bureaucrat into a prescient prophet whose ideas, rooted in a more realistic ecological vision of the region's arid limitations, might have saved the West from many of its disastrous land policies. This book reflected the advice he later would give about the links between past and present: seeing the West's land and water in crisis, he told a historical parable through Powell.[4]

Like many westerners of his Waspy social class in those postwar years, Stegner wanted to preserve the West of Powell and his own, sometimes nostalgic, memory—a memory that forgot most of the West's residents of color and too easily assumed American colonialism. Indeed, his omissions have inspired an entire book, *Why I Can't Read Wallace Stegner and Other Essays: A Tribal Voice*, by Elizabeth Cook-Lynn, a Dakota scholar from the Crow Creek Sioux Tribe.[5] We must remember his erasures and ways he minimized the West's Indigenous cultures and other people of color, even while we recognize the crucial ways Stegner challenged corporate and government business as usual.

Stegner built out from his personal interest in being outdoors to engage politically with conservation, his first critical foray into activism during the Echo Park campaign in the early 1950s.[6] He joined other wilderness advocates to block the Bureau of Reclamation's designs to build a dam that would flood part of Dinosaur National Monument on the Utah-Colorado border at a time when such river development proceeded with few objections. Stegner edited a protest volume, *This Is Dinosaur: Echo Park Country and Its Magic Rivers*, a lovely essay in words and images that every member of Congress received.[7] Stegner's fiction and nonfiction oeuvre legitimated his voice; his conservation work provided political bona fides. This campaign alerted Congress to the powerful and growing constituency of wilderness advocates and outdoor recreationists across the West and nation. Congress listened, not only stopping the Echo Park Dam but also initiating the Outdoor Recreation Resources Review Commission (ORRRC) to advise legislators of the public's needs, especially on public lands. A cynical view of the ORRRC is that it was a delaying tactic, one of those studies politicians institute so they can postpone decisions.[8] The truth in that underplays the significance and power of the public record the ORRRC produced, including what Stegner contributed.

On December 3, 1960, Stegner wrote to the commission's member charged with studying wilderness, David E. Pesonen. What has become known as simply the "Wilderness Letter" offered an eloquent appeal for wilderness as understood by Stegner and many others at that time who saw it as both an idea and a place that "helped form our character." His "our" here shows how Stegner understood wilderness from the perspective of his whiteness, and likely too his maleness, although white women also erased Native peoples' traces in the putative pristine wilderness.[9] For Stegner, wilderness was a spiritual salve, a reserve, a place needed more than ever in 1960 since urban-industrial civilization had replaced the frontier: "The more urban [the United States] has become, and the more frantic with technological change, the sicker and more embittered our literature, and I believe our people, have become." This transition saddened Stegner, whose love of a romantic frontier never quite shook loose, yet he believed in hope—for literature and for Americans—resting in the land itself. Wilderness held the key to recapture some fundamental goodness, some hope for righting the ship he saw running aground. Closing his letter to the ORRRC, Stegner wrote, "We simply need that wild country available to us, even if we never do more than drive to its edge and look in. For it can be a means of reassuring ourselves of our sanity as creatures, a part of the geography of hope."[10]

A hope-filled geography rested at least in part in people's dreams, with laws of Congress, and on the ground where conflict smashed those ideals together. To consider hope in the land, then and now, is to reckon with the past and history's claims to the public spaces of the American West, public spaces where not all the public has always felt welcomed.[11] Although Stegner here focused on wilderness, that need not be the sole focus. To consider hope in the land is to reflect on the stories past peoples told about places—the triumphs and failures; the dreams, the compromises, and the mixed results—if only to help us step thoughtfully into the present's uncertainty to chart pathways toward a future that is more equitable for our species and others. In 1979 he riffed on hope, hitting all these themes: "Angry as one may be

12. The wilderness Wallace Stegner named in his "Wilderness Letter." Lower Roost Canyon, Arthur Ekker Ranch. Dr. A. L. Inglesby, 1943. Used by permission, Utah State Historical Society.

at what careless people have done and still do to a noble habitat, it is hard to be pessimistic about the West. This is the native home of hope. When it fully learns that cooperation, not rugged individualism, is the pattern that most characterizes and preserves it, then it will have achieved itself and outlived its origins. Then it has a chance to create a society to match its scenery."[12] This, then, is how Stegner framed so much work—a tension between past sins and future hopes, between individualism and community, between people and place.

With the "geography of hope," his final rhetorical turn, Stegner offered a shorthand phrase others have adopted for their own purposes. Some have used it to mean wilderness; others have used it to refer to farms; others apply it to their cultural imaginings.[13] As we do, Stegner wrangled with the term himself, expanding and adjusting meanings as outside events prompted him to adapt and evolve his thinking.

LCC (February 5–6 and March 6, 2019)

Stegner indeed contended throughout his lifetime with the phrase he famously coined in 1960. Clever, pithy, and abstract, he originally wanted it to punctuate his points about the need for and the role of wilderness in American society in the emergent moment of legally codifying it in public lands management. But, by the end of his life, the phrase came to mean something broader about the American West. The trajectory of his thoughts about "the geography of hope" encapsulates his very personal aspirations for and concerns about the region he had come to believe embodied both the best and the worst of American society.

Stegner first framed wilderness as the geography of hope, in a similar vein as historian Frederick Jackson Turner's frontier, as the thing Americans needed to be American. Both men portrayed the frontier in terms of wild lands devoid of humans, despite the reality that these places were and continue to be the homelands of North America's Indigenous peoples. Both believed wild lands had created conditions during colonization—the opportunity for improvement, the power of the individual and Western civilization, and the hope for a better life—that endowed the nation with unique characteristics that would be lost in the face of development. Both worried that without these wild lands that had shaped American bodies and American thoughts, the nation would become something else, something lesser or more ordinary. But where Turner viewed the process of conquest (though he said "civilization") as the mechanism that created hope, Stegner believed in the transformative power and abiding comfort of place. For Stegner, the value of lands that Americans could continue to perceive as wild lay in how the land itself had historically contained "our hope and our excitement" and how that sentiment for the future was inscribed in these places and could be perpetuated by passing it on to future generations, "Americans who never saw any phase of the frontier." But he was adamant that this was only possible so long as we, meaning the American people specifically and humanity broadly, kept "the remainder of our wild as a reserve and a promise."[14]

Although Stegner's conflation of wilderness and the frontier, as you said, ignored the presence of Indigenous peoples and the process by which the United States dispossessed Indigenous peoples of their homelands, it also revealed a real and tangible desire for natural places seemingly unspoiled by human vagaries. His "Wilderness Letter," with its poignant closing, served as a clarion call to support not only the need for outdoor recreational spaces but also the deliberate delineation and dedicated protection of wild places on the nation's public lands, especially in the American West, a region Stegner believed to be still salvageable from industrial processes. Although Stegner perpetuated the narrative of Indigenous dispossession in his portrayal of wilderness, there is value in considering his ongoing attempts to rectify his relationship to the land as a descendant of settlers and as someone who moved constantly throughout his life. Stegner's hope is more than cultural; it is material. In lieu of a homeland, Stegner looked to the wilderness.[15]

In the aftermath of the passage of wilderness legislation in 1964, Stegner's phrase took on new meaning. The author revisited his phrase every time the geography in which he placed his hope was threatened, whether by bureaucratic processes, industrial or urban development, or the Sagebrush Rebellion. He evolved the place of his geography and the nature of his hope to grapple with these challenges. Stegner was driven by a love for the region of which he wrote. Writer and environmental lawyer Brett J. Olsen wrote that Stegner "held to a unique environmental ethic, drawing little from contemporary theological discussion, scientific ecology, economic or other environmental philosophies. Rather, he derived his primary understanding of the land from the empirical, practical fact of growing up in the West."[16] Historian Beth LaDow echoed this assessment, writing, "In dubbing western aridity 'the geography of hope' he coined the best phrase anybody could imagine for a desert full of dreams, and of the deadly combination of aridity and hope." She argued, "The graceful, tightly-wound phrase was Stegner's stock-in-trade. But at its best, Wallace Stegner's environmentalism was based on intuitive identification and intimacy with place."[17] Stegner's willingness to interrogate his own words and let the phrase flex and change over time is a testimony to how much he believed in the power of place.

In 1969 Stegner published his "Wilderness Letter" as part of a compilation of essays in *The Sound of Mountain Water: The Changing American West.* The compilation, Stegner said, was "not a volume of conservation essays or literary essays," but rather "a book of confrontations (not in a contemporary sense!) with the West, a series of responses and trial syntheses." The "Wilderness Letter" appeared at the end of the first section of the book, dedicated to discussion of land and place, as a "Coda" to Stegner's "personal responses to landscape—or perhaps one should say geography." Concluding with his "Wilderness Letter" provided "a personal expression of faith in the importance of geography, and especially wilderness, to human personality and culture." Stegner reiterated, "In making wilderness the geography of hope, I have undoubtedly revealed myself: there is nothing so desperately demoralizing to a New World optimist as the sight of the New World floundering toward total reunion with Europe's cynicism, belligerence, and despair."[18]

Nearly a decade after first penning the phrase, Stegner's geography was expanding. Though he did not yet explicitly state that the nation's public lands as a whole were the places in which he placed his hope, Stegner's continued emphasis on wilderness alluded to the context in which protected wild places existed. In addition, the context of public lands, the majority of which existed in the American West, extended this framework of the geography of hope to the region itself. From wilderness to public lands to the American West, Stegner viewed hope as widening from the most protected of wild places to the entirety of the western United States.

This perspective was born out in an interview of Stegner by the editor of the *Great Lakes Review* journal in the mid-1970s. The interviewer asked Stegner, "Your books are also into that theme of the

West as a geography of hope; and yet at the same time, rootlessness in the West creates a situation where culture can't quite be." Stegner responded, "I'll tell you one of the reasons why I think the West is the geography of hope; it's partly because it's so terribly vulnerable, that it doesn't heal. . . . I suppose one of the principal reasons why we're the geography of hope is that we come last and therefore there may be certain restraints operative here that weren't in other parts of the country."[19] Stegner went on to explain how the region's fragility offered an opportunity for Americans to respond differently to their environment. "That's one kind of hope," he wrote, "that somehow we could learn to live with the earth a little more intelligently, as people have done in the past. And even though it has been the place that historically was raided for its immediate resources, it may turn out, in the long run, to be stabler and healthier."[20]

Hope, for Stegner, involved restraint. "I don't go around waving my little white flag of hope saying the world is going to be better every day," he stated, "but I think there's more hope in a place like this than in some parts of the United States."[21] In the American West, public lands and the wilderness areas they contained represented a shared national geography, an antithesis to private land ownership that restrained urban and suburban development and limited industrial development. In Stegner's view, as long as this restraint governed Americans' behavior, there would be hope.

In 1980, on the twentieth anniversary of his "Wilderness Letter," he revisited the phrase again, stating, "I find that my opinions have not changed. They have actually been sharpened by an increased urgency." Writing at the height of the Sagebrush Rebellion, Stegner worried that wilderness was in danger, that public lands were in danger, and that the American West was in danger. The energy crisis of the 1970s had created a "national anxiety about energy sources" and prompted increased strip mining and oil and gas drilling, those signifiers of the worst kind of industrial development, throughout the American West. "Economic temptation begets politicians willing to serve special economic interests," he complained, "and they in turn bring on a new wave of states'-rights agitation, this time nicknamed the Sagebrush Rebellion. . . . The Sagebrush Rebellion is the worst enemy not only of long-range management of the public lands, but of wilderness. . . . It [the American West] is in danger of being made—of helping to make itself—into a sacrifice area."[22]

The Sagebrush Rebellion undermined the environmental protection efforts of an entire generation of environmentalists. It felt like a kick in the gut. During this discouraging moment, historian Richard Etulain interviewed Stegner and asked him about the shadow the Sagebrush Rebellion had cast on the protection of wild places, public lands, and the American West. Etulain queried, "When you speak of wilderness as the 'geography of hope,' might you not imply that a shrinking wilderness would bring disillusionment and despair?" Stegner answered:

> Well, it brings at least dissatisfaction and anxiety. . . . There are, what, a few million acres in wilderness that are permanently set aside unless Mr. [James] Watt succeeds in undoing them. Just a few million acres is not by any means enough, but they do give you some sense of a line beyond which you don't have to fall back. . . . That's, of course, speaking of wilderness in its purest form. There are also all the national parks, national monuments, and national historical sites, lakeshores, seashores, and recreational areas. There's quite a lot of federal land, besides all of the state land put aside in parks.[23]

As long as these places remained, Stegner's hope was maintained, but during the Sagebrush Rebellion it was not clear that they would.

In his darkest moment, Stegner nearly gave up hope for his most beloved region and the public lands that made it unique. Writing in *The American West as Living Space* in 1987, Stegner lamented the inadequate protections offered wilderness areas, national parks, national monuments, and all the other protected spaces by the land management agencies that oversaw them. "The protection provided by these various agencies is of course imperfect," he said. "Every reserve is an island, and its boundaries are leaky. Nevertheless this is the best protection we have, and not to be disparaged. All Americans, but especially Westerners whose backyard is at stake, need to ask themselves whose bureaus these should be."[24] Were these lands for the benefit of corporate extractive industries, livestock operators, the larger recreating public? Or were they for some higher purpose, existing for their own sake? Stegner wrote the beauty of the West's rivers and streams, forests and grasslands, mountains and valleys, geologic and cultural wonders had led him, "in a reckless moment, to call the western public lands part of the geography of hope."[25] "What should one make of facts as depressing as these?" he cried. "Sad to say, they make me admit, when I face them, that the West is no more the Eden that I once thought it than the Garden of the World that the boosters and engineers tried to make it; and that neither nostalgia nor boosterism can any longer make a case for it as the geography of hope."[26]

It may seem that in penning this, Stegner abandoned his optimism for the American West and traded hope for despair. However, to believe that is to deny Stegner's love of the landscape of his heart. He could no more abandon the geography of hope than he could abandon the American West, its public lands, or its wild places. These spaces were stitched into the very fabric of his being. So when the young, brash historian Patricia Nelson Limerick published *The Legacy of Conquest: The Unbroken Past of the American West* in the same year as his lament and shattered the tired Turnerian tropes of the frontier myth, Stegner found reason to renew his hope. Stegner, as did so many other scholars of the American West, found hope in the story Limerick told about the West's past, in the way her work moved beyond the frontier myth into the harsh, but truthful, reality of the conquest and exploitation of the region.

Limerick and Stegner traded letters, and their cross-pollinated ideas mutually invigorated their work.[27] In 1988 Limerick and noted lawyer and writer Charles Wilkinson asked Stegner to deliver the keynote address at a symposium hosted by the newly formed Center of the American West titled "A Society to Match the Scenery." Taken from Stegner's *The Sound of Mountain Water*, the title of the symposium alluded to future possibilities and optimistic outcomes for the American West. Responding to Limerick's request, Stegner returned to his place of faith. He wrote of his keynote address, "My inclination is to call it 'The West: the Geography of Hope.'" "What I want to talk about," he said, "is the relation of fantasy to fact and of both to the future. Hope in the West is so entangled with fantasy that it's hard to talk about it without knocking it. I guess what I would like to do is to sort out some fantasies from some facts in western history (stealing from you shamelessly), and then see if I can project into the future any viable hope that the symposium's 'society to match the scenery' is achievable. So maybe 'The Geography of Hope' is not too far off . . ."[28]

The lecture Stegner delivered at the University of Colorado Boulder in 1990 marked the recommitment of the preeminent western writer to both the geography of the American West, its public lands and wilderness areas, and his hope for the region's future. "Once I said in print," he began, "that the remaining western wilderness is the geography of hope, and I have written, believing what I wrote, that the West at large is hope's native home, the youngest and freshest of America's regions, magnificently endowed and with the chance to become something unprecedented and unmatched in the world." He went on to state, "I was shaped by the West and have lived most of a long life in it, and nothing would gratify me more than to see it, in all its subregions and subcultures, both prosperous and environmentally healthy, with a civilization to match its scenery."[29]

In revisiting his iconic phrase once more, Stegner emphasized that he meant the "interior West" was the nation's geography of hope, that empty quarter that contained the vast majority of the region's public lands. Stegner also qualified his enthusiasm for the hope part of the phrase. He wrote, "I curb my enthusiasm . . . I say yes, the West *is* the native home of hope, but there are varieties and degrees of hope, and the wrong kind, in excessive amounts, goes with human disappointment and environmental damage as bust goes with boom."[30] Scholars responded to Stegner's revitalized hope for the region. Geographer Charles Little wrote: "Some years ago, the eminent historian and novelist of the American West, Wallace Stegner, described his beloved region as 'a geography of hope.' Stegner was not romantic about the West; he understood the forces of change. And he knew better than most the destruction that change brought in his lifetime. Still, so long as there were choices to be made about the future of the West—and there are—there is always hope."[31]

Stegner contended his entire life with what hope meant for the American West, its public lands, and its precious wild places, from a position of power, defining what it means in these spaces. He has influenced countless scholars, including myself. In this context what Stegner has taught me is that hope is easily accessible when it is charismatic and riding a tide of popular support, as was the case when Stegner coined the "geography of hope" as a phrase. It is much more difficult when oppositional forces erode what is precious. At the end of his writing career, Stegner chose to maintain hope for the American West despite the pummeling he saw the region, its public lands and wilderness areas, endure in the 1980s. Stegner's choice is a reminder that, in writer Rebecca Solnit's words, "To hope is to gamble. It's to bet on the future, on your desires, on the possibility that an open heart and uncertainty is better than gloom or safety."[32] Stegner's geography of hope was entirely aspirational and evolutionary; he recognized the importance, the centrality of wilderness areas and public lands within the American West and how they embodied hope because of all they represented, to both those who would exploit the land and those who would preserve it.

AMS (March 11–13, 2019)

Your deep grounding of Stegner's "geography of hope," showing how he morphed and broadened the idea the longer he sat with it and responded to shifting political and cultural currents, is essential. That specificity is important and clarifying, especially for reminding us how a phrase or concept can become so useful as to become ubiquitous and then, if we are not careful, banal.

Your sense that public lands are aspirational spaces is also a crucial insight. Our nation wrote its aspirations onto this land and continues to do so. From the Land Ordinance (1785) to the John D. Dingell, Jr. Conservation, Management, and Recreation Act (2019), the American public through Congress and executive agencies has pinned its hopes onto these public spaces. Where private lands reveal the owners' imagination and actions, public lands illuminate something else, something I would characterize as grander—a social vision for the land, a place where something beyond capitalist accumulation and maximization can (sometimes) find expression.

Of course, the American public has never been monolithic or the polity unanimous, and so the social vision for the public's land has always been contested. The policy reversals and adjustments over the decades have inspired among some citizens celebration and just as often confusion and anger among others.[33] When Stegner and his allies rallied support for the Wilderness Act, millions of American praised the action, while miners and loggers worried about their future livelihoods; when the desert tortoise was listed as an endangered species, ranchers felt one more turn of the screw, and some resisted with threats of violence and by withholding grazing fees; when President Donald Trump hacked off 85 percent of Bears Ears National Monument, Native peoples who led the advocacy mourned while oil and gas companies cheered.[34] Winning produces losers, and compromises leave dreams on cutting-room floors. That is the nature of public lands policymaking; it is democracy's genetic code. We owe attention to the historical record's public statements and cultural expressions that give shape to wilderness's contours.

Earlier and more thoroughly than most areas of American life, decisions about these places and the policies that govern them faced public scrutiny. For half a century, public hearings have been required for many management decisions, opening avenues for exercising citizenship and revealing our collective aspirations for these places—just as Stegner shared in the ORRRC process. At countless public hearings in high school gyms and American Legion halls, people stood up and spoke out, leaving us no doubt about what wilderness meant, not equivocating or theorizing as scholars learn to do when interrogating concepts such as "wilderness." Consider, for instance, the following statement: "The Nez Perce tribesmen of today would be recreant sons of noble ancestors if we did not stand up and be counted on the side of preserving the last great vestiges of primitive America. We want our children and our children's children to see the heritage of our forefathers preserved for us as best they could through treaties which created reservations."[35] This remark was delivered in 1961 by Angus A. Wilson, the chair of the Nez Perce Tribal Executive Committee, during a hearing before the House Subcommittee on Public Lands held in McCall, Idaho. Wilson offered the official tribal perspective about the wilderness bill, and the statement expressed Nez Perce aspirations, rooted equally in the past and future. The statement helps us see how individuals and groups positioned themselves in the continuum of time. Not unlike Stegner, Wilson and the Nez Perces rooted their appreciation for wilderness in the past; they paid a debt to their ancestors in supporting wilderness preservation. And they planted their future hopes, for generation after generation, in these lands. Not only did they see themselves as part of the place but a part of time, too. Wilson's comment reinforces the point you made: that hope evolves.

Americans' writing and thinking about public lands reveal a good deal of disagreement. And community has not always integrated with hope in the context of wilderness and the broader public land system. In 1968, while the Wilderness Act remained fresh, an iconic book was published by an iconoclastic writer, Edward Abbey. Once a student of Stegner's, Abbey worked for the National Park Service at Arches National Monument (or "Money-mint" from his caustic pen), and he constructed perhaps the most famous account of public lands with *Desert Solitaire: A Season in the Wilderness*.[36] To move through the pages of *Desert Solitaire* is to be seduced by Abbey into the desert and into a rugged, unpeopled, wild view of life. His prose pulled people to Moab, Utah, when it was a mining town, not today's outdoor recreation mecca full of backpackers, mountain bikers, and chugging pickup trucks towing hulking trailers larger than Abbey's home at Arches. Abbey's essays were a bible for the solitary. After all, he explained, echoing Stegner: "We need wilderness whether or not we ever set foot in it. We need a refuge even though we may never need to go there. I may never in my life get to Alaska, for example, but I am grateful that it's there. We need the possibility of escape as surely as we need hope."[37] This passage, one that is frequently quoted, testified to a dominant strain of public lands writing. It is a place we need, a refuge that might heal us if we ail. But mostly, it is an escape, a place apart. And that escape provided Abbey with hope, and because Abbey attracted so many acolytes to the desert, they learned to align hope with escape.

But the story he told, the persona he constructed, and the way he constructed hope here requires a rejoinder, and recently one appeared in a little book called *Desert Cabal: A New Season in the Wilderness* by Amy Irvine. In singing, searing, and searching prose, Irvine wrote directly and intimately to Abbey while meditating on his classic memoir on its fiftieth anniversary. Irvine admired Abbey but also criticized him. She singled out his celebration of rugged individualism—so prevalent in *Desert Solitaire* and the followers it inspired—as most needing revision today. Humans are not by nature solitary, she explained, but a cabal: "A group gathered around a panoramic vision. A group gathered to conspire, to resist."[38] Irvine continued: "Our most precious resource now is wonder. What we wonder about ignites our imagination, unleashes our empathy, fuels our ferocity. We fold in on ourselves, a thunderous, galloping gathering, a passionate, peopled storm, nearly indistinguishable from the ground on which it rains, on which it sprinkles seeds. *This is how hope takes root.*"[39] Irvine knew that we cannot make a society out of singletons. Abbey's country, an appellation applied to the red rock lands in southern Utah and one that annoyed Irvine, needs fewer Abbeys. There was no community there. There was no hope. Hope lay not in escape but in coming together, with ordinary people imagining together, working together.[40]

Finally, one of the most forceful writers about community is another Stegner student, Wendell Berry, and it is worth a brief detour to his Kentucky farm to observe his thoughts about cultivating an ethical sense of place against modern forces of fragmentation, indifference, and violence. Berry loved small communities "devoted to protecting or saving things of value that are endangered," because, as he once put it, "they are the basis of our worldly hope. They are the basis of our *right* to hope that our own greatly endangered species may somehow be saved, if not from extinction, at least from the necessity of recognizing itself as the ultimate parasite, deserving extinction." The premise of all of Berry's work is that communities could knit us back together and provide "the hope and the purpose" needed to withstand the disintegrating forces that treat local communities and land as interchangeable parts in a relentless economic system.[41] Stegner saw wilderness as a source of sanity; Berry sees community the same way.

LCC (March 21–April 30, 2019)

I appreciate your distillation of Edward Abbey's perspective as a common vision of public lands, but one that is antithetical to cultivating hope. His individualism, the societal iconoclasm, and the subversive protest he preached are appealing but not truly satisfying. Stegner did not share Abbey's perspective. According to Olsen, "Abbey's own environmentalism fell prey to the influence of frontier romanticization and myth so detested by Stegner. As a transplanted easterner, Abbey was easily captured by the mythic individualism and the western landscape." Stegner, Olsen wrote, "had little patience for Abbey and the ecoterrorist position." According to him, Abbey's "arguments for defiant ecoterrorism, as well as those of his heirs in the ecodefense movement, reflected the same exaggerated sense of 'cowboy' individualism prevalent among nineteenth-century vigilantes, modern day cowboys, and 'Sagebrush Rebels.'"[42]

The hope afforded by wilderness, public lands, and the larger American West is as much about how these lands can serve as a forum for fostering community across time and space as it is about nature nurturing an individual spirit. They are good for nurturing the collective spirit. They are places that help teach us empathy, not just for nature but for each other.

Your invocation of Wendell Berry's work speaks to this. His sense of hope was located in the nation becoming a "healthy people in a healthy land."[43] He advocated adopting "nature as a measure of economic life," using the health of the land and the people upon it as the standard of success rather than industrial-scale economic productivity.[44] Berry's emphasis on communities grounded in place and intertwined with their environment speaks to the relational aspects of hope. This is what Stegner meant by a society or civilization in the West to match the scenery. LaDow reminded us of this aspect of Stegner's environmental ethos, one that I too frequently forget. She wrote: "Stegner's wilderness may contain human beings—even cattle ranchers, he goes on to say— yet is pristine, separate, set apart. Despite his impassioned paean to the 'wilderness idea,' he frequently argued for wise-use conservation and once decried environmentalists of a 'sentimental fringe' with a bent toward 'blind preservationism in all circumstances,' regardless of people's lives."[45] It mattered to Stegner that people grounded deeply in where they resided were as healthy as the land upon which they lived; both intertwined made for the kind of society he so desired. But as Potawatomi ecologist Robin Wall Kimmerer has wondered, "How can we begin to move toward ecological and cultural sustainability if we cannot even imagine what the path feels like?"[46]

That hope is relational, between ourselves and others as much as between ourselves and the land, is crucial. Along with hope being aspirational and evolutionary, it must by necessity also be relational. Too often middle-class descendants of settlers such as myself have been taught to see wilderness and public lands as Abbey saw them, as static, singular, and in solitude. Likewise, we are trained to see the West and its wilderness as the photographer Ansel Adams saw it. When I look at magnificent photographs Adams produced, it is as if he visualized Abbey's perspective. Adams was a master at capturing the magnificence and enduring majesty of landscapes devoid of people. So many other photographers of public lands, both professionals and amateurs like myself, have done the same. We strive for our own solitary moment in these magnificent landscapes. However, as appealing as it is, this is not an accurate portrayal of public lands. Rather, the more accurate images are those that include landscapes dotted with the detritus of long gone human habitation and industry, clusters of cattle and sheep in mountain and desert valleys, oil and gas derricks adjacent to wilderness areas, and most especially the other visitors alongside us at scenic pullouts along roads and trails that connect natural wonders.

I have been camping and hiking in Yosemite National Park since 1977 (since I was six years old). It is a family tradition. My Armenian grandmother, who grew up in Fresno, California, used to vacation in Yosemite with her church group in the late 1930s. She took my mother there in the 1950s and 1960s, and my parents took me in the 1970s and 1980s. Her pictures of Yosemite were of her friends and other tourists hiking and laughing against a backdrop of brilliant granite and tall pines. My parents took photographs of me, my brother, and my sister hiking, playing in the Merced River, riding our bikes between campsites, and climbing giant boulders, often with the children of other families camped nearby who were there, like us, to experience the wonder of Yosemite Valley. My pictures, however, were of long vistas across the valley, waterfalls, and granite peaks; I worked hard to eliminate people from the photos. I hated the crowds at Yosemite Falls and Mirror Lake.

Several years ago I had an epiphany at Tunnel View on the western edge of Yosemite Valley. The parking lot was packed full, and visitors were elbow-to-elbow at the wide edge of the most iconic view of the park. Annoyed at the crush of bodies and cameras, I stopped at the back of the crowd and watched as family after family took photo after photo, the same photo that Adams popularized decades earlier but with loved ones included. It struck me then that my experiences in Yosemite have been only in part about capturing this iconic landscape. The other aspect of my experiences has been about being a visitor alongside hundreds of other visitors.[47] This is the real Yosemite. It is at once both a magnificent landscape and a community of visitors. Against the backdrop of soaring granite peaks and stately pine trees, I snapped images of park visitors gazing through their camera lenses,

pointing, and talking to each other about this spectacular place. These visitors are not annoyances to be endured but rather my companions in appreciation and reverence of this incomparable valley.

Your recent work in *Environmental History* on Hannah Arendt's metaphor of a table described and organized the relational experiences of public lands users. The table separates us and allows us to have individual experiences, but it also creates a relationship and a common connection between us. You wrote: "The American public lands constitute such an Arendtian table. Their condition reveals the vibrancy of our democracy and the resilience of our ecological health."[48] In ascribing this metaphor to our public lands, you combine Berry's ethos that nature ought to be our measure with Arendt's useful organization of our relationship to each other via public lands. Many Americans like to believe that our democracy is predicated on the health of our relationship to each other in the civic arena. The ecological health of our public lands is both the measure of our relationship to nature and the measure of our civic health.

The beautiful wordsmith Terry Tempest Williams famously penned a speech at the University of Utah in 2003 that reminds us of this connection. Williams wrote: "In the open space of democracy, the health of the environment is seen as the wealth of our communities. We remember that our character has been shaped by the diversity of America's landscapes and it is precisely that character that will protect it." She prefaced this declaration with a description of what the open space of democracy looks like: a place that has room for dissent and room for difference. Later in the published work that contains this speech and offers an explanation of its content, she remarked that "public lands are our public commons," grounding the open space of democracy in the land itself.[49] This is how a society that matches the

13. (*opposite top*) Half Dome, Yosemite National Park, June 22, 2015. Courtesy Leisl Carr Childers.

14. (*opposite bottom*) Tunnel View, Yosemite National Park, June 22, 2015. Courtesy Leisl Carr Childers.

scenery functions—it recognizes that there are differences and dis-agreements between people, but what ties them together is their love of this region, this land, this place. This is why the relational nature of hope matters so much, and the stories historians tell about our relationship to nature and each other reinforce either hope or despair.

AMS and LCC (May 5–7, 2019, with a Postscript from June 8 and 30, 2021)

One of our entry points to this topic, in the way we have explored it, was the marvelous essayist Rebecca Solnit. Her website and book jacket biographies describe her, in order, as a "writer, historian, and activist."[50] In our ongoing conversation here, we have been considering the legacy of another westerner, Wallace Stegner, who might be described in sim-ilar terms: a writer first, a historian often, and an activist when called for (though one suspects that is not how he saw himself).[51] Besides both living in the Bay Area (at least for a time in Stegner's case) and writing histories and essays about the West and its landscapes, Solnit and Stegner cared about hope. Solnit, perhaps, thought more deeply about the concept, and her position includes greater relevance for the twenty-first century and the challenges for public lands and more.

Never denying inequality or oppression—the "dark" part of her title—Solnit, again similar to Stegner, nevertheless refuses to only dwell in the dark. *Hope in the Dark* chronicles achievements, "grounds for hope" in her words—the fall of the Berlin Wall, the Zapatistas' chal-lenge to the North American Free Trade Agreement, the various causes that brought people together to challenge those in power. In the new edition's preface, she wrote, "We need litanies or recitations or mon-uments to these victories," the moments of real joy and connection to each other and to the land, "so that they are landmarks in everyone's

15. (*opposite top*) El Capitan, Yosemite National Park, June 22, 2015. Courtesy Leisl Carr Childers.

16. (*opposite bottom*) Road to Half Dome, Yosemite National Park, June 22, 2015. Courtesy Leisl Carr Childers.

mind."[52] Solnit's insistence that Americans remember that all is not lost, that we have the power to change, the power to hope, is reminiscent of writer Ursula K. Le Guin's famous remarks when she was feted with a lifetime achievement award at the National Book Awards in 2014: "We live in capitalism, its power seems inescapable—but then, so did the divine right of kings. Any human power can be resisted and changed by human beings. Resistance and change often begin in art. Very often in our art, the art of words."[53] Solnit has quoted Le Guin approvingly.[54] From hope comes resistance; from resistance, change.

Like Stegner, Solnit does not abandon hope while the world burns. She does not demand we forget or overlook all the tragedies and injustices that have unfolded and are unfolding against the earth and people marginalized by power. Hope is not, she writes, "the belief that everything was, is, or will be fine. . . . It's also not a sunny everything-is-getting-better narrative." Hope counters despair, compels action. "Hope locates itself in the premises that we don't know what will happen and that in the *spaciousness of uncertainty* is room to act," she argues.[55] As historians, we know that contingency is a powerful and unpredictable factor that shaped the past. What is contingency if not the recognition that, as history unfolds amid the "spaciousness of uncertainty," trajectories of change alter? So hope is a choice, a worldview that encourages clear-eyed action and eschews inertia and indifference. Solnit and Stegner both saw history as something more than inert stories of the things long established.

The work of New Western Historians (whom Stegner respected) and environmental historians bears this out. So many tragedies, once buried, have become unearthed by them, by us, so that we can begin to reckon with this history, including those histories of how public lands have come to be, what public lands preserve and what they obscure. Historians must tell stories of the injustices so that we can repair them, and, just as importantly, we must also tell the stories of victory, the times people confronted and beat back the forces of war, exploitation, and discrimination and replaced them with peace, fairness, and equality. In this way, public lands history can be both a story of Indigenous dispossession and erasure and a story of nurturing species and democracy. Armed with the right stories and fuller accounts, the culture and then our politics can shift. Historians and writers, then, can help rig up that line Stegner wrote about in 1967 between past and present with an aim toward the future.

Recently in *The Atlantic*, the Ojibwe writer David Treuer wrote a provocative article whose title encapsulated its argument: "Return the National Parks to the Tribes." Noting that "for Native Americans, there can be no better remedy for the theft of land than land," and that the 90 million acres stripped from tribal control under the 1887 Dawes Act roughly matched the 85 million acres of national parks, Treuer's case follows a hopeful and clear logic.[56] This is not a scenario, we suspect, that Stegner could have imagined. It is, however, the type of reckoning Solnit describes. In the twenty-first century, new stories must be forged from hopes long suppressed and silenced to shape a future more just and less fear-filled. It is a lot to ask, but the ways forward on the public's land must embrace a reading of the past and present that incorporates all the nation's people, not only those who have for so long controlled the stories.

We have nothing to lose. As Terry Tempest Williams reminds us, "The integrity of our public lands depends on the integrity of our public process within the open space of democracy."[57] Our geography of hope depends upon us evolving our aspirations for the American West and the public's land, of attending to the relationships between ourselves as individuals and our communities and with these places. In a tribute to his former teacher, Wendell Berry praised Stegner's "instructive humility" and regional integrity: "He has the care and the scrupulousness of one who understands remembering as a duty, and who therefore understands historical insight and honesty as duties."[58] As Berry recognized and Stegner long understood, storytelling about the West is a duty that demands not only factual accuracy but also a sensitivity to all that lay in the region's sometimes-troubled heart. Only with new stories, new hopes, and better relationships can we change our society to match the scenery.

Notes

1. The touchstone essay for environmental historians about the complicated moral power of the shape of historical narratives is William Cronon, "Place for Stories: Nature, History, and Narrative," *Journal of American History* 78, no. 4 (March 1992): 1347–76.
2. Rebecca Solnit, *Hope in the Dark: Untold Histories, Wild Possibilities*, 3rd ed. (Chicago: Haymarket Books, 2016), xvi.
3. Wallace Stegner, "History, Myth, and the Western Writer," in *The Sound of Mountain Water: The Changing American West* (New York: Doubleday, 1969; rpt., New York: Vintage Books, 2015), 195.
4. Wallace Stegner, *Beyond the Hundredth Meridian: John Wesley Powell and the Second Opening of the West* (Boston: Houghton Mifflin, 1954; rpt., New York: Penguin, 1992).
5. Elizabeth Cook-Lynn, *Why I Can't Read Wallace Stegner and Other Essays: A Tribal Voice* (Madison: University of Wisconsin Press, 1996); "Elizabeth Cook-Lynn," Hanksville.org, accessed June 4, 2019, http://www.hanksville.org/storytellers/cooklynn/.
6. Mark W. T. Harvey, *A Symbol of Wilderness: Echo Park and the American Conservation Movement* (Seattle: University of Washington Press, 2000).
7. Wallace Stegner, *This Is Dinosaur: Echo Park Country and Its Magic Rivers* (New York: Alfred A. Knopf, 1955); Mark W. T. Harvey, *Wilderness Forever: Howard Zahniser and the Path to the Wilderness Act*, Weyerhaeuser Environmental Books (Seattle: University of Washington Press, 2005), 182–83.
8. Steven C. Schulte, *Wayne Aspinall and the Shaping of the American West* (Boulder: University Press of Colorado, 2002), 117.
9. Historian Glenda Riley shows some complexity to this claim, highlighting a handful of women whose environmental ideas and reform agendas included better conditions for Native Americans. This exception, though, may well prove the rule. Glenda Riley, *Women and Nature: Saving the "Wild" West*, Women in the West (Lincoln: University of Nebraska Press, 1999), 154–70.
10. Wallace Stegner, "Coda: Wilderness Letter," in *The Sound of Mountain Water: The Changing American West* (New York: Doubleday; rpt., New York: Vintage Books, 2015), 140, 144, 147.

11. A growing body of writing has emerged about people of color and their relationship with the American outdoors. See, for a start, Alison H. Deming and Lauret E. Savoy, eds., *Colors of Nature: Culture, Identity, and the Natural World* (Minneapolis: Milkweed, 2011); Carolyn Finney, *Black Faces, White Spaces: Reimagining the Relationship of African Americans to the Great Outdoors* (Chapel Hill: University of North Carolina Press, 2014); J. Drew Lanham, *The Home Place: Memoirs of a Colored Man's Love Affair with Nature* (Minneapolis: Milkweed, 2016); and Lauret Savoy, *Trace: Memory, History, Race, and the American Landscape* (Berkeley CA: Counterpoint, 2015).

12. This comes from Stegner, "Introduction: Some Geography, Some History," in *Sound of Mountain Water*, 32.

13. A federal report extended the concept of "geography of hope" almost opposite of what we do, focusing instead on private farms. United States Department of Agriculture (USDA), National Resources Conservation Service, *America's Private Land: A Geography of Hope* (n.p.: USDA, 1996), https://www.nrcs.usda.gov/sites/default/files/2022-09/GeogHope.pdf.

14. Stegner, "Coda: Wilderness Letter," 142.

15. Krista Comer, *Landscapes of the New West: Gender and Geography in Contemporary Women's Writing* (Chapel Hill: University of North Carolina Press, 1999), 44.

16. Brett J. Olsen, "Wallace Stegner and the Environmental Ethic: Environmentalism as a Rejection of Western Myth," *Western American Literature* 29, no. 2 (Summer 1994): 125.

17. Beth LaDow, "The Astonishing Origins of Wallace Stegner's Environmental Genius," *Montana: The Magazine of Western History* 52, no. 3 (Autumn 2002): 71.

18. Stegner, "Introduction: Some Geography, Some History," 5.

19. Wallace Stegner, "Interview," *Great Lakes Review* 2, no. 1 (Summer 1975): 16.

20. Stegner, "Interview," 17.

21. Stegner, "Interview," 17.

22. Wallace Stegner, "Saga of a Letter: The Geography of Hope," quoted in Robert Wyss, *The Man Who Built the Sierra Club: A Life of David Brower* (New York: Columbia University Press, 2016), 88–89.

23. Wallace Stegner and Richard W. Etulain, *Stegner: Conversations on History and Literature* (Reno: University of Nevada Press, 1996), 178. It is worth noting that Stegner did not invoke any of the national forests managed by the U.S. Forest Service or lands managed by the Bureau of Land Management, all of which were managed under the multiple-use concept, in this list of protected places.

24. Wallace Stegner, *The American West as Living Space* (Ann Arbor: University of Michigan Press, 2001), 42.

25. Stegner, *American West as Living Space*, 43.

26. Stegner, *American West as Living Space*, 60.

27. Philip L. Fradkin, *Wallace Stegner and the American West* (Berkeley: University of California Press, 2009), 291.

28. Wallace Stegner to Patricia Nelson Limerick, August 26, 1988, series 3, folder 2, Patricia Nelson Limerick Papers, Denver Public Library, Denver CO.

29. Wallace Stegner, *Where the Bluebird Sings to the Lemonade Springs: Living and Writing in the West* (New York: Modern Library, 2002), xxi. The quote is from the introduction and was adapted from "A Geography of Hope," the lecture Wallace Stegner delivered at the University of Colorado at Boulder in 1990. The lecture itself is published in Wallace Stegner, "A Geography of Hope," in *A Society to Match the Scenery: Personal Visions of the Future of the American West*, ed. Gary Holthaus, Patricia Nelson Limerick, Charles F. Wilkinson, and Eve Stryker Munson (Boulder: University Press of Colorado, 1991), 218–29.

30. Stegner, "Geography of Hope," 218; emphasis in the original.

31. Charles E. Little, "Redeeming the Geography of Hope," *Natural Resources Journal* 43 (Winter 2003): 1.

32. Solnit, *Hope in the Dark*, 4.

33. Your case study focusing on Nevada's Fallini family captures how dependency on public lands generates frustration and uncertainty when policies change. See Leisl Carr Childers, "The Angry West: Understanding the Sagebrush Rebellion in Rural Nevada," in *Bridging the Distance: Common Issues in the Rural West*, ed. David Danbom (Salt Lake City: University of Utah Press, 2015), 269–315.

34. The best account of public land management after the Wilderness Act is James Morton Turner, *The Promise of Wilderness: American Environmen-*

tal Politics since 1964 (Seattle: University of Washington Press, 2012). *High Country News*, a biweekly western news magazine, provides coverage of public land conflicts, such as the issues alluded to here. President Joe Biden restored Bears Ears National Monument and appointed the first Indigenous woman to a cabinet position. Secretary of the Interior Deb Haaland oversaw that restoration.

35. *Wilderness Preservation System: Hearings before the Subcommittee on Public Lands of the Committee on Interior and Insular Affairs, House of Representatives, Eighty-Seventh Congress, First[-Second] Session, on S. 174 [and Other] Bills to Establish a National Wilderness Preservation System for the Permanent Good of the Whole People, and for Other Purposes* (Washington DC: Government Printing Office, 1962), 184.

36. David Gessner, *All the Wild That Remains: Edward Abbey, Wallace Stegner, and the American West* (New York: W. W. Norton, 2015) tackles both men (and his own relationship with their ideas and landscapes).

37. Edward Abbey, *Desert Solitaire: A Season in the Wilderness* (New York: Ballantine Books, 1968), 148–49.

38. Amy Irvine, *Desert Cabal: A New Season in the Wilderness* (Torrey House Press, 2018), 78.

39. Irvine, *Desert Cabal*, 78–79; emphasis added.

40. I try to suggest this in Adam M. Sowards, "Sometimes, It Takes a Table," *Environmental History* 23, no. 1 (January 2018): 143–51.

41. Wendell Berry, "The Purpose of a Coherent Community," in *The Way of Ignorance and Other Essays* (Berkeley: Counterpoint, 2005), 69–79, quotations from 71, 79; emphasis in the original.

42. Olsen, "Wallace Stegner," 136–37.

43. Wendell Berry, "The Agrarian Standard," in *The World-Ending Fire: The Essential Wendell Berry* (Berkeley: Counterpoint, 2019), Kindle.

44. Wendell Berry, "Nature as Measure," in *World-Ending Fire*.

45. LaDow, "Astonishing Origins," 69.

46. Robin Wall Kimmerer, *Braiding Sweetgrass: Indigenous Wisdom, Scientific Knowledge, and the Teachings of Plants* (Minneapolis: Milkweed Editions, 2013), 6.

47. Visitation to national parks has steadily increased throughout most of the system's history. As of 2015, visitation consistently exceeded 300 million, and it took a global pandemic to stem it. See "Visitation Numbers,"

National Park Service, https://www.nps.gov/aboutus/visitation-numbers
.htm.

48. Sowards, "Sometimes, It Takes a Table," 144.
49. Terry Tempest Williams, *The Open Space of Democracy* (Eugene OR: Wipf and Stock, 2004), 8, 59.
50. Rebecca Solnit, "Biography," accessed January 3, 2019, http://rebeccasolnit .net/biography/.
51. Olsen, "Wallace Stegner," 136. Stegner found 1960s activists distasteful. Still, it is hard to deny his "Wilderness Letter" or *This Is Dinosaur* editorial duties as anything other than activism.
52. Solnit, *Hope in the Dark*, xxi.
53. Ursula K. Le Guin's speech of November 19, 2014, is available on YouTube, https://www.youtube.com/watch?v=Et9Nf-rsALk; the full text can be found at "Ursula K Le Guin's Speech at National Book Awards: 'Books Aren't Just Commodities,'" *The Guardian*, November 20, 2014, https:// www.theguardian.com/books/2014/nov/20/ursula-k-le-guin-national -book-awards-speech.
54. Rebecca Solnit, "Why Climate Change Is Not Inevitable," *The Nation*, December 23, 2014, https://www.thenation.com/article/archive/why -climate-change-not-inevitable/.
55. Solnit, *Hope in the Dark*, xiii, xiv quotations, respectively; emphasis added.
56. David Treuer, "Return the National Parks to the Tribes," *The Atlantic*, May 2021, https://www.theatlantic.com/magazine/archive/2021/05/return -the-national-parks-to-the-tribes/618395/.
57. Terry Tempest Williams, *The Hour of Land: A Personal Topography of America's National Parks* (New York: Sarah Crichton Books, 2016), 267.
58. Wendell Berry, "Wallace Stegner and the Great Community," in *Wendell Berry: Essays, 1969–1990*, ed. Jack Shoemaker (New York: Library of America, 2019), 673. The essay first appeared in Berry's 1990 collection *What Are People For?*

Possibility

We're all tougher than we think we are.
We're fixed so that almost anything heals.

—Wallace Stegner, *Crossing to Safety*

9

The Education of
Wallace Stegner   MELODY GRAULICH

A Western Education

In *Beyond the Hundredth Meridian* Stegner makes the Harvard-educated pessimist Henry Adams into the foil for his optimistic, energetic John Wesley Powell, who, like many others in the biography and in Stegner's work more broadly, goes west with only the kind of "home-made education" Stegner approved and believed he himself possessed.[1] To understand the West "took an education of a special kind. To grow up with the West, or to grow with and through it into national prominence, you had to have the West bred in your bones, you needed it facing you like a dare."[2] Stegner wrote repeatedly about the value of what he called a "western education, . . . with all the forming and shaping and the dynamics of special challenge and particular response that such an education implied." "The thing that many western boys called their education," he added, "would have seemed to Adams a deprivation, so barren was it of opportunities and so pitiful were its methods and equipment."[3]

Yet as others in this volume suggest, Stegner sometimes took contradictory positions on topics he returned to frequently. In an assessment of another western writer and friend, Walter Van Tilburg Clark, he describes his own "western education" in the terms he ascribes to Adams, recognizing the handicaps of a "western education": he grew up "culturally undernourished," "a western boy who came hungrily toward civilization from the profound barbarism of the frontier."[4]

Stegner's many ruminations about education throughout his work generally focus on frontier circumstances, or their remnants, and they sometimes reveal a typical western "chip on the shoulder" about the cultural dominance of the East Coast, perhaps most prevalent in his portrayal of Susan Ward and especially Thomas Hudson in *Angle of Repose*.[5] But at their heart they address issues of class and privilege, certainly pertinent in our political life today when every Supreme Court justice in 2021 attended Harvard or Yale, while we paradoxically have a billionaire (maybe) ex-president who depended upon and stirred up ignorance of what most educated people call "facts" and put our democracy in danger by encouraging a riot at our Capitol and trying to steal an election.

The title of Henry Adams's landmark autobiography offers me a way into thinking about "The Education of Wallace Stegner," a lifelong theme in almost all of his work. The stories he tells about the role of education in shaping our private values and public lives continue to be relevant today, as are his sometimes contradictory descriptions of what defines and constitutes a "usable" education in today's world.

The Five-Foot Shelf of Books:
On Which I Display My Own Chip on the Shoulder

"History is a pontoon bridge. Every man works at its building end, and has come as far as he has over the pontoons laid by others he may never have heard of."[6]

Stegner offers me a bridge, many bridges in fact, to thinking about my own western—and eastern—educations.

Like Stegner, I grew up "culturally undernourished."[7]

Like Stegner, I am the first person in my family to go to college.

Like Stegner, "I was a western [kid] who came hungrily toward civilization from the profound barbarism of the frontier and was confronted with the fairly common task of would-be American writers—that of encompassing in one lifetime, from scratch, the total achievement of the race."[8]

I had never been further east than Reno—my parents would have loved Bo's casino—when my father, well aware of class symbolism, insisted in 1968 that I go to Stanford rather than Berkeley. I didn't take a class from Stegner, who had just expressed his opinion of 1960s Stanford students in *All the Little Live Things* (1967). But I did meet my future—and now ex—husband there, Brock, who grew up on Philadelphia's posh Main Line.

Brock's ancestors lived in Salem, Massachusetts, so far back that one (Ann Putnam) accused another (Susannah Martin) of being a witch.

At his eight-bedroom ancestral family home in New Hampshire, built in 1888 by a Harvard graduate, Harry Peirce Nichols, and since inhabited, in the summer at least, by the descendants of the witch, the living room is graced with stained glass windows of the Harvard and Bryn Mawr shields. (Yes, the same family as philosopher Charles Sanders Pierce, whose privilege rivaled that of Henry Adams.)

At our bicentennial wedding in 1976, in the aforementioned ancestral home, Brock's father, an English teacher with an MA from Columbia and headmaster of The (always capped) Haverford School, wore gray flannel trousers, his Princeton tie, and, of course, a tweed jacket.

My father, who dropped out of high school at sixteen and ran away to join the merchant marines to avoid the kind of whippings Bo wailed on Bruce, wore fluorescent yellow polyester slacks, white loafers and a white belt, and a yellow-and-white-checked sport coat that resembled an oilcloth table spread. He was a ray of sunshine dancing across the somber lawns of tradition.

And here I finally get to my title for this section: Brock's ninety-some-year-old grandmother, who graduated from Bryn Mawr in 1906, as did his other (Putnam) grandmother, and said of their graduation speaker, William James, "He wrote like a novelist while his brother wrote like a philosopher," gave us as part of our wedding present The Harvard Classics or Dr. Eliot's Five-Foot Shelf of Books, inherited from her minister father, the ancestral home builder (Harvard 1870-something).

There was a time in my life when I would have assumed everyone but me knew about the Harvard Five-Foot Shelf. The shelf was Dr. Eliot's idea of what any "educated person" with a "liberal education" would have read, ranging from Greek tragedies to Emerson, Hawthorne, and Henry James.

I no longer own the shelf because when we moved from New Hampshire to Utah, I refused to move the fifty-one volumes, claiming that neither of us had ever opened them, which was not exactly true since I had checked to see if there were U.S. authors (very few) and any women at all (two, Jane Austen and George Eliot).

The shelf now resides in the ancestral home, along with collected editions of Hawthorne, Longfellow, Prescott, Parkman, Holmes, and even some of Sarah Orne Jewett's children's books. They take up many dusty shelves. The millennials never open them.

While Stegner's "culturally undernourished" years took place in that migrant childhood in the U.S.-Canadian borderlands, he taught at Harvard in the 1940s. Yet as he writes in "Finding the Place," "At Harvard, lapping up ideas and enjoying associations of the kind I always hungered for . . . I could never forget who I was and where I came from."[9] Working on *The Big Rock Candy Mountain* led him to this conclusion: "I began to write my life and my life was all western."[10]

Many years later Stegner would write critically about Harvard in *The Uneasy Chair*, his biography of his close friend Bernard DeVoto. In that biography he retells his own childhood education through his description of DeVoto's, as he did writing about Clark. Yet he also makes very clear his view that DeVoto, unlike himself, was handicapped by his effort to prove himself to the eastern elite and to his Harvard colleagues. And in a telling detail, he compares DeVoto's unease at Harvard to his own experience: "Not inappropriately, [DeVoto's] first tutee was as blue-blooded and blue-stockinged as all of Boston could produce: George Homans, the son of Henry Adams's favorite niece. I imagine DeVoto feeling as I felt when, a frontier boy born without history, I accepted a Fulbright appointment in Greece and carried culture back to Athens."[11] It is one of the paradoxical contradictions in Stegner's life that it ended while he was living in the East, in Vermont.

Although I feel certain Stegner would never have given away the Harvard Classics, the western borderlands childhood he describes in *The Big Rock Candy Mountain* and *Wolf Willow* does not contain the Five-Foot Shelf of Books, though one of the most poignant moments is when Bo gives Elsa a collected Shakespeare, which Bruce carries across the border to the ranch in Montana in the summers, reading while manning his gopher traps. He describes the cultural traditions of his childhood in Eastend, Saskatchewan, and in Montana as a "falling back mainly on oral traditions, on the things that can be communicated without books."[12] His hated father, Bo, was often the transmitter, engendering Stegner's interest in folklore and songs.

Like Stegner, I come from a storytelling family; my much beloved North Dakota–born grandfather often repeated the line, "While I never lie, it might be that I sometimes pre-var-i-cate." Like Bo Mason, he recited Canadian Robert Service's poetry and sang songs.

There once was a girl I knew
Her name was Duckfoot Sue
She was chief engineer at the shirttail factory
Down by the river Sioux.

Also like Bo, my grandfather was violent and brutalized his family.

Yet the boy Stegner re-creates eagerly sought books, "read whatever books [he] could lay his hands on" (from Shakespeare to "Tarzan" to B. M. Bower), but, he says, "almost everything I got from books was either at odds with what I knew from experience or irrelevant to it or remote from it. Books didn't enlarge me; they dispersed me."[13] I never encountered a portrayal of a western woman I could admire until Barbara Stanwyck's Victoria Barkley in *The Big Valley* television show in the late 1960s.

Eastend, fictionalized as Whitemud, Stegner emphasizes, had no library.

My hometown, Salinas, California, did, where I spent many hours during my teenage years. It was named when I was sixteen or so for an author Stegner admired, hometown boy John Steinbeck, who had just died, after locals refused, despite the alliterative temptation of "Steinbeck Street," to rename Main Street after that "communist." Today Salinas's central avenue is still called Main Street, though it now dead ends into the Chamber of Commerce—created Steinbeck Center, less a tribute than a tourist draw.

Stegner's reading dispersed him partially because there was no one to guide it. "We were not lucky enough to have in Whitemud one of those eccentric men of learning who brought good libraries to so many early frontier towns," he says, "and who lighted fires under susceptible village boys."[14]

Growing up in the 1960s as an all-too-susceptible village girl, I did read every Steinbeck novel I could, and my mother, perhaps not fully thinking of the implications, pointed out the location of Cathy's whorehouse from *East of Eden*, but I can't say Steinbeck lighted a fire under me. He couldn't compete, at least, with Jim Morrison.

But when I finally found Stegner, long after leaving Stanford, certainly never reading him at that school of gentlemen, at the Harvard of the South where I attended graduate school, the University of Virginia, he did light that fire.

Another of his images captures what he offered me: "At its best [literature] is a bolt of lightning from me to you, a flash of recognition and a feeling within the context of a shared culture."[15]

Although over forty years younger than he, and thus not so fully the product of the *young* West, I also began where Stegner began: "The civilized tradition of books, ideas, poetry, history, philosophy, all the instruments and residue of human self-examination, all the storage and retrieval possibilities of human experience, I knew only in school, and most imperfectly."[16]

Stegner offers me a way to read myself and my history "within the context of a shared culture." He lends me a usable literary and cultural past. In his long career as fiction writer, historian, biographer, folklorist, essayist, environmentalist, and critic, he became one of those "eccentric men of learning" who provided later western cultural historians with books that countered our dispersal, books that brought other books into conversations with each other. Stegner's work challenges the easy categorization of the PS, GV, and HJ classification system. He could have been writing about his own work when he described DeVoto's as "cultural criticism," quoting his insistence that "no manifestation of American life is trivial to the critic of culture."[17] Particularly in his biographies, essays, and *Angle of Repose*, he built us all a library, an interdisciplinary library, a western pontoon bridge to a relevant "civilized tradition."[18]

Educating Good Citizens

Given Stegner's recurrent attention to education, it is fitting that I have turned to him frequently to educate the next generations of students, particularly about social and cultural responsibilities. I often assigned upper-level students to research a "quirky little detail" from *Angle of Repose* to develop that insatiable sense of curiosity about our culture and history that will keep them reading and engaged in learning about what I now call, in the political climate of 2021, our democratic processes.[19] I conclude with another assignment I often used in nature or environmental writing classes to illustrate how Stegner can also map trails for general education students. This assignment originates in his advocacy for conservation and environmental issues, particularly in the West. He admired Powell as "the personification of an ideal of public service"[20] and DeVoto for taking on causes, for being what we would now call a "public intellectual," a figure routinely derided for the past decade by U.S. politicians. DeVoto, he said, "galvanized" him "the moment [he] showed signs of being an activist."[21] Twenty years after writing his "Wilderness Letter" in 1960, Stegner acknowledged in "The Geography of Hope" that he was probably inspired to do so by the activism of Sierra Club president David Brower, who "cattleprod[ded]" him into action. Environmental historian Dan Flores echoes Stegner, calling the "Wilderness Letter" a "worldwide classic of environmental history, . . . a galvanizing document."[22] I assign the letter hoping my students will be galvanized by reading it, as students have been in the past, hoping students will recognize that for any hope to exist for our futures we must accept public responsibility.

Stegner shows us the importance of turning words into deeds. In class we talk about the coalition between Stegner and Brower that led to the book *This Is Dinosaur: Echo Park Country and Its Magic Rivers* (1955), distributed to all members of Congress as a lobbying tool to prevent a dam from flooding the canyon; it served as a template for later books such as Stephen Trimble and Terry Tempest Williams's *Testimony: Writers of the West Speak on Behalf of Utah Wilderness* (1996), also distributed to all congressional members to help protect the red rock desert. Nothing could be more relevant today, particularly as we attempt to address the effects of climate change. We also discuss Stegner's later regret that in saving Dinosaur from flooding, they had sacrificed Glen Canyon, exploring the inevitable consequences of our actions. In *his* actions, as well as in passages such as this one, Stegner illuminates for the next generation what he saw as the responsibility of the writer:

> You speak of the writer's involvement in his society. I think too many writers are far too little involved. They sit in the middle of their own skulls, or their endocrines, and snipe at the saints, politicians, working people, housewives, and bureaucrats who have to keep the world running. This doesn't mean I am anti-literary. The highest thing I can think of doing is literary. But literature does not exist in a vacuum. . . . We are neither detached nor semi-detached, but are linked to our world by a million interdependencies. To deny the interdependencies, while living on the comforts and services that they make possible, is adolescent when it isn't downright dishonest.[23]

After reading Stegner's letter and discussing its influence and how it laid the groundwork for his work with Stewart Udall at the Department of the Interior and numerous conservation successes, my students write a letter themselves, about a social or political or cultural issue they care strongly about, to a *real* person or agency or group that has some influence over their chosen topic; then they must find an address and mail the letter.[24] One day in class they all read their letters aloud, and we talk about the rhetorics of advocacy, about differences between polemics and persuasion, between Abbey's and Stegner's writing on red rock country. (Later we get to Terry Tempest Williams.) Sometimes they have actually received a reply they can share. Students have written letters to county officials about the desecration of runoffs into Bear Lake, to the National Park Service about snowmobiles in Yellowstone, to whoever it is—I have forgotten, but the student knew—who dispenses licenses to fish in the Logan River, to potential donors for a Humane Society in Cache County. One student managed to get policies changed in the Utah State University Dairy Bar, where she worked. (Sadly, despite my persistent pushiness, none of them have managed to get the Styrofoam containers and plastic utensils removed from the student union.) As they listen to each other, I ask them to think about another of Stegner's recurring concerns: "the bonds that make individuals into a society."[25] Or as he said in a talk at the dedication to the Utah State Library, "Except as we belong to a tradition and a community . . . we are nothing."[26] These themes are especially resonant as I revise this essay during the summer of 2021, when the pandemic and political divisions have crippled social discourse, when the foundations of our democracy have been attacked.

I tell my students I don't really care what they write about, what position they take, one of my grandfather's "prevarications," though I always write a letter myself as well. But this assignment reaches beyond environmentalism. I want to train students to be insightful lifelong readers, but I also feel it's my responsibility, especially at a public land grant university with many first-generation college students, to encourage them to become good citizens. "Responsibility," now that's one of Stegner's favorite words. "I'm quite sure that what I least like about some kinds of people is irresponsibility," he groused to Richard Etulain. "I don't give a damn what their morals are or anything else, but their irresponsibility to something larger than themselves, to some kind of social stability or common tradition and standard, does seem to me a kind of delinquency."[27]

This line resonates in 2021, when delinquents seem to rule the airwaves. His past, he says,

> probably leads me to take a moralistic view of writing, to think of it not only as an art, but also as a kind of cultural function. I suppose I'm constantly trying to bear in mind that having been very lucky, I also am very responsible, and that the only thing that makes civilization go forward is the responsibility of individuals, whether gifted or otherwise, small or large. All of us have the obligation somehow to have some kind of concern for the species, for the culture, for the larger thing outside of ourselves. I'm sure that's buried not too deeply in most of the books I've written.[28]

That's a lesson I have hoped my students learned from reading Stegner, and it's one many members of our democracy, including members of Congress, still need to learn.

The "Wilderness Letter" ends with that audacious phrase Stegner used elsewhere as well, so often quoted, "the geography of hope," an ideal hard to achieve in 2021, our hottest summer ever, with brush fires raging across the West, and young Black men (and women) routinely endangered, a subject Stegner addressed only in *One Nation*. Yet he argued that individual acts mattered, and he recognized that taking responsibility is a way of addressing our society's failings. I think it's important that he leaves today's young people with that message and that hope.

When I became editor of *Western American Literature* in 1997, I remembered one of my favorite Stegner lines: "Culture is a pyramid to which each of us brings a stone."[29] He regularly grounds his discussions of culture in such organic metaphors. We decided to make our logo a cairn. In western American studies, Stegner is one of our most significant cairns. I've dropped rocks there before, and I bring another today.

Notes

1. Wallace Stegner, *Beyond the Hundredth Meridian: John Wesley Powell and the Second Opening of the West* (New York: Penguin, 1992), 10. For a biographical treatment of Stegner and his work, see Jackson Benson, *Wallace Stegner: His Life and Work* (New York: Penguin, 1996); and Curt Meine, "Wallace Stegner, Geobiographer," in *Wallace Stegner and the Continental Vision: Essays on Literature, History, and Landscape*, ed. Curt Meine (Washington DC: Island Press, 1997), 121–36.

2. Stegner *Beyond the Hundredth Meridian*, 9.

3. Stegner, *Beyond the Hundredth Meridian*, 9.

4. Wallace Stegner, "Walter Clark's Frontier," in *Walter Van Tilburg Clark: Critiques*, ed. Charlton Laird (Reno: University of Nevada Press, 1983), 58.

5. Wallace Stegner, *Angle of Repose* (1971; rpt., New York: Penguin, 1992).

6. Wallace Stegner, *Wolf Willow: A History, a Story, and a Memory of the Last Plains Frontier* (1962; rpt., New York: Penguin, 2000).

7. Wallace Stegner, "Finding the Place: A Migrant Childhood," in *Where the Bluebird Sings to the Lemonade Springs: Living and Writing in the West* (New York: Modern Library, 2002), 3–21. Stegner first published this essay in *Growing Up Western*, ed. Clarus Backes (New York: Alfred A. Knopf, 1989).

8. Stegner, "Walter Clark's Frontier," 53–70.

9. Stegner, "Finding the Place," 20.

10. Stegner, "Finding the Place," 19.

11. Wallace Stegner, *The Uneasy Chair: A Biography of Bernard DeVoto* (1987; rpt., Lincoln: University of Nebraska Press, 2001), 90.

12. Stegner, *Wolf Willow*, 26.

13. Stegner, *Wolf Willow*, 26.

14. Stegner, *Wolf Willow*, 27.

15. Wallace Stegner, "Coming of Age: The End of the Beginning," in Stegner, *Where the Bluebird Sings*, 135–42. Stegner first published this essay in 1990.

16. Stegner, "Walter Clark's Frontier," 57.

17. Stegner, *Uneasy Chair*, 381. See Wallace Stegner, "Fiction: A Lens on Life," in *On Teaching and Writing Fiction*, ed. Lynn Stegner (New York: Penguin, 2002), 1–10. Stegner originally published this essay in 1982.

Also see Stegner, "History, Myth, and the Western Writer," in *The Sound of Mountain Water: The Changing American West* (1969; rpt., New York: Penguin, 1997), 186–201.

18. Stegner, *Angle of Repose.*

19. For a discussion of this assignment, see Melody Graulich, "Quirky Little Things and Wilderness Letters: Using Wallace Stegner to Teach Cultural Studies and the Responsibilities of Citizenship," in *Teaching Western American Literature*, ed. Brady Harrison and Randi Lynn Tanglen (Lincoln: University of Nebraska Press, 2020), 41–60. The remainder of this essay has been adapted and updated from this earlier piece.

20. Wallace Stegner, *Beyond the Hundredth Meridian: John Wesley Powell and the Second Opening of the West* (1954; rpt., New York: Penguin, 1992), vii.

21. Wallace Stegner and Richard Etulain, *Wallace Stegner on Western History and Literature*, rev. ed. (Salt Lake City: University of Utah Press, 1990), 170; John L. Thomas, *A Country in the Mind: Wallace Stegner, Bernard DeVoto, History, and the American Land* (New York: Routledge, 2000).

22. Dan Flores, "Bioregionalist of the High and Dry: Stegner and Western Environmentalism," in Meine, *Wallace Stegner*, 113. Wallace Stegner's 1960 "Wilderness Letter" has been published in many venues. Stegner wrote about the phrase in "The Geography of Hope," originally published in *The Living Wilderness* (December 1980).

23. Wallace Stegner, quoted in Philip L. Fradkin, *Wallace Stegner and the American West* (New York: Knopf, 2008), 208.

24. Fradkin, *Wallace Stegner*, 213–14.

25. Stegner and Etulain, *Wallace Stegner*, 197.

26. Stegner and Etulain, *Wallace Stegner*, 285.

27. Stegner and Etulain, *Wallace Stegner*, 197.

28. Stegner and Etulain, *Wallace Stegner*, 196–97.

29. Wallace Stegner, "Living Dry," in Stegner, *Where the Bluebird Sings*, 59. Stegner first published this essay in *The American West as Living Space* (University of Michigan Press, 1987).

10

Revisiting "The Marks of Human Passage"

Lessons from the
Dinosaur and Bears Ears
National Monument
Controversies

ROBERT B. KEITER

A place is nothing in itself. It has no meaning, it can hardly be said
to exist, except in terms of human perception, use, and response. . . .
It is legitimate to hope that there may be left in Dinosaur the special
kind of human mark . . . simply the deliberate and chosen refusal to
make any marks at all.

—Wallace Stegner, 1955

Protection of the Bears Ears area will preserve its cultural, prehistoric, and historic legacy and maintain its diverse array of natural
and scientific resources, ensuring that the prehistoric, historic, and
scientific values of this area remain for the benefit of all Americans.

—President Barak Obama, 2016

Wallace Stegner was a reluctant but influential conservationist. He was
drawn into conservation advocacy during the contentious mid-1950s
battle over the proposed Echo Park dam inside Dinosaur National
Monument, where his compelling essay titled "The Marks of Human
Passage" helped defeat the dam proposal, launching him into the
spotlight within conservation circles. A student of the American West

227

and familiar with many of its special places, Stegner was uniquely qualified to assume the preeminent conservation scribe mantle. His "Wilderness Letter" remains a seminal piece in the list of influential conservation writings, while his books and stories about the American West have promoted a richer understanding of the region—its exploration, settlement, development, and preservation. But Stegner is just part of the Dinosaur story, which also laid the groundwork for the modern conservation movement. The battle over Dinosaur National Monument provided momentum for passage of the Wilderness Act and confirmed advocacy tactics that have since been deployed repeatedly to challenge ill-advised development proposals and to preserve special places. It represents a major turning point in American conservation history, marking the beginning of a remarkable growth period during which the nation has protected vast tracts of public land in the form of new national parks, monuments, refuges, and wilderness areas.

An earlier turning point in conservation history involved adoption of the Antiquities Act of 1906, which empowers presidents, with the stroke of a pen, to declare a national monument and put those lands off-limits to industrial development. Since then nearly every president has employed the Antiquities Act to protect important historic and scientific sites, including large landscapes such as the Grand Canyon and the Olympic Mountains. Although the Antiquities Act was adopted, in part, to prevent damage to Native American ruins and artifacts that were being rampantly looted across the Southwest, Indian people themselves never sought to invoke the act to protect their ancestral lands or heritage. That changed in 2015, when the Bears Ears Inter-Tribal Coalition presented President Barak Obama with a proposal to protect 1.9 million acres in southeastern Utah to preserve a stunning landscape overflowing with cultural and historic significance to the tribes. A year later the president obliged and set aside 1.35 million acres as the Bears Ears National Monument, establishing a new precedent in conservation history, one marked by tribal involvement in the creation and management of the new monument.

Another turning point awaited, however. In 2017 President Donald Trump employed the Antiquities Act to reshape radically this new Indian-driven national monument. Asserting that the area was too large and already protected, President Trump shrank the Bears Ears National Monument to less than two hundred thousand acres in size, broke it into two disconnected pieces, and renamed each piece—the first time a president had used the Antiquities Act in such a manner. Trump's overtly political action presented a challenge not dissimilar to the one that engaged Stegner and his allies at Dinosaur. A determined coalition of Bears Ears supporters proceeded to mount an aggressive, multi-pronged campaign to restore Obama's groundbreaking conservation achievement that had enshrined a new, more active Native American presence on the public lands. And they too succeeded in convincing President Joe Biden to reestablish the original monument, marking yet another step forward in conservation history and social justice.

Dinosaur National Monument

In 1909 paleontologist Earl Douglass discovered a trove of dinosaur bones in the remote Uinta Basin in northeastern Utah, representing one of the largest caches of dinosaur fossils yet found in North America.[1] Douglass, who was sponsored by the Carnegie Museum, proceeded to develop the site, which ultimately yielded the remains of four hundred Jurassic dinosaurs. He shipped the fossils to Pittsburgh and elsewhere, to the dismay of local residents, who hoped to capitalize on public interest in this remarkable find. In 1915, in an effort to stop the fossils from falling into private hands, President Woodrow Wilson set aside eighty acres of federal land as the Dinosaur National Monument to protect "an extraordinary deposit of Dinosaurian and other gigantic reptilian remains of the Juratrias period, which are of great scientific interest and value."[2] A year later, the newly created National Park Service assumed management of the monument site but continued allowing Carnegie Museum to remove the skeletons, soon leaving the monument with few remaining fossils and no real attraction to draw tourists to the area. Despite the protective national monument designation, the region's public lands had been plundered of a valuable resource, depriving local residents of the economic boost they had hoped would follow the national monument designation.

But this isolated, lightly populated region on the Utah-Colorado border offered another valuable resource: its spectacular scenery. The original monument boundaries rested near the confluence of the Yampa and Green Rivers, which flowed through the deep, breathtaking Yampa and Lodore Canyons. It was rugged country little changed since settlers first arrived, and was known to the outside world primarily through John Wesley Powell's account of his 1869 journey down the Colorado River and his resulting Arid Lands report.[3] By the 1920s local interest flared again to rekindle tourism as a source of new revenue in this chronically depressed region. That interest then peaked in 1928, when A. G. Birch, a *Denver Post* newsman, floated through Yampa Canyon and reported, "There is nothing like the Yampa river canon that I have ever seen."[4] He further explained his awe: "Imagine seven or eight Zion canons strung together, end-to-end; with Yosemite valley dropped down in the middle of them; with half a dozen 'pockets' as weird and awe-inspiring as Crater Lake; and a score of Devil's towers plumbed down here and there for good measure."[5]

As interest in the area's tourism potential mounted, the National Park Service undertook a study for a possible national park designation. The study, conducted by Roger Toll, who was Yellowstone's superintendent, described Yampa Canyon as having "a scenic individuality that is different from any other area and it is outstandingly beautiful, rugged, and picturesque."[6] He similarly extolled Echo Park (also known as Pats Hole), where the Yampa and Green Rivers joined, creating a setting that had captivated Major Powell on his river journey: "Pats Hole is one of the most beautiful and impressive places in the area. . . . The same scene that [early explorers] saw is there today, unchanged. . . . Across the river stands Steamboat Rock, a great sentinel, with a smooth cliff that suggests a small El Capitan."[7] The report also noted evidence of an early Native American presence, other historic features, and the area's plentiful wildlife, ultimately recommending that the Park Service

17. Steamboat Rock in Echo Canyon, Dinosaur National Monument, 1950s. Used by permission, Uintah County Library Regional History Center, all rights reserved.

protect the setting as a national monument. Following the report, local support, including politicians from both Utah and Colorado, grew even stronger for the proposed national monument, with residents convinced that it would bring curious tourists to the area.

In 1938 President Franklin Roosevelt signed a terse proclamation expanding Dinosaur National Monument by 203,000 acres to encompass the rivers' confluence and the country extending along the river corridors.[8] However, the proclamation included potential dam sites on the Green and Yampa Rivers coveted by the Bureau of Reclamation and the Federal Power Commission for power generation—a matter of considerable importance to the surrounding states.[9] In deference

18. Green River at Echo Park, Dinosaur National Monument, 1939. Used by permission, Uintah County Library Regional History Center, all rights reserved.

to these two powerful agencies, Roosevelt's proclamation included provisions that preserved the dam options, an unusual but necessary political concession the Park Service was essentially forced to accept. The revised monument, which retained the misleading "Dinosaur" name, significantly expanded the fledgling national park system, but the "national monument" (rather than "national park") designation did little to attract the attention of potential tourists. Moreover, the area remained remote without major road connections, another factor that detracted from visitation and left the new monument without a broad constituency prepared to safeguard it.

The national mobilization effort during World War II brought major economic and social changes to the West, including to the upper basin Colorado River states. Demand for water and power escalated as more people and money poured into the area during and after the war.[10] To support this regional growth, the Bureau of Reclamation conceived the Colorado River Storage Project designed to develop the river and support the influx of people and businesses.[11] Two sites inside Dinosaur National Monument were identified by the bureau as ideal dam locations: Echo Park, situated at the confluence of the Yampa and Green Rivers, and Split Mountain, situated further downstream from the confluence.[12] Both dam sites were soon thrust into the limelight in what became an epic struggle between a nascent conservation movement intent on protecting the integrity of this remote national park unit and development interests committed to harnessing the river. Lurking in the background was the earlier, turn-of-the-century battle over Hetch Hetchy Valley in Yosemite National Park, which saw politically powerful development interests in San Francisco prevail over John Muir and his preservationist allies, securing approval for a dam on the Tuolumne River inside the park.[13] The same story seemed on the verge of repeating itself at Echo Park in Dinosaur.

But that did not occur. Instead, an assortment of committed individuals and organizations managed to muster the political strength to block construction of the proposed Echo Park dam by introducing Congress and the nation to Dinosaur National Monument's little-known wonders. In the process Wallace Stegner emerged as an important figure, using his literary skills to produce a large-format book titled *This Is Dinosaur*, which brought alive the stunning canyon scenery that would be flooded by the proposed dam.[14] Stegner edited the volume, which contained striking photographs and incisive textual descriptions of the rugged Dinosaur country, including his own introductory essay titled "The Marks of Human Passage."[15] Asserting that "we cannot describe a place except in terms of its human uses," Stegner traced the human history of Dinosaur beginning with the prehistoric people who left their mark in the form of pictographs and petroglyphs on the area's rock faces.[16] He then described the marks left by the early Spanish explorers, fur trappers, gold rush travelers, John Wesley Powell's expedition, and finally Earl Douglass, the paleontologist who discovered the dinosaur graveyard that led to the initial monument designation—another distinctive mark of human passage.

19. Cover of *This Is Dinosaur*, edited by Wallace Stegner. Courtesy of the University of Utah Marriott Library Special Collections.

Stegner continued his account by noting the 1938 monument expansion as another mark. But Stegner cautioned that this more recent mark and, indeed, the entire Dinosaur landscape were now imperiled: "To this moment, at least, the Green and Yampa canyons have been saved intact, a wilderness that is the property of all Americans, a 325 square mile preserve that is part schoolroom and part playground and part—the best part—sanctuary from a world paved with concrete, jet propelled, smog-blanketed, sterilized, over-insured, aseptic, a world mass-produced with interchangeable parts, and with every natural beautiful thing endangered by the raw engineering power of the twentieth century."[17] He then asked: "How much wilderness do wilderness-lovers want?" And he answered: "*Enough so that there will be in the years ahead a little relief, a little quiet, a little relaxation, for any of our increasing millions who need and want it.*"[18] He went on to

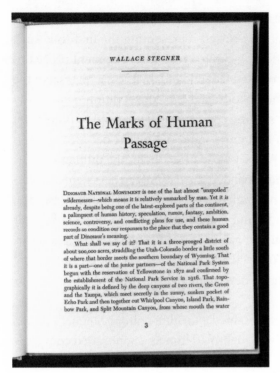

20. Wallace Stegner's introductory essay in *This Is Dinosaur*. Courtesy of the University of Utah Marriott Library Special Collections.

urge that Dinosaur be left with "the special kind of human mark, the special record of human passage that distinguishes man from all other species. . . . It is simply the deliberate and chosen refusal to make any marks at all. Sometimes we have withheld our power to destroy, and have left . . . a threatened beauty spot like Yosemite or Yellowstone or Dinosaur scrupulously alone."[19] Finally, Stegner astutely observed: "If we preserved as parks only those places that have no economic possibilities, we would have no parks."[20]

A copy of *This Is Dinosaur*, the brainchild of a young David Brower who had recently assumed leadership of the Sierra Club, was distributed to all members of Congress in hopes that it would convince them to protect the area from the imminent dams.[21] At the same time, Brower and his allies were busy building political coalitions and encouraging supporters to lobby Congress to oppose the dams.[22] In the end they succeeded, and Congress voted to exclude the Dinosaur dams from the Colorado River Storage Project, representing the first time such an effort had succeeded in blocking a major development project to safeguard previously protected federal lands.[23] It was a reversal of the Hetch Hetchy result and encouraged the conservation community to take the offensive by seeking congressional approval to protect yet more federal acreage in its natural state. Within the decade Congress passed the Wilderness Act, set aside more than nine million acres as "instant" wilderness, and expanded the national park system by sixty-eight units, adding such wonders as Canyonlands, North Cascades, Redwood, Virgin Islands, and Guadalupe Mountains.[24] As Stegner hoped, a new mark of human passage was imprinted on the landscape, one written in law and protective boundaries that put certain special places off limits to intensive development by preserving them in their natural condition.

The Dinosaur battle represented a turning point in Stegner's career, too. The book and his essay identified him as a committed conservationist willing to employ his formidable writing skills in the cause. Five years later Stegner penned his famous "Wilderness Letter."[25] Drawing upon some of the ideas expressed in his Dinosaur essay, he eloquently endorsed the wilderness idea for its spiritual, contemplative, and character-building value, opining that "something will have gone out of us as a people if we ever let the remaining wilderness be destroyed."[26] Stegner went on to serve on the Wilderness Society's national council, the National Parks Advisory Board, and as a special assistant to Secretary of the Interior Stewart Udall.[27] He also wrote numerous essays promoting and defending the preservationist impulse, including his well-known essay on the national parks, which he memorably characterized as "America's Best Idea."[28] Along the way he made clear, in the "Wilderness Letter" and other writings, that southern Utah's red rock and desert country deserved legal protection: "It is a lovely and terrible wilderness, such as wilderness as Christ and the prophets went out into; harshly and beautifully colored, broken and worn until its bones are exposed, its great sky without a smudge of taint from Technocracy, and in hidden corners and pockets under its cliffs the sudden poetry of springs."[29] Stegner, the dedicated conservationist, would plainly have been pleased by the recent presidential actions under the Antiquities Act preserving southern Utah's Grand Staircase–Escalante and Bears Ears country as expansive, new national monuments. And he would have been dismayed at their abrupt but temporary demise.

The Antiquities Act

By the dawn of the twentieth century, the American West was settled, the frontier closed, and the region's original Native American inhabitants relegated to reservations. Through an array of treaties, the federal government owned vast tracts of land across the West that it eagerly sought to transfer into private hands via homesteading, mining, and other laws designed to attract new inhabitants to the vast landscape.[30] Congress, having witnessed rampant destruction of valuable timber lands during the nation's relentless march westward, introduced a new conservation concept during the latter part of the nineteenth century. First, in 1872, Congress created Yellowstone National Park and then established forest reserves beginning in 1891, soon to become the national forest system.[31] Meanwhile, as white settlement intensified, Native American ruins and sites across the Southwest were being extensively looted and desecrated, partly in response to a burgeoning commercial market in original Indian artifacts. A cadre of professional archeologists, increasingly concerned about the loss of these irreplaceable historic remains and objects, approached Congress for assistance in protecting this disappearing heritage.[32]

In 1906, after several futile attempts at legislation, Congress adopted the Antiquities Act in an effort to safeguard these important archeological resources from theft and destruction. Passage of this protective legislation is generally credited to the joint efforts of archeologist Edgar Lee Hewett, who earlier served as the first president of New Mexico Normal University, where he learned about the region's abundant Native American sites, and Iowa congressman John Lacey, who introduced the bill after Hewett exposed him to the destruction occurring across the region.[33] The act is quite short: it vests the president with the discretionary authority to designate "historic landmarks, historic and prehistoric structures, and other objects of historic or scientific interest" situated on federal lands as national monuments but requires the designation be "confined to the smallest area compatible with the proper care and management of the objects to be protected."[34] The act represented a compromise between competing factions; the professional archeologists wanted to limit such designations to ancient ruins no more than 320 acres in size, while the Park Service endorsed a more expansive approach that sought to protect "scenic beauty and natural wonders" without any size limitation. The final version split the difference by adopting the "historic and scientific objects" standard and the "smallest area compatible" language rather than an explicit acreage limitation.[35]

Since its inception the Antiquities Act has been used to protect an array of historic sites and landscapes. It has received a broad interpretation both by the presidents who have invoked it and by the courts that have reviewed their actions. President Theodore Roosevelt, who signed the act into law, first used it to protect Devil's Tower in Wyoming and soon followed with seventeen more national monument designations, including the eight-hundred-thousand-acre Grand Canyon National Monument.[36] Roosevelt's use of the act to protect the Grand Canyon as an "object of historic and scientific interest" was challenged in court as exceeding his statutory authority. The U.S. Supreme Court, however, upheld the new national monument, concluding that the Grand Canyon afforded "an unexampled field for geologic study" and represented "one of the great natural wonders."[37] Since then nearly every president has used the act to establish new national monuments, including Mount Olympus, Bryce Canyon, Glacier Bay, Death Valley, and Jackson Hole.[38] Several of these national monuments, though controversial at the time of designation, were later converted by Congress into revered national parks, such as Olympic National Park and Grand Teton National Park.[39] In 1996, drawing upon the precedent established by these earlier expansive national monument designations, President Bill Clinton proclaimed the 1.7-million-acre Grand Staircase–Escalante

National Monument in southern Utah, followed a few years later by several other landscape-scale national monuments.[40] Clinton's handiwork was challenged in several lawsuits, but the courts consistently sustained his actions.[41] In one notable case the court ruled that "the inclusion of such items as ecosystems and scenic vistas in the Proclamation did not contravene the [Antiquities Act]," observing that the Supreme Court has held that the act "is not limited to protecting only archeological sites."[42]

Although the Antiquities Act has been used primarily to protect federal lands, a few presidents have modified national monuments created by their predecessors. Congress too has occasionally adopted legislation eliminating or modifying earlier national monuments. In both cases these revisionary actions have generally been driven either by a later-discovered mistake in the original designation, such as boundary errors straying outside the federal estate, or a nationally compelling reason, such as wartime necessity.[43] President Wilson, for example, reduced Olympic National Monument in size by half to secure access to its valuable timber that was being used during the First World War in aircraft production.[44] With few exceptions these monument revisions have been modest in size, and none has occurred since 1963. More often Congress has converted presidentially decreed national monuments into national parks, as in the case of the Grand Canyon, Death Valley, Grand Teton, Zion, and numerous others.[45] In short, the Antiquities Act has served as an important legal tool available to presidents to protect invaluable scientific and historic sites on federal lands from development or exploitation.

Bears Ears National Monument

It was against this backdrop that President Obama, in December 2016, proclaimed the 1.35-million-acre Bears Ears National Monument in southeastern Utah, responding to an official proposal from local tribes to protect their ancestral lands and cultural heritage.[46] It was the first time in more than 110 years that any Native American individual or entity had looked to the Antiquities Act for protection.[47] It was also

21. July 2015 meeting of tribal leaders and Obama administration officials in Bears Ears meadow. © Tim Peterson.

the first time these five tribes had come together in such a common cause. And it represented an unusual coalition between the tribes and majority-dominated conservation organizations that had long sought wilderness protection for this remote and spectacular landscape. According to the Bears Ears Inter-Tribal Coalition, "perhaps nowhere in the United States are so many well-preserved cultural resources found within such a striking and relatively undeveloped natural landscape."[48] Earlier, Wallace Stegner described the Bears Ears country as a place that "fills up the eye and overflow[s] the soul."[49] The area, though, had long been looted for its Native American artifacts, a practice deeply troubling to the tribes but that nonetheless continued. The chronically underfunded Bureau of Land Management (BLM), the federal agency responsible for much of the area, simply did not have the staff or resources to prevent these desecrations.

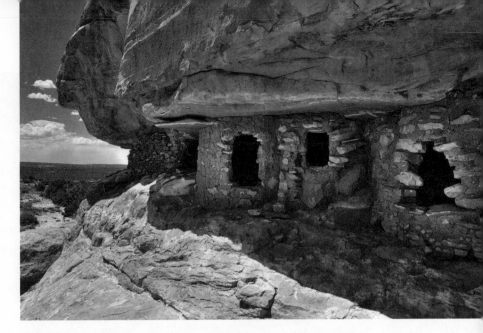

22. Granaries in Bears Ears National Monument. © Tim Peterson.

23. The Bears Ears Buttes with the background peak known as Navajo Mountain to the USGS, Naatsis'áán to Diné people, and Toko'navi to Hopi people. © Tim Peterson.

24. Alcove in the Bears Ears National Monument high country. © Tim Peterson.

25. Petroglyphs and contemporary vandalism on Bears Ears National Monument canyon wall. © Tim Peterson.

The Intertribal Coalition's petition to the president presented a compelling case for federal protection of this landscape, which held special significance for the tribes. Mostly under BLM management, the area was subject to extensive livestock grazing, mining, and oil and gas exploration as well as escalating recreational use. The petition envisioned different management priorities for the area, one responsive to the tribes' longstanding relationship with the land. Citing the federal-tribal government-to-government relationship, the petition sought a new national monument designation that "will honor the worldviews of our ancestors and Tribes today and their relationships with this landscape."[50] It quotes extensively from tribal members to explain how they view and interact with the Bears Ears country. Malcolm Lehi, a Ute Mountain Ute, observes, "We can still hear the songs and prayers of our ancestors on every mesa and in every canyon."[51] Phillip Vicenti, a Zuni, explains, "The importance of Bears Ears for our people is through our ancestral sites. . . . When we visit Bears Ears, we connect with our migration history immediately without doubt. With that, we must preserve, manage and educate our future generations."[52] To ensure themselves a voice in administration of the new monument, the petition proposed a new, groundbreaking collaborative management arrangement between the tribes and the BLM, which would give both of them an equal voice in resource and cultural management decisions.[53]

Sensitive to this unprecedented tribal request and underlying social justice concerns, President Obama established the Bears Ears National Monument. His lyrical proclamation evoked the unique historical and scientific dimensions of the landscape as well as the tribes' centuries-old relationship with it. The proclamation begins by describing the prominent twin buttes—Bears Ears—that overlook the area, and continues: "For hundreds of generation, native peoples lived in the surrounding deep sandstone canyons, desert mesas, and meadow mountaintops, which constitute one of the densest and most significant cultural landscapes in the United States. Abundant rock art, ancient cliff dwellings, ceremonial sites, and countless other artifacts provide an extraordinary archaeological and cultural record that is important to us all, but most notably the land is profoundly sacred to many Native American tribes."[54] After fully reviewing the area's various resources, President Obama concludes, "Protection of the Bears Ears area will preserve its cultural, prehistoric, and historic legacy and maintain its diverse array of natural and scientific resources, ensuring that the prehistoric, historic, and scientific values of this area remain for the benefit of all Americans."[55]

The proclamation acknowledges the special Native American connection with the land and their deep knowledge about the area. It largely adopts the tribe's collaborative management proposal by establishing a Bears Ears Commission consisting of one member selected by each of the five tribes "to provide guidance and recommendations on the development and implementation of management plans and on management of the monument."[56] It also instructs federal officials, in developing the management plan, to "carefully and fully consider integrating the traditional and historical knowledge and special expertise of the Commission or comparable entity."[57] To ensure monument managers take tribal proposals seriously, the proclamation requires them to provide a written explanation if they choose not to incorporate specific recommendations.[58] In short, the monument was envisioned as a living cultural landscape, marking a new, more integrated relationship between the federal land management agencies and the tribes whose ancestors called the Bears Ears country home.[59] It represented a bold new legal mark on the landscape, one that Stegner would surely approve of.

This new, unique Bears Ears National Monument, however, proved short-lived. Soon after assuming office, President Trump instructed his secretary of the interior to review President Obama's numerous national monument designations.[60] Responding to Utah's congressional delegation, which was upset with the large-scale Bears Ears designation and the impact on potential mineral development opportunities, President Trump specifically called for a prompt review of that monument. Upon receiving Secretary Ryan Zinke's report, the president invoked the

Antiquities Act and proceeded to dramatically alter Bears Ears National Monument.[61] He not only reduced the monument by 85 percent to a mere two hundred thousand acres but also divided it into two separate units, only one of which was connected to Native American concerns. Noting that the Antiquities Act requires that monument designations be confined to the smallest area compatible with protection of the designated objects, President Trump's revised proclamation asserted that some of Obama's protected objects were not of significant scientific or historic interest, that existing federal law already protected much of the landscape and objects, and that no real threat existed to many of the objects.[62] He concluded that the area's historic and scientific objects could be adequately protected with a smaller designation and proceeded to break the Obama monument into two much smaller protected areas.[63] The Trump monument revisions represented another mark on the landscape, albeit one that was patently disrespectful of the area's original inhabitants, its cultural significance, and Stegner's Dinosaur admonition.[64]

Not surprisingly, President Trump's action greatly dismayed the tribes and the new monument's other supporters. The Intertribal Coalition and its allies responded immediately, filing three lawsuits in federal court and arguing that the president did not have the authority to take such an action.[65] The litigation presented a novel legal question yet unanswered by the courts: whether the president has the authority under the Antiquities Act to eliminate or modify a national monument. Presidents prior to 1963 assumed such authority, but their actions were generally not controversial and went unchallenged.[66] The Antiquities Act expressly authorizes the president to establish national monuments to protect "historic and scientific objects" confined to the smallest area compatible with their protection, but it is silent regarding a president's authority to revoke or modify an existing monument. President Trump's supporters, citing past presidential practice, argued that a modification power can be inferred from the act's language and that his actions were consistent with the act's "smallest area compatible" language.[67] Proponents of the Obama monument argued that

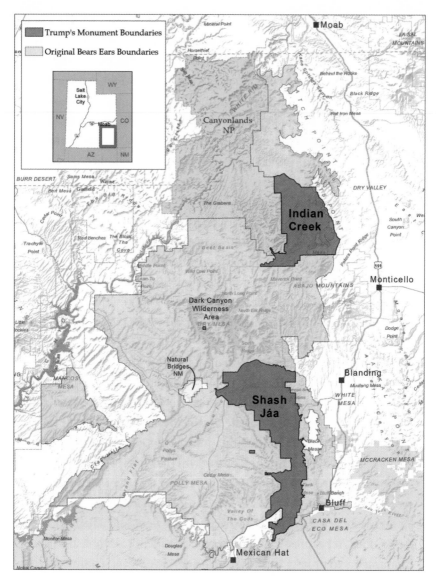

26. Map showing original boundaries of Bears Ears National Monument as established by President Obama and the revised boundaries per President Trump's December 2017 modification proclamation. In 2021 President Biden restored the original monument boundaries while also including additional acreage in the Indian Creek area. Courtesy of Creed Murdock/Southern Utah Wilderness Alliance.

the act's lack of express modification language negates its existence, and they contended that the Federal Land and Policy Management Act of 1976 clearly intended to prohibit presidents from revoking or modifying an existing national monument.[68] They also noted that prior presidential alterations of national monuments did not approach the scale of the Trump modification or rest upon the same "smallest area compatible" rationale.[69] As a legal matter, under the U.S. Constitution's property clause, Congress always has the authority to revoke or modify a national monument, but it has chosen not to speak in this matter.[70] And it appears that the courts will not be heard from either on this issue.

Following his 2020 election, President Joe Biden reversed Trump's downsizing decision and reestablished the initial Bears Ears National Monument, putting yet another legal mark on the landscape. In Proclamation 10,285, President Biden explains that "restoring the Bears Ears National Monument honors the special relationship between the Federal Government and Tribal Nations, correcting the exclusion of lands and resources profoundly sacred to Tribal Nations, and ensuring the long-term protection of, and respect for, this remarkable and revered region." Describing the Bears Ears area landscape as "a sacred land of spiritual significance, a historic homeland, [and] a living, breathing landscape," the Biden proclamation concludes that it is "an object of historic and scientific interest" and the original boundaries represent the smallest area necessary to protect these objects. The proclamation also observes that the Bears Ears region "conveys the story of westward expansion of European Americans" and remains "one of the most ecologically intact and least-roaded regions in the contiguous United States." The proclamation explains that the area contains extensive geological, archeological, and paleontological objects that tell "the stories of epochs past" and concludes by reestablishing the Obama monument as well as the original Bears Ears Commission that gave the tribes a meaningful role in its management. By law, the remarkable yet contested Bears Ears landscape is once again protected, at least for now.[71]

Another Mark of Human Passage

In the "Marks of Human Passage," Wallace Stegner described in detail the progression of physical marks humans made upon the Dinosaur National Monument landscape. He concluded his essay observing that the monument designation represented a new approach to this special landscape, one that involved "simply the deliberate and chosen refusal to make any marks at all."[72] Although Stegner evidently saw the creation of national monuments and parks as reflecting the absence of more human marks on the landscape, it actually represents a new type of mark on the land—one that is legal in nature and quite powerful. It is captured in the new, legally significant boundary line designed to protect the land from intensive human use. Viewed from this perspective, resolution of the Dinosaur controversy acknowledged the importance of this invisible yet tangibly powerful legal mark. It also heralded the advent of a new era in federal land conservation, an era that has seen the nation preserve more than 110 million acres of wilderness while also more than doubling the size of both the national park and national wildlife refuge systems.[73]

These changes are part of the larger changes that have come to the West since the Echo Park dam was defeated, leaving Dinosaur National Monument undisturbed by a new human-engineered encumbrance. On the federal lands the preservation impulse has taken hold, as have new ideas about landscape conservation, ecosystem management, dam removal, and the like.[74] These new commitments put biodiversity and ecological restoration on a coequal footing with the extractive uses— mining, logging, drilling, and livestock grazing—that long dominated federal public land policy. These policy changes reflect larger social and economic changes afoot across the region, including dramatic population growth, increased urbanization, and new economic realities that have elevated the importance of tourism and recreation for western state economies.[75] Change is also evident among the West's original Native American inhabitants; the tribes are effectively asserting their sovereignty, securing important new legal rights, developing their own natural resource management capacities, and seeking a more engaged role in federal land management decisions.[76] And for the first time, President Biden has appointed a Native American to serve as secretary of the interior and as director of the National Park Service. These changes have not come without controversy, and the region still has a long road ahead before it obtains, in Wallace Stegner's immortal words, "a society to match its scenery."[77]

The 2016 Bears Ears National Monument designation represented another important step forward, seeming to signal the beginning of a new era in federal public land policy and Native American relations. President Obama's precedent-setting proclamation envisioned a living monument that preserved, at a landscape scale, the area's natural and cultural heritage. The new monument also responded to historic social injustices and ensured the region's Native American residents an important managerial role in overseeing their cultural patrimony. While these aspirations appeared lost following President Trump's unprecedented monument modification order, President Biden's 2021 proclamation has now restored the original monument. Of course, either Congress or another president could reverse the reestablished monument, and litigation challenging Biden's actions is pending. But by any measure, the restored Bears Ears monument stands as a powerful new mark in the progression of our relationship with the land and with each other. There is good reason to expect, over the passage of human time, that this new mark will ultimately prevail and endure, which would certainly please Stegner.

Notes

1. Mark W. T. Harvey, *A Symbol of Wilderness: Echo Park and the American Conservation Movement* (Albuquerque: University of New Mexico Press, 1994), 7. See also Richard G. Beidelman, *Administrative History: Dinosaur National Monument* (National Park Service, n.d.), http://npshistory.com /publications/dino/adhi.pdf.

2. President Woodrow Wilson, Presidential Proclamation No. 1313 (October 4, 1915), reprinted in National Park Service, "Foundation Document:

Dinosaur National Monument" (July 2015), 51, http://npshistory.com
/publications/foundation-documents/dino-fd-2015.pdf.

3. John Wesley Powell, *The Canyons of the Colorado* (Meadville PA: Flood and Vincent, 1895); Powell, *Report on the Lands of the Arid Region of the United States*, ed. Wallace Stegner (Washington DC: Government Printing Office, 1879).

4. Harvey, *Symbol of Wilderness*, 11.

5. Harvey, *Symbol of Wilderness*, 11.

6. Harvey, *Symbol of Wilderness*, 11.

7. Harvey, *Symbol of Wilderness*, 11–12.

8. President Franklin Roosevelt, Proclamation No. 2290, 53 Stat. 2454 (1938).

9. Harvey, *Symbol of Wilderness*, 16–20.

10. Harvey, *Symbol of Wilderness*, 22, 25–26

11. Mark Reisner, *Cadillac Desert: The American West and Its Disappearing Water* (New York: Viking, 1986), 145–50.

12. Harvey, *Symbol of Wilderness*, 22, 29.

13. Robert W. Righter, *The Battle over Hetch Hetchy: America's Most Controversial Dam and the Birth of Modern Environmentalism* (New York: Oxford University Press, 2006).

14. Wallace Stegner, ed., *This Is Dinosaur: Echo Park Country and Its Magic Rivers* (New York: Alfred Knopf, 1955).

15. Wallace Stegner, "The Marks of Human Passage," in Stegner, *This Is Dinosaur*, 3.

16. Stegner, "Marks of Human Passage," 15.

17. Stegner, "Marks of Human Passage," 14.

18. Stegner, "Marks of Human Passage," 14; emphasis in original.

19. Stegner, "Marks of Human Passage," 17.

20. Stegner, "Marks of Human Passage," 17.

21. Philip Fradkin, *Wallace Stegner and the American West* (New York: Alfred Knopf, 2008), 184–90.

22. Harvey, *Symbol of Wilderness*, 256–59.

23. Harvey *Symbol of Wilderness*, 283–85.

24. National Wilderness Preservation System, September 3, 1964, 16 U.S.C. §§ 1131–36; Doug Scott, *The Enduring Wilderness: Protecting Our Natural Heritage through the Wilderness Act* (Golden CO: Fulcrum, 2004), 57;

Robert B. Keiter, *To Conserve Unimpaired: The Evolution of the National Park System* (Washington DC: Island Press, 2013), 237–38.

25. Wallace Stegner, "Wilderness Letter" (1960), reprinted in Wallace Stegner, *The Sound of Mountain Water* (Lincoln: University of Nebraska Press, 1985), 145–53.

26. Stegner, "Wilderness Letter," 146.

27. Fradkin, *Wallace Stegner*, 167. While working at the Interior Department, Stegner assisted Secretary of the Interior Stewart Udall in writing a book on conservation. Stewart Udall, *The Quiet Crisis* (New York: Holt, Rinehart, & Winston, 1963); Fradkin, *Wallace Stegner*, 207–9.

28. Wallace Stegner, "The Best Idea We Ever Had," in *Marking the Sparrow's Fall: The Making of the American West* (New York: Henry Holt, 1998), 135.

29. Stegner, "Wilderness Letter," 153; Wallace Stegner, introduction to Utah Wilderness Coalition, *Wilderness at the Edge: A Citizen's Proposal to Protect Utah's Canyons and Deserts* (Salt Lake City: Utah Wilderness Coalition, 1991), 3–6.

30. Charles F. Wilkinson, *Crossing the Next Meridian: Land, Water, and the Future of the American West* (Washington DC: Island Press, 1993), 15–27.

31. Alfred Runte, *National Parks: The American Experience*, 2nd ed. (Lincoln: University of Nebraska Press, 1987), 29–41; Wilkinson, *Crossing the Next Meridian*, 120–24.

32. Hal Rothman, *America's National Monuments: The Politics of Preservation* (Lawrence: University Press of Kansas, 1994), 6–30.

33. Raymond Harris Thompson, "Edgar Lee Hewett and the Politics of Archaeology," in *The Antiquities Act: A Century of American Archaeology, Historic Preservation, and Nature Conservation*, ed. David Harmon, Francis P. McManamon, and Dwight T. Pitcaithley, (Tucson: University of Arizona Press, 2006), 35–47; Rebecca Conrad, "John F. Lacey, Conservation's Public Servant," in Harmon et al., *Antiquities Act*, 58–61.

34. Antiquities Act of 1906, Pub. L. No. 59-209, 34 Stat. 225 (1906), 16 U.S.C. § 431, re-codified, 54 U.S.C. § 320301 (2014).

35. Ron F. Lee, *The Antiquities Act of 1906* (Washington DC: National Park Service, 1970), rpt., *Journal of the Southwest* 42, no. 2 (2000): 198–269, https://www.nps.gov/archeology/pubs/lee/Lee_FPM.htm; Conrad, "John F. Lacey," 58–61.

36. Runte, *National Parks*, 66–68; Mark Squillace, "The Antiquities Act and the Exercise of Presidential Power: The Clinton Monuments," in Harmon et al., *Antiquities Act*, 132n50.
37. Cameron v. United States, 252 U.S. 450 (1920).
38. Harmon et al., *Antiquities Act*, 288–97.
39. Runte, *National Parks*, 127–28; Rothman, *America's National Monuments*, 214–22.
40. President William Clinton, "Proclamation Establishing Grand Staircase–Escalante National Monument, Proclamation No. 6920," 61 Fed. Reg. R 50,223, 50,225 (1996); Mark Squillace, "The Monumental Legacy of the Antiquities Act of 1906," 37 *Georgia Law Review* 473, 509–10 (2003); Sanjay Ranchod, "The Clinton National Monuments: Protecting Ecosystems with the Antiquities Act," 25 *Harvard Environmental Law Review* 535, 555–73 (2001).
41. Mountain States Legal Foundation v. Bush, 306 F.3d 1132 (D.C. Cir. 2002); Tulare County v. Bush, 306 F.3d 1138 (D.C. Cir. 2002); Utah Association of Counties v. Bush, 316 F. Supp. 2d 1172 (D. Utah 2004), appeal dismissed, 455 F.3d 1094 (10th Cir. 2006).
42. Tulare County v. Bush, 306 F.3d 1138, 1142 (D.C. Cir. 2002).
43. John C. Ruple, "The Trump Administration and Lessons Not Learned from Prior National Monument Modifications," 43 *Harvard Environmental Law Review* 1, 74–76 (2019).
44. Ruple, "Trump Administration," 70–74.
45. Runte, *National Parks*, 102–4; Brad Barr and Katrina Van Dine, "Application of the Antiquities Act to Oceans," in Harmon et al., *Antiquities Act*, 257.
46. President Barak Obama, "Proclamation No. 9558—Establishment of the Bears Ears National Monument," 82 *Federal Register* 1139 (January 5, 2017); Bears Ears Inter-Tribal Coalition, "Proposal to President Barak Obama for the Creation of Bears Ears National Monument," October 15, 2015, https://www.bearsearscoalition.org/wp-content/uploads/2015/10/Bears-Ears-Inter-Tribal-Coalition-Proposal-10-15-15.pdf.
47. Charles Wilkinson, "'At Bears Ears We Can Hear the Voices of Our Ancestors in Every Canyon and on Every Mesa Top': The Creation of the First Native National Monument," 50 *Arizona State Law Journal* 317, 323 (2018).

48. Bears Ears Inter-Tribal Coalition, "Cultural & Archaeological Significance," https://bearsearscoalition.org/archaeological-significance/.

49. Stegner, *Sound of Mountain Water*, 18.

50. Bears Ears Inter-Tribal Coalition, "Proposal to President Barack Obama," 2. See also Rebecca Robinson, *Voices from Bears Ears: Seeking Common Ground on Sacred Land* (Tucson: University of Arizona Press, 2018); Jacqueline Keeler, ed., *Edge of Morning: Native Voices Speak for the Bears Ears* (Salt Lake City: Torrey House Press, 2017).

51. Keeler, *Edge of Morning*, 3.

52. Keeler, *Edge of Morning*, 10.

53. Bears Ears Inter-Tribal Coalition, "Proposal to President Barack Obama," 28–34; Wilkinson, *At Bears Ears*, 331–32.

54. Obama, "Proclamation No. 9558," 1.

55. Obama, "Proclamation No. 9558," 5.

56. Obama, "Proclamation No. 9558," 7.

57. Obama, "Proclamation No. 9558," 7.

58. Obama, "Proclamation No. 9558," 7.

59. Sarah Krakoff, "Public Lands, Conservation, and the Possibility of Justice," *Harvard Civil Rights–Civil Liberties Law Review* 212, 216 (2018) (arguing that "Bears Ears National Monument and other recent monuments constitute a step toward repairing past injustices and reintegrating disenfranchised groups with the landscape").

60. "Review of Designations under the Antiquities Act," Executive Order no. 13,792, 82 Fed. Reg. 20,429 § 2 (April 26, 2017).

61. Ruple, *Trump Administration*, 22–23; Memorandum from Ryan Zinke, secretary of the interior, to President Trump, "Final Report Summarizing Findings of the Review of Designations under the Antiquities Act" (August 24, 2017), https://www.eenews.net/assets/2017/12/05/document_pm_01.pdf; President Donald Trump, "Proclamation No. 9681—Modifying the Bears Ears National Monument," 82 *Federal Register* 58081 (December 8, 2017).

62. Trump, "Proclamation No. 9681."

63. Trump, "Proclamation No. 9681."

64. In addition, President Trump also used the occasion to reduce the size of the Grand Staircase–Escalante National Monument by roughly one million acres. Trump, "Proclamation 9682—Modifying the Grand Staircase–

Escalante National Monument," 82 *Federal Register* 58089 (December 8, 2017).

65. Ruple, *Trump Administration*, 4n8.

66. Ruple, *Trump Administration*, 39–74.

67. Todd Gaziano and John Yoo, "Presidential Authority to Revoke or Reduce National Monument Designations," 35 *Yale Journal on Regulation* 617 (2018); Richard H. Seamon, "Dismantling Monuments," 70 *Florida Law Review* 553 (2018). See also Massachusetts Lobstermen's Ass'n v. Raimondo, 592, U.S. 141 S.Ct. 979, 981 (2021) (C. J. Roberts) (suggesting, in a statement attached to the court's order denying a certiorari petition, that the Antiquities Act's "smallest area compatible" language may have been stretched too far by past presidents in establishing large-sized national monuments).

68. Mark Squillace et al., "Presidents Lack the Authority to Abolish or Diminish National Monuments," 103 *Virginia Law Review Online* 55 (2017); Ruple, *Trump Administration*, 23–34; 43 U.S.C. § 1714(j) (providing that "the Secretary [of the Interior] shall not . . . modify or revoke any withdrawal creating national monuments under [the Antiquities Act]"). The legislative history behind this provision states that it "would also specifically reserve to the Congress the authority to modify and revoke withdrawals for national monuments created under the Antiquities Act. . . . These provisions will insure that the integrity of the great national resource management systems will remain under the control of the Congress." H.R. Rep. No. 94-1163 (May 15, 1976), 9.

69. Ruple, *Trump Administration*, 75–76.

70. U.S. Constitution, art. IV, § 3, cl. 2.

71. President Joseph Biden, "Proclamation No. 10,285—A Proclamation on Bears Ears National Monument," 86 *Federal Register* 57,321 (October 15, 2021). The Biden proclamation also increases the original Bears Ears National Monument in size by 11,200 acres, representing new acreage that Trump included in his proclamation modifying the monument. It describes in detail the various discrete areas and resources found within the original Bears Ears designation, an apparent effort to clearly demonstrate why these expansive lands merit protection under the Antiquities Act as "objects of historic or scientific interest."

72. Stegner, "Marks of Human Passage," 17.

73. Robert B. Keiter, "Toward a National Conservation Network Act: Transforming Landscape Conservation on the Public Lands into Law," 42 *Harvard Environmental Law Review* 61, 65–77 (2018).

74. Robert B. Keiter, *Keeping Faith with Nature: Ecosystems, Democracy, and America's Public Lands* (New Haven CT: Yale University Press, 2003), 312–27; Bruce Babbitt, *Cities in the Wilderness: A New Vision of Land Use in America* (Washington DC: Island Press, 2005), 137–42; Keiter, "National Conservation Network Act," 93–104.

75. Robert B. Keiter and Matthew McKinney, "Public Land and Resources Law in the American West: Time for Another Comprehensive Review?" 49 *Environmental Law* 1, 6–35 (2019).

76. Charles Wilkinson, *Blood Struggle: The Rise of Modern Indian Nations* (New York: Norton, 2005).

77. Stegner, *Sound of Mountain Water*, 38.

11

The Geography of
Hope in an Age
of Uncertainty

PAUL FORMISANO

Since the publication of Wallace Stegner's missive to David Pesonen on the occasion of the Outdoor Recreation Resources Review Commission report, the 1960 "Wilderness Letter" has become a foundational text of western environmentalism. Indeed, as Beth LaDow suggested at the founding of the Wallace Stegner Society in 2001, his "Wilderness Letter" is "perhaps the most eloquent and widely quoted plea for wilderness in the twentieth century."[1] Among the many provocative passages in the letter is Stegner's closing paragraph wherein he reaffirms the value of wilderness outside of economic interests and leaves readers with perhaps his most iconic of phrases. He concludes: "These are some of the things wilderness can do for us. That is the reason we need to put into effect, for its preservation, some other principle than the principles of exploitation or 'usefulness' or even recreation. We simply need that wild country available to us, even if we never do more than drive to its edge and look in. For it can be a means of reassuring ourselves of our sanity as creatures, a part of the geography of hope."[2] The last three words, the "geography of hope," have become a mantra, a rallying cry for many writers, environmental advocates, and nature lovers who view the Earth's wild places as a remedy to combat the instability and chaos seen in our built and natural environments. A quick internet search reveals the range of Stegner's memorable wordsmithing to include a 2008 publication about the climate crisis by a British author; the NGO Geography of Hope, which seeks to provide underprivileged youth with outdoor experiences; and a report on an iconic Colorado-based ultramarathon.[3]

While Stegner's idea has inspired such a diverse range of activities, the geography of hope has most powerfully resonated with those thinking, living, recreating, and writing about the American West. Ken Burns's celebrated series on the West, a collection of Colorado poetry, the Alaska Wilderness League's event series, and Stephen Trimble and Terry Tempest Williams's chapbook *Testimony*, destined for members of Congress to preserve and expand Utah's wilderness areas, all draw upon Stegner's passage either to title their work or provide the driving force for the project.[4] In the case of *Testimony*, Trimble and Williams address their desire to change the tenor of public land deliberations, to inspire legislators to see the inherent values—similar to those articulated by Stegner in his "Wilderness Letter"—that make Utah's desert and mountainscapes worthy of protection. They close, stating, "We live in the geography of hope."[5]

Such a declaration, especially considering the context in which it is uttered, reflects a long-standing tradition of wedding the wilderness, as a tonic to civilization's despair, with the American West. We can look back to Frederick Jackson Turner's 1893 frontier thesis as perhaps the most famous of Western paeans, but its roots reach much farther back to the earliest exploration narratives of the Western Hemisphere by European settlers. In this vein Stegner, too, becomes part of the western mythmaking machine as the wilderness he experienced in places west of the hundredth meridian such as the Colorado Plateau's labyrinthine canyons, the Uintah's majestic peaks and lakes, and Saskatchewan's windswept prairies led him to hail wilderness as "the thing that has helped to make an American different from and, until we forget it in the roar of our industrial cities, more fortunate than other men. For an American, insofar as he is new and different at all, is a civilized man who has renewed himself in the wild."[6] Like Turner's frontier thesis, Stegner's "Wilderness Letter" places American exceptionalism and identity squarely within the West's hinterlands, suggesting that wilderness is an essential and necessary part of American identity and will be for generations to come.[7]

Yet now two decades into the twenty-first century, we might well wonder if the ideals expressed in the "Wilderness Letter," and more specifically as they resonate within "the geography of hope," are still relevant. Do today's deep cynicism, political tumult over race relations and a global pandemic, toxic discourse, and widespread environmental degradation threaten Stegner's vision in our age of uncertainty, or do they still offer a path forward through which we can address the complicated environmental and cultural issues of our day? Is the wilderness-West-hope triad—or the "hope trope," as literary critic Krista Comer calls it—still relevant when postwestern studies and New Western History have presented a much more complicated and, depending on the perspective, pessimistic vision of the region?[8] And in that vein, can we view the American West and its celebrated wilderness as that "spatial container of American optimism," in light of a history of land dispossession and genocide that constitute, in historian Margaret Jacobs's words, "the disquieting truth of America's founding crimes?"[9] The obvious answer would seem to be a resounding "no."

Such skepticism about Stegner's representation of the West as the geography of hope is not new, however. In 1996 Elizabeth Cook-Lynn published *Why I Can't Read Wallace Stegner and Other Essays*, its titular essay condemning Stegner for promoting a narrative of the West based on the popular notion of the "vanishing Indian" rather than acknowledging the West's Indigenous peoples such as the Dakotas—her people—and their diverse cultures and traditions, which persist despite centuries of dispossession and death.[10] Of Stegner she writes, "There is, perhaps, no American fiction writer who has been more successful in serving the nation's interests of a nation's fantasy about itself than Wallace Stegner."[11] And yet, "Because I am an Indian born and raised on a northern plains Indian reservation in this century," Cook-Lynn writes, "I argue with Stegner's reality."[12] Comer picks up Cook-Lynn's critique of Stegner's construction of the West and its "fondly remembered colonial past" in *Landscapes of the New West* in 1999, wherein she traces his ideas about the West throughout his career. She notes how early on "it did not occur to Stegner that indigenous peoples and nonwhite immigrants of the nineteenth and twentieth century prospered amidst their own artistic, religious, sociopolitical, and cultural traditions."[13] But toward the end of his life, the optimism he so fervently located in the West dwindled as he came to understand that "the West's history of settlement by conquest necessarily meant that one man's geography of hope was another man's geography of the *end* of hope."[14] Comer further details how such realizations caused Stegner to renounce the West as his bastion for hope in the lectures he eventually published as *The American West as Living Space*.[15] Because of these and other critiques, Stegner's star has dramatically faded as many readers and scholars have concluded that his writings are too simplistic, too well-worn for discussion, too steeped in privileged racial and gendered discourses to be pertinent to our understanding of the American West's history and its present condition. Rare today are the university reading lists or academic conference proceedings that include Stegner and his work as important contributions to present-day western American concerns.

Our collective growing awareness of the West's complex and violent past and presence, and Stegner's own recognition that the "hope trope" fails in light of these realities, suggests that West as the geography of hope is best put to rest. Yet as I suggest in this chapter, notwithstanding these realities and the region's rapid and ongoing transformation to more urban and diverse cultures, Stegner's vision is relevant nonetheless as we confront the region's complex natural resource issues. In fact, Stegnerian hope—albeit with some important refashioning in line with his later reflections on the West and contemporary assessments of hope—is as pertinent and necessary now as when he first penned the words to advocate for the nation's system of wilderness preservation. Indeed, if the pandemic-induced mass exodus to the West's public lands in recent years—evident in overflowing trailheads and campsites—has taught us anything, the notion of the "West Cure" is as real today as it was for those in the nineteenth and early twentieth centuries seeking respite and rejuvenation from physical ailments.[16]

In making this case, I wish to shift our understanding of the geography of hope as it concerns the West's public lands so well addressed in Leisl Carr Childers and Adam M. Sowards's chapter to consider its application to western waters. That is, while the public land battles of the closing decades of the twentieth century inspired such works as Trimble and Williams's piece, as well as Robert Keiter's 1998 collection *Reclaiming the Native Home of Hope* that celebrates Stegnerian ideas on western lands, I would argue that the West's millennial drought beginning in 2000 has made water the defining western resource issue of the twenty-first century.[17] Of course, one cannot truly separate western lands from their waters. However, Stegner's ongoing preoccupation with aridity throughout his writing as "the West's ultimate unity" reminds us that water is central to understanding the geography of hope.[18] With aridity and its historic and current impacts on the region in mind, including the effects of climate change Robert M. Wilson outlines in his essay, I want to consider the value of the geography of hope within the context of the Colorado River watershed, a place often celebrated by Stegner in his writing, and which, today, faces numerous threats. To do so, I read the geography of hope within the context of Colorado River development history and Stegner's writings on aridity to suggest a more complex understanding of Stegner's wilderness-focused vision than that typically offered by conservationists. Then, I briefly turn to examine how contemporary writers grapple with Stegner's vision as they come to terms with the West's water challenges. Together, Stegner's writings and these more recent assessments demonstrate the resiliency of Stegner's metaphor, one that is "aspirational and evolutionary" as well as "relational," as Carr Childers puts it.[19] Thus, while certainly optimistic in its reach, the geography of hope also embraces the realities of the past and our current and pending challenges to offer a more complete vision of what this region and its waters can be for future generations.

Stegner's fascination with and commitment to the Colorado River Basin are evident in his numerous stories and essays that capture the river and its unique landscapes, peoples, and histories as well as his own adventures traveling through the region. Such works include his groundbreaking autobiography on John Wesley Powell, *Beyond the Hundredth Meridian* (1954), his advocacy for saving Echo Park evident in *This Is Dinosaur* (1955), and more musings on his western travels captured in collections such as *The Sound of Mountain Water* (1969) and *Where the Bluebird Sings to the Lemonade Springs* (1992). In *The Sound of Mountain Water*, in particular, Stegner's love of the Colorado and its tributaries is evident as he recounts his own experiences on the San Juan River, a primary tributary of the Colorado, and in Glen Canyon, now submerged under Lake Powell. In the chapter "San Juan and Glen Canyon," Stegner recounts a raft trip with the legendary river guide Norm Nevills. Upon leaving the San Juan as it merges with the Colorado, Stegner and his fellow travelers "turn our backs on the San Juan. But we do it regretfully. [The river is] a marvelous roadway into wonder."[20] Later, in "Glen Canyon Submerses," he "reluctantly and skeptically" returns to the Colorado to see how Lake Powell's rising waters have changed Glen Canyon.[21] Herein, he pens one of his more memorable statements about the transformations to the West's wildness. While he recognizes the value of Lake Powell, he nonetheless laments the loss of the free-flowing Colorado impeded by Glen Canyon Dam: "In gaining the lovely and the usable, we have given up the incomparable."[22] Such passages reinforce Stegner's preference for landscapes and waterways that embody "beauty, wonder, and the sort of silence in which you can hear the swish of falling stars."[23]

Stegner's nostalgic memorialization of time spent on the basin's free-flowing rivers starkly contrasts with his reaction to the river's transformation after dams such as Glen Canyon forever altered the Colorado. Such passages reinforce Stegner's preference for wild rivers and the hope they instill in those privileged to float on them in attempts to retreat from modernization's supposed insanity. Thus, when considered within the long history of conflict that has shaped western water policy and Colorado River management, more specifically, as states grapple to address rapid development, Stegner's geography of hope seems at first glance quite naive or historically amiss. In the case of Colorado River Basin, where tensions between various individuals, communities, states, and even nations have defined Colorado River development since Powell's first voyage down the Colorado in 1869, we might well describe the watershed as a geography marked by self-interest, peril, and legal battles rather than one that "reassur[es] ourselves of our sanity as creatures."[24] Instead, the Colorado Basin and the larger arid West have been described as a place where the oft-quoted phrase well applies: "whiskey is for drinking, water is for fighting." Writing of the many competing needs along the river, Marc Reisner posits in *Cadillac Desert* (1993), his widely acclaimed primer on western water development, "The Colorado's modern notoriety . . . stems not from its wild rapids and plunging canyons but from the fact that it is the most legislated, most debated, and most litigated river in the entire world."[25] This controversy stems from the basin's extensive aridity; the unpredictability of the river's flow regimes; the many urban areas dependent on its life-giving waters, actively asserting their water rights to protect the river, its flora and fauna; and cultural connections to the Colorado.

Much of the Colorado River's tumultuous history can be traced to its unique geography and the legal framework created over the years to manage the river. Flowing westward from its headwaters in Colorado's Rocky Mountain National Park, the river cuts through 1,450 miles of mountains, plateaus, canyons, and desert valleys before reaching its historic terminus at the Gulf of California. Seven states in the United States (Arizona, California, Colorado, Nevada, New Mexico, Utah, and Wyoming) and two in Mexico (Baja California and Sonora) compose the 246,000-square-mile river basin that constitutes some of the hottest and driest areas on the continent. In fact, the United States' five driest states are part of the Colorado Basin.[26] Despite these arid conditions, settlers, boosters, and politicians have looked to the Colorado and its tributaries as their geography of hope wherein to create their own slice of Eden. Of particular interest was the Colorado's delta comprising portions of southern California and Arizona and of northern Mexico.

For eons, the Colorado had deposited silt to create incredibly rich, fertile soil. It was here that the Spanish arrived in 1540 and encountered the Cocopahs among other Indigenous peoples, who, at the time of contact, had a population of over twenty thousand inhabitants and had been cultivating the delta's soils for generations.[27] However, not until the late nineteenth and early twentieth centuries did the delta come under large-scale, industrial cultivation by harnessing the Colorado's accessible waters. Not surprisingly, such transformations to these lands under corporate control had devastating impacts on the Cocopahs and other tribes.[28]

This early river development in the delta caused the Upper Basin states great concern.[29] Because the West's arid states subscribed to the principle of prior appropriation to govern water resources, a "first in time, first in right" system ensued. Developed in California's mining camps, this system ensured that those users who first filed for a water claim and then put it to beneficial use had priority over subsequent users even if the senior holder's use of a legal allotment denied the junior holders their portion.[30] In the case of the Colorado, the lion's share of early development occurred in the Lower Basin, and the Upper Basin states worried that their own attempts to use the river could be thwarted by this unique system of water governance. But it was not just Upper and Lower Basin states at odds with one another; naturally, competing visions between states also emerged. As Norris Hundley Jr. explains in his comprehensive study of the Colorado River negotiations, one of the primary challenges Colorado River Basin states faced in developing the river was that no "clear-cut interstate law of waters" existed.[31] Therefore, "state officials could regulate uses within their own state's borders; but when they were forced to protect their citizens from adverse developments elsewhere, they could invoke no readily agreed upon principles."[32] With no governing document or body to regulate interstate water use, the seven basin states "acted as if they were independent nations, adopting policies calculated to further their individual self-interest."[33] Any hope of reaching a unified approach to managing the river seemed futile under such conditions.

To avoid the inevitable conflicts prior appropriation would create between how best to develop the Colorado's waters as California steadily grew and Upper Basin states sought to play catch-up, the states initiated various gatherings to work toward an agreement that would ensure that all states had their needs met. Beginning in 1917 with the formation of the League of the Southwest, the states began the march toward compromise.[34] The intricacies of the ensuing proceedings are far beyond the scope of this chapter. Suffice it to say there were endless disagreements and posturing in the following years as each state vied for its piece of the water pie. In January 1922 then secretary of commerce Herbert Hoover was appointed to oversee what had become the proceedings of the Colorado River Commission.[35] Eleven months later, on November 24, 1922, after years of negotiations, the commission's representatives met in New Mexico to sign the Colorado River Compact. By signing the compact, the states agreed to divide the Colorado's water equally between the two basins, with each basin having the right to develop up to 7.5 million acre feet (maf). However, a key point of the compromise was that the Upper Basin would be required to make consistent deliveries to the Lower Basin, even in times of drought.[36]

But this guarantee was one the Upper Basin states were willing to concede in exchange for an "equal" share of the river's flow. For those who had worked for years to make a deal, the compact's historic signing was a beacon of hope for most of the officials as it demonstrated that states with vastly different geographies and needs could indeed compromise on how to best apportion Colorado River water. Of course, the compact did not resolve all issues, and in many ways it "set the stage for years of additional strife"[37]

Notwithstanding the momentum the states had made by signing the compact, it was little more than a symbolic gesture as it still had to be ratified by the states and accepted by Congress. Although the compact would eventually be signed into law in 1928 as part of the Boulder Canyon Act, Arizona refused to accept the terms, initiating a decades-long legal battle with California over how the two states would develop their legal allotments.[38] It took until 1944 for Arizona to accept how the Lower Basin's 7.5 maf would be divided and until 1963 for the landmark *Arizona v. California* case to settle the dispute between the states and to pave the way for the basin's tribes to receive their legal allotments. These various iterations and amendments to the original 1922 Compact have come to be known collectively as the "Law of the River." They reflect the very difficult and costly work of compromise evident in other such Colorado River provisions established between the United States and Mexico to ensure standards in both quantity and quality.[39] In sum, they are the basin's articulation of hope that these laws, declarations, minutes, and other expressions of responsibility to one another will ensure shared governance and management of this precious resource.

In the final decades of the twentieth century, much of the earlier controversy between the states and between the United States and Mexico had been settled. Throughout the 1980s and 1990s significant snowmelt throughout the basin ensured that reservoirs filled and that states had ample water to meet their needs. With the new millennium, however, old wounds have emerged once again, and the provisions outlined in the Law of the River have come under increasing stress as the region has experienced significant population growth that has coincided with the worst drought in over a thousand years.[40] The drought's effects have had unprecedented impacts on the river's major storage reservoirs, especially Lake Powell and Lake Mead, that have caused great concern for the region's water managers and communities that depend on reliable flows, cheap hydropower, and recreational dollars when storage is high.[41] Such conditions challenge earlier hopes that the arid West could be redeemed through such careful governance and investment in water infrastructure.

Of particular worry has been the looming specter of a shortage declaration by the federal government, precipitated when water levels at Lake Mead drop below the 1,075-foot-elevation mark. In response to increasing demands and the worsening drought in the early 2000s, the secretary of the interior mandated that the seven basin states work to address dropping reservoir levels. Beginning in 2005 the basin states met periodically to hash out how they might collaborate to avoid a shortage declaration and greater involvement by the federal government in dictating future river use. In 2007 the states finalized the Colorado River Interim Guidelines to articulate the consequences of water levels dropping below the 1,075-foot threshold at Lake Mead. Establishing a set of "tiers" that outline reductions based on how low Lake Mead levels drop, the Interim Guidelines show significant cuts to Arizona, Nevada, and Mexico first as they hold junior rights to California.[42] To avoid a potential shortage declaration by better managing Lake Mead and Lake Powell, the basin states, Mexico, and various water utilities finalized in 2019 the Colorado River Drought Contingency Plan Authorization Act. The overall goal of such measures is to "enhance conservation of water in the Colorado River System for the benefit of each of the Colorado River Basin States."[43] It is significant to note that these agreements to coordinate deliveries to prevent undue burdens on any one state or entity are purely voluntary "and in the interest of comity," as the document reads.[44] Put another way, James Eklund, Colorado's former Upper Colorado River commissioner, explains that "the states must hang together or we'll hang separately."[45] The collaboration evident in this recent legislation and in agreements with Mexico to ensure habitat restoration and predictable deliveries to communities south of the border reflect a hopeful response to the region's growing awareness that cooperation across borders is the best chance for dealing with the inevitable shortages that will occur as the number of needs throughout the system continues to grow and as climate change and drought reduce available water sources.

Reacting to the new normal of below average runoff, many stakeholders throughout the Colorado River Basin have worked together to find solutions to better spread the effects of drought equally rather than default to the terms under the 2007 Interim Guidelines that terminate at the end of 2025. Nonetheless, the process has not been without its challenges. In 2018 the Upper Basin states chastised Arizona for attempting to manipulate data to show that it needed higher releases from Lake Powell despite the shared-shortage burden agreements

27. Timothy R. Petty, assistant secretary of the interior for water and science, Brenda Burman, commissioner of the Bureau of Reclamation, and principals from each of the Colorado River Basin states signing the Drought Contingency Plan (DCP) at Hoover Dam. "Interior and states sign historic drought agreements to protect Colorado River," May 20, 2019. Courtesy the Bureau of Reclamation.

outlined in the Interim Guidelines. Writing to the Central Arizona Water Conservation District (CAWCD), the Upper Basin commissioners asserted that "CAWCD's statements run contrary to the spirit of interstate comity and cooperation."[46] The widespread media attention given to Arizona's questionable practices, along with the political pressure by the states, helped corral Arizona's maverick spirit despite the temporary "bruised relations" such actions caused.[47] Such conflicts are bound to surface again, however, as the impacts of drought and climate change are causing water managers to respond sooner than predicted to dropping reservoirs.

This was the case in August 2021, when the federal government issued its first ever shortage declaration.[48] Since this historic action, Lake Mead and other major reservoirs throughout the basin have con-

28. Lake Mead water level, February 16, 2022. Photo by Christopher Clark. Flickr, https://www.flickr.com/photos/usbr/52536334094/in/album-7217772 0304138328/. Licensed under https://creativecommons.org/licenses/by-sa/2 .0/legalcode.

tinued to drop, adding greater stress on the river system and threatening their generation of hydroelectricity for much of the American West. While the 2019 Drought Contingency Plan established a framework to address impeding water shortages, the shortage declaration and ongoing declines to the reservoirs prompted water managers to put further and more immediate measures in place. Following emergency water releases in late 2021 from upstream reservoirs to keep Lake Powell from dropping below 3,490 feet, basin officials convened in spring 2022 to develop the 2022 Drought Response Operations Plan that "establishes a coordinated and collaborative process" among many different river stakeholders to maintain Lake Powell's hydroelectric viability.[49] In the ensuing months, Bureau of Reclamation commissioner Camille Touton demanded that basin states curtail water use by 2–4 maf in 2023 in order to "protect the Colorado River system infrastructure and the long-term stability of the system."[50] This is just the latest in a long line of give-and-take between identifying problems and calls for change.[51]

As I write in May 2023, the historic snowfall that blanketed many parts of the Upper Basin this past winter is now filling reservoirs throughout the region after years of declining water levels. In the case of Lake Powell, the Bureau of Reclamation projects that the reservoir could rise by upward of fifty to nearly ninety feet by early summer.[52] However, despite the momentary relief that this runoff brings, water managers recognize that this year's exceptional conditions do not end the drought nor excuse them from continuing to plan for a future of increased water scarcity. While today's climate uncertainties have created conditions far different from those the signers of the Colorado Compact faced a century ago, there is nonetheless a resolve, perhaps even a hope, that working together we can find solutions to our most significant problems. As one river stakeholder commented after the 2021 shortage declaration, "The Colorado River can be a model for resiliency and sustainability but not without a concerted and significant effort by stakeholders in the region."[53] The persistence of drought throughout the region will continue to test water managers' resolve and the Contingency Plan's spirit of cooperation as it seeks to put individual interests aside for the greater good of the watershed.

The cycles of conflict and cooperation evident in these most recent developments along the Colorado River embody the sort of work Stegner knew had to be at the heart of successful, hopeful living in a region whose defining characteristic is aridity. Stegner's understanding of the water woes that have plagued the Colorado River and the West more broadly allowed him to see the imminent clashes between states and the federal government over water in the post–Colorado Compact years. Writing about the federal government's involvement in western water management in his essay "Living Dry," Stegner anticipates the day when the secretary of the interior would be required to issue a shortage declaration, acknowledging "that unless the states arrive at some relatively uniform set of rules, order will have to be imposed on western water by the federal government."[54] Stegner came to understand this fraught relationship between the federal government and the western states through his pioneering work on John Wesley Powell and Powell's efforts to steer the states away from the clashes that would occur in the twentieth century. As Stegner outlines America's confrontation with the Great American Desert in *Beyond the Hundredth Meridian*, he lauds Powell's prophetic views regarding western reclamation and the region's pervasive aridity. Of Powell's findings captured in his Arid Lands Report, Stegner writes, "It was clear that individual initiative and individual labor and individual capital were inadequate to develop the irrigation works."[55]

Despite the individualism celebrated through the frontier myth, working to reclaim a desert and make it "blossom as the rose" was something only intense cooperation and collaboration could achieve. Looking to the Native, Hispano, and Mormon settlements that had made a successful stand in the arid West, Powell promoted a vision of the region delineated by what has recently become a symbolic representation of a more environmentally sound way of western living. His revolutionary watershed map redrew geopolitical borders to align with hydrographic basins so that water would be kept within watersheds unlike today where, in the case of the Colorado River, it is transported under mountains and through deserts to places such as Denver, Salt Lake City, Albuquerque, San Diego, and Los Angeles—all outside of the Colorado Basin. Such transbasin diversions have been highly contentious, and plans for these massive delivery systems continue to surface today.[56] Summing up Powell's address to a Montana delegation during his western tour with the Senate's irrigation committee in 1889, Stegner captures the difficulties of deploying Powell's revolutionary approach to western settlement and resource development: "What [Powell] suggested was so radical that it could not possibly have any effect on the delegates . . . , so rational that it could not possibly come to pass short of heaven, so intelligently reasoned from fact that it must have sounded to Montana's tradition-and-myth-bound constitution-makers like the program of a crank."[57] In the end Montana, like every other western

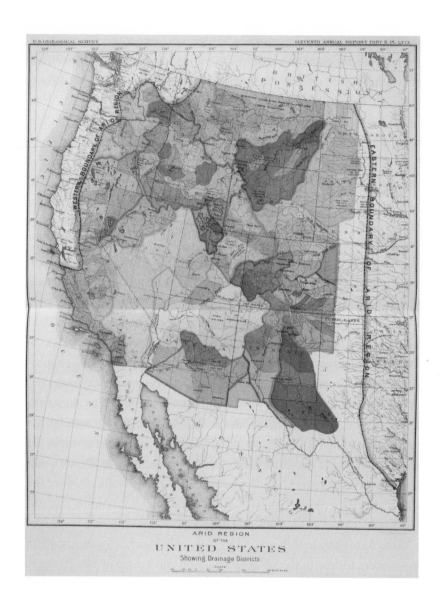

29. John Wesley Powell, "Arid Region of the United States Showing Drainage Districts." *Eleventh Annual Report of the Director of the United States Geological Survey, Part 2—Irrigation: 1889–1890*, plate LXIX. Courtesy the Government Information Collection, Special Collections and Archives, Utah State University Libraries.

state, chose to draw its boundaries, as Stegner writes, "according to the tried-and-true patterns of more than a hundred years, with county lines marking none but the political basins, and county seats competitively chosen in the atmosphere of deal, coup, and horse-trade."[58] The communities and governments of the late nineteenth-century West would not heed Powell's hope for wise western settlement. Eventually boosterism, self-interest, and greed won out as western development advanced on the belief that individual communities and states could engineer their way out of reality.

Stegner's experiences living and traveling throughout the West and his comprehensive study of Powell's life and ideas impressed upon him the significance of aridity as a, or perhaps *the*, defining western characteristic. And it is within an understanding and acceptance of this fact that the geography of hope thrives. In "Thoughts in a Dry Land," Stegner reinforces this relationship as he reflects on the impact aridity has had on the West's human history. Noting that "the primary unity of the West is a shortage of water," he recounts the efforts to reclaim the land and make it productive, suggesting, "We have acted upon the western landscape with the force of a geological agent."[59] Invoking the Anthropocene long before it became part of everyday parlance, Stegner emphasizes the drastic impacts humans have had in reengineering western waterways to make the land agriculturally productive and home to millions, many of whom have gone west in search for the geography of hope.

But to truly find this hope, Stegner urges readers to rethink assumptions about the West. "You have to get over the color green; you have to quit associating beauty with gardens and lawns," he argues.[60] In this memorable passage Stegner reminds his audience that the West is not the East or any other well-watered land, and to see it as such is to approach the region under false pretenses. Rather, he argues for a shift in perception, a greater awareness of the ways in which humans have shaped and are continuing to impact the region, its resources, and inhabitants today. This passage likewise invites readers to contemplate the ways in which aridity might be shaping individuals and entire societies. While we have gone to herculean efforts to reclaim the arid West, evident in the incredible engineering projects that have transformed areas such as the Colorado River Basin, "aridity has made a lot of difference in us, too," as it "still calls the tune, directs our tinkering, prevents the healing of our mistakes; and vast unwatered reaches still emphasize the contrast between the desert and the sown."[61] Despite our best efforts to redeem the desert from its supposed fallen state, aridity continues to dictate our relationship to the region.

Stegner's acknowledgment of the defining impact of aridity on the West combined with the recent examples of collaboration from the Colorado River Basin enrich our understanding of the West and its varied landscapes as the geography of hope. While the geography of hope, and the "Wilderness Letter" of which it is a part, nonetheless evoke to a certain degree Turnerian individualism where we can "see ourselves single, separate, vertical and individual in the world," this hope embraces community and restraint where we are also "part of the environment of trees and rocks and soil, brother to the other animals, part of the natural world, and competent to belong in it," as he writes in the letter.[62] If we accept Stegner's assessment of our relationship to wild nature—and by extension, the West—we acknowledge that our belonging to them is predicated on our ability to sustainably live among these entities. And as Stegner's writings about Powell and western water issues demonstrate, such living demands our forbearance, our ability to adapt to the conditions surrounding us. In the closing words to "Living Dry," he observes of aridity: "You may deny it for a while. Then you must try to engineer it out of existence or adapt to it," while in "Thoughts in a Dry Land" he remarks: "The Westerner is less a person than a continuing adaptation. The West is less a place than a process."[63] Stegner's recognition of the West as a place of flux and change requiring continual adaptation anticipates Susan Kollin's postwestern understanding of the West by a couple of decades when she writes that "we understand the region not as a closed system or a bounded space but as a continually changing entity in both content and form."[64] Indeed the Colorado River Basin is perpetually in motion; it is an unfolding process both materially in its rapidly changing hydrology and the way that hydrology is managed as well as conceptually in how we understand the river, its histories, and many cultures.

If we approach both the region and our experience within it as a process, as a continually developing relationship, we begin to see the outlines of the geography of hope. It becomes something far different than a nostalgic longing for yesterday's attitudes and practices or an unqualified invitation to head out to the hills, to eschew modernity, and the cities and its masses as it often seems to be interpreted, evident in Edward Abbey's writing, as Carr Childers and Sowards remind us. Rather, this hope becomes something akin to what Sarah Jaquette Ray calls "critical hope," which "[links] positive prospects for the future with social change."[65] Under these terms the West as the geography of hope is no Pollyannaish rejection of reality, some overly idealistic wishful thinking that current circumstances will improve if only we believe hard enough or ignore the problems outright. For as John Parsi, a contributor to the field of hope theory, suggests, "hope is an active process. Dreams and optimism are just belief structures."[66] Instead of wishful thinking about what the West and the future of the Colorado River could be, Stegnerian hope today demands humility, restraint, and a continual adaptation to ever-changing circumstances. A geography of hope for the twenty-first century resides in a persistent effort to create more sustainable and equitable solutions throughout the watershed.

Such are the themes evident in works by contemporary scholars and artists who grapple with current environmental challenges and the role that hope might play in addressing these uncertainties. In her foreword to the third edition of *Hope in the Dark*, Rebecca Solnit writes, "Hope locates itself in the premises that we don't know what will happen and that in the spaciousness of uncertainty is room to act. . . . Hope is an embrace of the unknown and the unknowable, an alternative to the certainty of both optimists and pessimists."[67] A great deal of uncertainty exists about how to address future water issues throughout the region. But such was the case for those who negotiated compacts, treaties, and agreements over the last century. Like them, we need to continue to foreground the value of collaboration and cooperation, to do the difficult work of compromise. Yet unlike those meeting in 1922, today's circumstances require a more open approach to water management, one in which all users have a voice at the bargaining table.

These themes are front and center in Jennifer Price's work about Los Angeles and its river as she challenges traditional binaries between nature and culture to argue for heightened engagement on pressing environmental issues within the city. Writing to address the misperceptions that Los Angeles—one of the cities that relies heavily on the Colorado River—is void of nature and therefore nature writing, Price outlines thirteen different ways in which to see the metropolis as the paramount example for understanding how nature (even wild nature) is part of our everyday lived experiences. Channeling Stegner's position that the geography of hope is grounded in our intimate relationship to the natural world, Price urges us to reconsider Los Angeles as a place "that imagines nature not as the opposite of the city but as the basic stuff of modern everyday life."[68] At the same time, we see Stegnerian hope emerge in her assessment and celebration of the Los Angeles River, long viewed as a stain on the cityscape. Echoing Stegner's belief that the West is a "process," Price encourages us to resee the channelized, concrete restrained semblance of a river as a potent site for restoration. As such, the river becomes for her the axis mundi of American nature writing as its history and presence powerfully weave together the highly diminished yet still-there riparian ecosystem awash in the detritus of American consumerism to speak to the manifold ways in which water and our human activities are inseparable. To bring about this change, she channels Ray's activist hope and Parsi's focus on effort to urge readers to adopt and tell new stories about LA, its river, and, by extension, nature everywhere. At the confluence of the Arroyo Seco and the Los Angeles River, the site where Los Angeles was born, Price explains, "Here, we say, lies at once the most hopeless and the most hopeful spot on the L.A. River."[69] Despite the river's recent past as a slurry for LA's waste, its future is one that holds great promise as stakeholders work with "great reserves of faith and patience" to restore some of its former glory, a transformative process that will enable an increasing number of city dwellers to interact more closely and more humanely with the natural world.[70] Price's vision for the Los Angeles River offers important considerations for the larger Colorado River system, whose vast urban centers, rangeland, farms, and fields should be as valued as its more iconic wilderness.

Another writer grappling with the mantle of Stegner's geography of hope as it relates to the Colorado River is Paolo Bacigalupi. His novel *The Water Knife* (2015) takes the reader to a far darker, more pessimistic West than Price's portrayal of LA. Set in the future when extreme drought throughout the American West has caused regional economic collapse and severe water shortages, *The Water Knife* portrays the worst of human behavior when faced with such realities. Rampant violence abounds not only between individuals but also between communities and states as the Southern Nevada Water Authority seeks to secure water rights with mercenary armies and assassins known as water knives. Climate refugees from places such as Arizona ("Zoners") and Texas ("Merry Perrys") attempt to flee across state borders now walled off from one another and patrolled by state militias. Cities throughout the Colorado River Basin are in ruins. To Angel, the chief water knife at the center of the unfolding drama, "It was striking . . . how similar every town looked after it lost its water. It didn't matter whether it was at the top of the Colorado River or the bottom. It could be Las Vegas or Phoenix, Tucson or Grand Junction, Moab or Delta. In the end there was always the same: traffic lights swinging blind on tumbleweed streets; shadowy echoing shopping malls with shattered window displays; golf courses drifted with sand and spiked with dead trees."[71] Such depictions of the watershed seem a world away from Stegner's geography of hope. However, when considered in light of Ray's "critical hope" and the uncertain future for which it allows, Bacigalupi's apocalyptic vision becomes a powerful means by which to marshal the possibilities of climate fiction to imagine a world when nearly all hope is lost and what it means to disregard Stegner's observations about aridity. At the same time, Bacigalupi's bleak potentialities are not void of hope. Despite the many dark themes and events that transpire throughout the text, hope does prevail in the end, at least for Phoenix, as the novel's protagonists locate senior water rights to the Colorado River by which the city can survive.

Together, Price's and Bacigalupi's texts carry on the legacy of Stegner's geography of hope even as they address places and circumstances where optimism seems impossible. As Stegner recognized the West's complexity, the need to be more fully integrated with the natural world and to recognize its limits, these authors challenge our assumptions about the West and what it may become either through activism and a desire to make a positive change or through greed and neglect. Their works also remind us, as does Solnit, that when confronting the environmental challenges of our day, understanding the past is essential to shaping the future.

Responding to Walter Brueggeman's thoughts on hope and memory, Solnit explains: "Though hope is about the future, grounds for hope lie in the records and recollections of the past. We can tell of a past that was nothing but defeats and cruelties and injustices, or of a past that was some lovely golden age now irretrievably lost, or we can tell a more complicated and accurate story, one that has room for the best and worst, for atrocities and liberations, for grief and jubilation."[72] Price and Bacigalupi are but two contemporary authors joining a host of other artists and scholars whose work engages western water issues in their work to reimagine future possibilities while being cognizant of past injuries. Percival Everett's novel *Watershed* (2003) upends the traditional wilderness recreation plot as his protagonist, a Black hydrologist gone fishing, finds himself supporting a nearby tribe in their quest for environmental justice, whereas Cree scholar Stephanie Fitzgerald attends to Indigenous women's present-day environmental justice activism as they work to preserve and protect lands and waters sacred to tribal peoples.[73] In fact, many of the more hopeful considerations of the West's lands and waters derive from the proliferation of Native authors over the last few decades who give powerful witnesses to their ongoing presence and important contributions to the West. They include Cook-Lynn, Sherman Alexie (Spokane), Leslie Marmon Silko (Laguna), Ofelia Zepeda (Tohono O'odham), and Natalie Diaz (Mohave).[74] These voices capture not only the historic relationships to the West's lands and waters but also their present fight to secure resources and projections for what a greater involvement in the West's natural resource deliberations might look like. For example, Diaz's poems "The First Water Is the Body" and "How the Milky Way Was Made" from her recent collection *Postcolonial Love Poem* express her intimate connections to the Colorado, challenge stereotypes of Indigenous peoples, and urge her readers to reassess their use of the threatened river.[75]

These authors and their contributions offer alternative stories to those that have shaped western water management since the end of the nineteenth century to showcase the value of historically marginalized voices to water governance and to account for past injustices—to make the story of the West more complete. Whether employing poetry, nature writing, climate fiction, or environmental justice scholarship, these authors are highly cognizant of the West's difficult and complicated past and recognize, as Stegner did to varying degrees, that there is ample space for us to work through yesterday's wrongs as well as the future's possibilities as we negotiate and adapt to the unique conditions aridity creates for the West and its diverse inhabitants.[76]

Stegner's extensive travels on foot and by car, boat, and pen through the American West helped him understand how successful relationships between scarce resources and communities must endure. In the introduction to *The Sound of Mountain Water* he writes: "Angry as one may be at what heedless men have done and still do to a noble habitat, one cannot be pessimistic about the West. This is the native home of hope. When it fully learns that cooperation, not rugged individualism, is the quality that most characterizes and preserves it, then it will have achieved itself and outlived its origins. Then it has a chance to create a society to match its scenery."[77] Here, Stegner's optimism in the power of the West's beauty and potential is unquestioned. And it is true that such declarations are aimed toward readers, as Cook-Lynn observes, "made up of the children and offspring of pioneer settlers."[78] Yet, it is for this reason that Stegner's geography of hope should not be jettisoned but reimagined by this audience. As I argue in this essay, Stegner's profound statement is rich in its application and use today when considered in light of the region's complex natural resource issues and historically marginalized voices as they remind us that despite the past's challenging, unsavory, and even traumatic realities, the region's future can be a geography of hope for all. Today and into the future such a geography will be less a quality or type of landscape but a feeling, a spirit of dwelling in place where we know the stories of the past, where we possess a "watershed consciousness" in which we see ourselves as part of a bigger system and in partnership with those who have always possessed these feelings and knowledge.[79] With drought and climate change drastically impacting available water resources, "summoning hope amid so much loss will be our deeper spiritual challenge," and yet the answer to preserving any optimism and generating hope amid such conditions necessitates our willingness to welcome a sense of "sufficiency," as the contributors to this thematic section remind us.[80] Such a geography of hope encourages us to see beyond the borders of our own backyards or neighborhoods, or even our respective states to see how our attitudes about and actions toward the land and rivers impact others who also rely on these resources. It embraces cooperation and a willingness to act, to put aside historic divides between states, the Upper and Lower Basins, tribal and nontribal communities, and nations, to work together to mitigate drought. Stegner's geography of hope relies on our ability to reassess our surroundings, to welcome the limits aridity imposes, and to create new stories where restraint, respect, and reconciliation are the region's hallmarks. In sum, a twenty-first-century geography of hope becomes a vast place of potential, an expansive territory of the mind and heart that knows no boundaries and yields endless possibilities as we come together to solve the pressing resource challenges of our day.

Notes

1. Beth LaDow, "The Astonishing Origins of Wallace Stegner's Environmental Genius," *Montana: The Magazine of Western History* 52, no. 3 (2002): 67, https://www.jstor.org/stable/i406168.
2. Wallace Stegner, "Coda: Wilderness Letter," in *The Sound of Mountain Water: The Changing American West* (New York: Penguin, 1992), 153.
3. Chris Turner, *Geography of Hope: A Tour of the World We Need* (Toronto: Vintage, 2008); "About," Geography of Hope, accessed August 31, 2022, https://www.geographyofhope.org/what-we-do; Andy Jones-Wilkins, "The Geography of Hope," *AJW's Taproom*, iRunFar, July 9, 2015, https://www.irunfar.com/the-geography-of-hope.
4. *The West*, episode 7, "The Geography of Hope," directed by Stephen Ives, PBS, aired September 1996; "Geography of Hope," Alaska Wilderness Series, 2022, https://alaskawild.org/geography-of-hope/; David J. Rothman, ed., *The Geography of Hope: Poets of Colorado's Western Slope* (Denver CO: Conundrum Press, 1998); Stephen Trimble and Terry Tempest Williams, "An Act of Faith," in *Testimony: Writers of the West Speak on Behalf of Utah Wilderness* (Minneapolis: Milkweed, 1996).
5. Trimble and Williams, "An Act of Faith," 7.
6. Stegner, "Coda: Wilderness Letter," 148.
7. Stegner, "Coda: Wilderness Letter," 148.
8. Krista Comer, *Landscapes of the New West: Gender and Geography in Contemporary Women's Writing* (Chapel Hill: University of North Carolina Press, 1999), 44.
9. Comer, *Landscapes of the New West*, 44; Margaret D. Jacobs, *After One Hundred Winters: In Search of Reconciliation on America's Stolen Lands* (Princeton NJ: Princeton University Press, 2021), 7.
10. Elizabeth Cook-Lynn, "Why I Can't Read Wallace Stegner," in *Why I Can't Read Wallace Stegner and Other Essays: A Tribal Voice* (Madison: University of Wisconsin Press, 1996), 32.
11. Cook-Lynn, "Why I Can't Read Wallace Stegner," 29.
12. Cook-Lynn, "Why I Can't Read Wallace Stegner," 30.
13. Comer, *Landscapes of the New West*, 42.
14. Comer, *Landscapes of the New West*, 45.

15. Comer, *Landscapes of the New West*, 44; Wallace Stegner, *The American West as Living Space* (Ann Arbor: University of Michigan Press, 1987). The three essays in this collection, "Living Dry," "Striking the Rock," and "Variations on a Theme by Crèvecoeur," were later published in Wallace Stegner, *Where the Bluebird Sings to the Lemonade Springs: Living and Writing in the West* (New York: Penguin, 1992).

16. I experienced this firsthand while camping in southeastern Utah on Bureau of Land Management lands in spring 2020. With national parks shut down because of COVID-19, nearby public lands and state parks were inundated with those, like me, looking to get outside and social distance. Certainly, the irony and problematic nature of my interests in "getting away" were not lost on me. See Colorado State University's Public Lands History Center website, https://publiclands.colostate.edu /2020/04/public-landemic/, for more on what the center observes as a "Public Landemic."

17. Robert B. Keiter, *Reclaiming the Native Home of Hope* (Salt Lake City: University of Utah Press, 1998). Keiter is the Wallace Stegner Professor of Law at the University of Utah and the director of the Wallace Stegner Center for Land, Resources, and the Environment. *Reclaiming the Native Home of Hope* was the result of symposia hosted by this center.

18. Wallace Stegner, introduction to *Where the Bluebird Sings to the Lemonade Springs: Living and Writing in the West* (New York: Penguin, 1992), 15.

19. Leisl Carr Childers and Adam M. Sowards, "Hope in Public Lands: A Conversation," chapter 8 in this publication.

20. Wallace Stegner, "San Juan and Glen Canyon," in *The Sound of Mountain Water: The Changing American West* (New York: Penguin, 1980), 116.

21. Wallace Stegner, "Glen Canyon Submerses," in Stegner, *Sound of Mountain Water*, 121.

22. Stegner, "Glen Canyon Submerses," 128.

23. Stegner, "Glen Canyon Submerses," 136.

24. Stegner, "Coda: Wilderness Letter," 153.

25. Marc Reisner, *Cadillac Desert: The American West and Its Disappearing Water* (New York: Penguin, 1993), 120.

26. Oishimaya Sen Nag, "States That Receive the Least Amount of Rain," WorldAtlas, accessed August 30, 2022, https://www.worldatlas.com /articles/the-10-driest-states-in-the-united-states-of-america.html.

The five states are Nevada, Arizona, Utah, New Mexico, and Wyoming, respectively.

27. Norris Hundley Jr., *Water and the West: The Colorado River Compact and the Politics of Water in the American West* (Berkeley: University of California Press, 2009), 19. For a more extended treatment of the Spanish encounter with the Cocopahs and their reliance on Cocopah knowledge, food, and labor, see chapter 2, "Beach Encounters," in Damon B. Akins and William J. Bauer Jr., *We Are the Land: A History of Native California* (Berkeley: University of California Press, 2021), 46–53.

28. Western water boosters such as William Smythe saw the Cocopahs as a willing labor force to transform the delta's soils under the control of corporate agriculture. As Smythe argued, the Cocopahs "are peaceful work-loving folk, who have earned their living by rude farming for generations. There are about two thousand of them in this locality, and they will make a useful class of laborers when the country is developed." Quoted in Evan Ward, *Border Oasis: Water and the Political Ecology of the Colorado River Delta, 1940–1975* (Tucson: University of Arizona Press, 2003), xxi–xxii.

29. The Upper Basin states are Colorado, New Mexico, Utah, and Wyoming.

30. Hundley, *Water and the West*, 66–69.

31. Hundley, *Water and the West*, 73.

32. Hundley, *Water and the West*, 73–74.

33. Hundley, *Water and the West*, 74.

34. Hundley, *Water and the West*, 55.

35. Hundley, *Water and the West*, 138.

36. The Upper Basin agreed to deliver an aggregate of 75 maf every ten years regardless of how much water flowed down the Colorado. The federal government built Glen Canyon Dam, whose reservoir, Lake Powell, acts as a water savings account to ensure that the Upper Basin can meet its Colorado River Compact obligations downriver.

37. Hundley, *Water and the West*, 215.

38. Arizona wanted to build the Central Arizona Project to move water from the Colorado River to the Phoenix and Tucson areas.

39. In 1944 Mexico was granted a 1.5 maf guarantee. In 1973 the United States agreed to address salinity issues in deliveries to Mexico. This addition to the Law of the River is known as Minute 242.

40. Bureau of Reclamation, "Another Dry Year in the Colorado River Basin Increases the Need for Additional State and Federal Actions," *News and Multimedia*, May 9, 2018, https://www.usbr.gov/newsroom/newsroomold /newsrelease/detail.cfm?RecordID=62170.

41. Lake Mead, created by the construction of Hoover Dam as part of the 1928 Boulder Canyon Act, was intended primarily to provide flood control for the Lower Basin.

42. Bureau of Reclamation, "Record of Decision—Interim Guidelines for the Operation of Lake Mead and Lake Powell," December 13, 2007, https:// www.usbr.gov/lc/region/programs/strategies/RecordofDecision.pdf; Bureau of Reclamation, "Reclamation Announces 2022 Operating Conditions for Lake Powell and Lake Mead," August 16, 2021, https://www .usbr.gov/newsroom/news-release/3950. In a tier 1 shortage, Arizona's allocation would be reduced from 3 to 2.48 maf, and Nevada's would drop from 300,000 acre feet (af) to 287,000 af. This is for levels below 1,075 but above 1,050 feet. These reductions equate to roughly 18 percent (512,000 af) and 7 percent (21,000 af), respectively, of the state's annual Colorado River allocation.

43. Bureau of Reclamation, "Agreement Concerning Colorado River Drought Contingency Management and Operations" (draft), October 5, 2018, 4, https://www.usbr.gov/dcp/docs/DCP_Agreements_Final_Review_Draft .pdf.

44. Bureau of Reclamation, "Agreement Concerning Colorado River Drought," 11.

45. Bureau of Reclamation, "Another Dry Year."

46. Upper Colorado Commission to Tom Buschatzke, Arizona Department of Water Resources, April 13, 2018, https://assets.documentcloud .org/documents/4438256/041318-Upper-Colorado-River-Commission -Letter-1.pdf.

47. Gary Pitzer, "As Colorado River Levels Drop, Pressure Grows on Arizona to Complete a Plan for Water Shortages," Water Education Foundation, June 15, 2018, https://www.watereducation.org/western-water /colorado-river-levels-drop-pressure-grows-arizona-complete-plan -water-shortages.

48. On August 31, 2021, Lake Mead stood at 1,067.92 feet. On August 29, 2022, Lake Mead dropped to 1,044.2 feet, reflecting almost a 24-foot drop

over the past year. See Bureau of Reclamation, Lower Colorado Region, "Archives of Daily Reservoir & River Conditions," August 2021, https://www.usbr.gov/lc/region/g4000/cy2021/08_2021.out; Lake Mead Water Database, "Water Summary," accessed August 30, 2022, http://lakemead.water-data.com/.

49. Bureau of Reclamation, "Drought Response Operations Agreement," *Colorado Basin Drought Contingency Plans*, May 3, 2022, https://www.usbr.gov/dcp/droa.html. In 2021 the Bureau of Reclamation released 161,000 af from Flaming Gorge and Blue Mesa Reservoirs. Initially the 2022 plan stipulated that Flaming Gorge Reservoir would release another 500,000 af. However, because of improving conditions in late 2022 and into 2023, Flaming Gorge released only 463,000 af between May 2022 and March 2023. See Bureau of Reclamation, "Attachment A: Summary of 2023 Drought Response Operations Plan," *Colorado Basin Drought Contingency Plans*, accessed May 24, 2023, https://www.usbr.gov/dcp/droa.html.

50. Camille Touton, "Statement of Camille Calimlim Touton, Commissioner, Bureau of Reclamation, U.S. Department of the Interior, Before the Senate Committee on Energy and Natural Resources," June 14, 2022, https://www.energy.senate.gov/services/files/6CB52BDD-57B8-4358-BF6B-72E40F86F510.

51. Another key response to the worsening drought has been Las Vegas's construction of the "third straw," a new point from which to draw water from Lake Mead. With dropping reservoir levels, the usual access point has been left high and dry, and new access points have been drilled to pull water from the very bottom of the lake to ensure reliable water deliveries for years to come. "Exposed Water Intake Demonstrates Necessity of Infrastructure Investment," *Las Vegas Review-Journal*, July 25, 2022, https://www.reviewjournal.com/brandpublishing/local/exposed-water-intake-demonstrates-necessity-of-infrastructure-investment/.

52. Bureau of Reclamation, "May 2023 24-Month Study Projections: Lake Powell and Lake Mead: End of Month Elevation Charts," accessed May 24, 2023, https://www.usbr.gov/uc/water/crsp/studies/images/PowellElevations.pdf.

53. The Nature Conservancy, "Shortage Declared for the Colorado River," August 16, 2021, https://www.nature.org/en-us/newsroom/drought-water-shortage-colorado-river/.

54. Wallace Stegner, "Living Dry," in *Where the Bluebird Sings to the Lemonade Springs: Living and Writing in the West* (New York: Penguin, 1992), 67.

55. Wallace Stegner, *Beyond the Hundredth Meridian: John Wesley Powell and the Second Opening of the West* (New York: Penguin, 1992), 228.

56. Brian Maffly, "Entrepreneur Revives Proposed Pipeline to Carry Green River Water from Utah to Colorado," *Salt Lake Tribune*, updated March 1, 2018, https://www.sltrib.com/news/environment/2018/02/27/entrepreneur -revives-zombie-pipeline-proposal-to-carry-green-river-water-from-utah -to-colorado/. A Colorado developer, Aaron Million, has proposed building a pipeline from the Flaming Gorge Reservoir in Utah and Wyoming that impounds water from the Green River to Denver.

57. Stegner, *Beyond the Hundredth Meridian*, 315.

58. Stegner, *Beyond the Hundredth Meridian*, 316.

59. Stegner, "Thoughts in a Dry Land," in Stegner, *Where the Bluebird Sings*, 47.

60. Stegner, "Thoughts in a Dry Land," 54.

61. Stegner, "Thoughts in a Dry Land," 47.

62. Stegner, "Coda: Wilderness Letter," 146–47.

63. Stegner, "Living Dry," 75; Stegner, "Thoughts in a Dry Land," 55.

64. Susan Kollin, "Introduction: Postwestern Studies, Dead or Alive," in *Postwestern Cultures: Literature, Theory, Space*, ed. Susan Kollin (Lincoln: University of Lincoln Nebraska, 2007), xi.

65. Sarah Jaquette Ray, "Coming of Age at the End of the World: The Affective Arc of Undergraduate Environmental Studies Curricula," in *Affective Ecocriticism: Emotion, Embodiment, Environment*, ed. Kyle Bladow and Jennifer Ladino (Lincoln: University of Nebraska Press, 2018), 309.

66. John Parsi, quoted in Maya Shrikant, "The Science of Hope: More Than Wishful Thinking," Arizona State University Knowledge Enterprise, June 14, 2021, https://research.asu.edu/science-hope-more-wishful-thinking.

67. Rebecca Solnit, "Grounds for Hope," *Tikkun* 32, no. 1 (2017): 33, https:// www.tikkun.org/grounds-for-hope/.

68. Jennifer Price, "Thirteen Ways of Seeing Nature in Los Angeles: Part I," *The Believer*, no. 33 (April 1, 2006), https://thebeliever.net/thirteen-ways -of-seeing-nature-in-la/.

69. Price, "Thirteen Ways."

70. Price, "Thirteen Ways."

71. Paolo Bacigalupi, *The Water Knife* (New York: Vintage, 2015), 51.

72. Solnit, "Grounds for Hope," 34.

73. Percival Everett, *Watershed* (Boston: Beacon Press, 2003); Stephanie Fitzgerald, *Native American Women and the Land: Narratives of Dispossession and Resurgence* (Albuquerque: University of New Mexico Press, 2015).

74. Elizabeth Cook-Lynn, *Aurelia: A Crow Creek Trilogy* (Boulder: University Press of Colorado, 1999); Sherman Alexie, "Powwow at the End of the World," Poetry Foundation, accessed January 13, 2020, https://www.poetryfoundation.org/poems/47895/the-powwow-at-the-end-of-the-world; Leslie Marmon Silko, *Gardens in the Dunes* (New York: Simon and Schuster, 1999); Ofelia Zepeda, "The Man Who Drowned in the Irrigation Ditch," in *Ocean Power: Poems from the Desert* (Tucson: University of Arizona Press, 1995), 29–33.

75. Natalie Diaz, *Postcolonial Love Poem* (Minneapolis: Graywolf Press, 2020).

76. A reading of Silko's, Zepeda's, and Diaz's work in relation to the Colorado River is found in Paul Formisano, *Tributary Voices: Literary and Rhetorical Explorations of the Colorado River* (Reno: University of Nevada Press, 2022). This study explores at greater length alternative narratives from the Colorado River Basin to foreground the fundamental role the environmental humanities can play in reorienting how we think about and use the river.

77. Wallace Stegner, introduction to *Sound of Mountain Water*, 38.

78. Cook-Lynn, "Why I Can't Read Wallace Stegner," 33.

79. A watershed consciousness, as considered within the humanities, draws from such work as Lawrence Buell's "watershed aesthetics" chapter in *Writing for an Endangered World: Literature, Culture, and Environment in the U.S. and Beyond* (Cambridge MA: Belknap Press of Harvard University Press, 2001) and Jack Loeffler and Celestia Loeffler's collection *Thinking Like a Watershed: Voices from the West* (Albuquerque: University of New Mexico Press, 2012), which borrows from Aldo Leopold's famous "Thinking Like a Mountain" selection in *A Sand County Almanac* (1949; rpt., New York: Oxford University Press, 1987).

80. See two chapters in this book: Leisl Carr Childers and Adam M. Sowards, "Hope in Public Lands: A Conversation," chapter 8; Robert M. Wilson, "The American West as Unlivable Space: Hope, Despair, and Adaptation in an Era of Climate Chaos," chapter 12.

12

The American West as
Unlivable Space
Hope, Despair, and
Adaptation in an Era of
Climate Chaos

ROBERT M. WILSON

Among the reoccurring themes in Wallace Stegner's work, few are as prominent as hope and adaptation. Stegner famously called the West the "native home of hope," and he returned to the topic of adaptation again and again, particularly in his nonfiction. For him, much of western American history was a tension between those who tried to adapt to the region's aridity and those who sought to circumvent it. This tension is the central conflict in *Beyond the Hundredth Meridian* (1953) and *The American West as Living Space* (1987), Stegner's reflection late in life on aridity, western history, and the region's future. Despite the tumultuous history of the West, he still hoped westerners could build a society to match the region's scenery.

Yet as we enter the third decade of the twenty-first century, the American West seems less like the native home of hope than a place cursed by climate chaos. In recent years climate change–exacerbated events, most notably megafires, have challenged westerners. Over the past four decades the area burned by wildfires in the West has doubled, and in California, it has increased fivefold. Smoke from massive blazes in California, Washington, and British Columbia have blanketed San Francisco and Seattle. These cities did not necessarily contend with wildfires directly. Instead, smoke from blazes hundreds of miles away darkened the skies and fouled the air. For a few weeks they had worse

30. Smoke from distant wildfires gives San Francisco a dystopian feel, September 2020. Frame capture from "San Francisco Looking Like Blade Runner / Mars / Chernobyl," https://www.youtube.com/watch?v=dSreOPz0Zcs&t=0s.

air quality than places in India and China, home to the cities with some of the worst air quality in the world. In the fall of 2020, light passing through the smoke-filled skies above San Francisco created an eerie orange, which gave the city a feeling reminiscent of the dystopian film *Blade Runner.* Infernos at the urban fringe have also incinerated parts of Sonoma, Malibu, Colorado Springs, Santa Barbara, and Superior, Colorado, a suburban community near Denver. Worst of all, the 2018 Camp Fire, the most destructive fire in California history, reduced much of Paradise, California, to ash and killed eighty-six people.[1]

In June 2021 the Pacific Northwest experienced a once-in-a-millennium heat wave sending temperatures soaring above 100 degrees Fahrenheit for days on end in normally cool, rainy Portland and Seattle. In Lytton, British Columbia—a hamlet about a hundred miles north of the international border—it reached a 121 degrees Fahrenheit, shattering Canada's all-time temperature record. But the worst was yet to come. A day after breaking the temperature record, Lytton residents smelled smoke. With no time to load belongings, they fled the town as the blaze engulfed the village, and in less than an hour, the fire destroyed most of Lytton. Yet the word "destroyed" fails to convey the devastation wrought by the fire. With most of the buildings gone and with only foundations and chimneys left behind, it looked as if a malevolent force had vaporized the village.[2]

The searing heat and ferocious wildfire that incinerated Lytton were worsened by climate change, which in turn is driven by the relentless rise in greenhouse gasses in the atmosphere. Preindustrial carbon dioxide levels were about 280 parts per million (ppm). At the time of Stegner's death in 1993, CO_2 levels were almost 360 ppm. Now they are 419 ppm, levels not seen on Earth for four million years.[3] In short, we have added as much CO_2 to the atmosphere in the quarter century since Stegner died as we had in the seventy years prior to that. As the level of greenhouse gases in the atmosphere has risen, so too have global temperatures. They are a little over one degree Celsius higher than just prior to the Industrial Revolution, and much of that warming has occurred in the past few decades. Like a building retreating in the rearview mirror of a speeding car, the climate Stegner knew in the twentieth century is fading rapidly behind us. Meanwhile, we hurtle toward a warmer, drier, and more chaotic future.[4]

Do Wallace Stegner's nonfiction and fiction have anything to say about the warming West? Or are Stegner's writings relics from of a simpler time when multiple climate change–worsened disasters did not beset the region? After all, Stegner was a twentieth-century writer, perhaps the quintessential twentieth-century writer of the western United States. Born in 1909, his life and career spanned the time from the early twentieth century, when the West was, in the words of historian Richard White, "a poor, hardscrabble place full of resentments against the East," to the late twentieth century, when the region had become an economic behemoth.[5] It was also a period of relative climate stability, particularly in comparison with the climate disruption now underway and given what is in store these coming decades. Only with sustained political mobilization and the deployment of new technologies can nations limit global warming to 1.5 or 2 degrees Celsius above preindustrial levels. But we are on track for over 2 to 3 degrees of warming by the end of the century, which would subject the West to unfathomable environmental change.[6]

Even though climate change will create a very different West from the one Stegner knew, his writings still have much to teach us even in today's different political and environmental moment. Stegner's central preoccupation with adaptation also happens to be a key topic among climate activists and environmental professionals. Westerners must adapt as best they can to these new conditions because climate change is already underway and since more warming will come even if nations radically reduce their emissions. But how should the region adapt? Should westerners pursue a softer path of learning to live with a dynamic, changing environment or a rigid path where they try to better engineer their communities and water systems for this hotter, drier West? Stegner would have much to say about this, and his work can help guide us. He can also serve as a model for mustering hope in the face of a seemingly bleak climate future. Stegner had ample grounds for despair in the last decade of his life. His beloved West seemed hell-bent on growth and unwilling to learn the lessons of how heedless economic development had fouled the land and impounded rivers. How did he summon hope despite what he saw?

Adaptation in the Drying, Combustible West

Adaptation was a key theme in Stegner novels such as *The Big Rock Candy Mountain* (1943) and *Angle of Repose* (1971), one of his most celebrated books. It was an even more prominent topic in his nonfiction. For Stegner, western American history was a story of Americans coming to grips with the "implacable fact of aridity." Faced with this hard reality, Stegner said westerners had two choices: "either try to engineer it out of existence or adapt to it."[7] By and large western boosters, with the aid of the federal government, chose the engineering option. The U.S. Bureau of Reclamation and Army Corps of Engineers built dozens of mammoth multipurpose dams that impounded waters on the Colorado, Columbia, Sacramento, and other rivers, making it available for industrial agriculture and the region's metropolises. Also, cities such as San Francisco and Los Angeles extended their tentacles into California's hinterlands to appropriate distant water and redirect it to serve urban residents and businesses. What emerged is what Donald Worster called a hydraulic society, a brash region impatient with limits.[8]

Instead of valorizing the bureaucracies that reengineered the region's waterscape, Stegner admired the Mormons who used small-scale irrigation to foster close-knit communities. In *Beyond the Hundredth Meridian* he celebrated John Wesley Powell and his hard-fought but fruitless attempt to persuade the federal government to manage and settle the West by watershed. Powell understood how aridity made the West different from the East, and because of this, how the region needed be settled differently.[9] Stegner did not steadfastly oppose any sort of water management. Rather, for him, if "the unrestrained engineering of western water was original sin, as I believe, it was essentially a sin of scale."[10] Municipal, state, and federal water agencies failed to recognize any limits whatsoever, and in the process, this failure to adapt instead produced an unsustainable hydraulic civilization.

Stegner said western aridity was an implacable fact—the West's scant rainfall defined the region. Like quartzite, it was fixed and unchanging. Runoff from the snow and rain falling in the Cascade Mountains, Sierra Nevada, and Rocky Mountains enabled a civilization to prosper in the lowlands. Stegner saw the region's mountains as "fountains" that nourished the lands below with precious water. "When those fountains fail," Stegner wrote prophetically, "the lowlands suffer ruin."[11]

There are already ominous signs these fountains are failing. The warming climate has already diminished snowpack, the ultimate source of water for much of the West, and by later in the century the seasonal snow may disappear entirely.[12] Reduced rain and snowfall coupled with warmer temperatures is diminishing the reservoirs along the Colorado River, most notably at Lake Mead, where the water level has diminished considerably since 2000. In 2022 the West was deep in a megadrought, the worst in 1,200 years, and the reservoir was only at 27 percent capacity.[13] Hundreds of feet above the water, "bathtub rings" on the cliffs served as mute markers of higher lake levels in decades past. The low lake level was a consequence partly of upriver diversions by cities and agriculture but primarily because of worsened drought and higher temperatures, brought on by climate change, which led to greater evaporation. In the coming decades the river flow could diminish by 11 percent and up to 55 percent by the end of the century. Hoover Dam and Glen Canyon Dam were built to block the flow of the Colorado so growers and municipalities could divert the water for beneficial use. But the dams can only impound the water nature provides. With meager snowpack becoming more frequent in a warming world, the dams may become curious monuments built during a bygone wetter, cooler, twentieth-century West.[14]

Large-scale engineering projects such as multipurpose dams and aqueducts were often the solution to overcoming the West's aridity. Massive engineering might also serve as a desperate attempt by the United States and other nations to slow global warming. Solar geoengineering—the large-scale interference with the atmosphere to counteract climate change—was once considered an outlandish idea, more appropriate for science fiction movies than a serious response to climate change. But even though all the world's nations signed the 2015 Paris Climate Accord, carbon emissions continue to rise, increasing the likelihood that global temperature will surpass the two-degree Celsius target considered the threshold for dangerous climate change.[15] Given this grim situation, the United States, China, and other major carbon-emitting countries are investigating altering Earth's thermostat through artificial means. These include technologies to reflect sunlight, such as by using jet airplanes to spray sulfate aerosols high in the atmosphere. Such a plan would mimic the cooling properties of aerosols ejected from volcanoes during eruptions. Other geoengineering schemes would suck carbon from the atmosphere rather than block solar radiation. Scientists have created experimental machines to directly capture the air and store carbon underground. While technologically feasible, making a dent in greenhouse gas levels would require constructing thousands of these plants around the world.[16]

What might Stegner make of such grandiose engineering schemes? He was deeply critical of the Bureau of Reclamation's decades-long effort to impound the West's rivers instead of encouraging the region's residents to adapt to aridity. Given this, he would probably view these geoengineering schemes with great suspicion. They are a way to circumvent the need to reduce greenhouse gas emissions and ensure a livable climate for us and our children. He might also see them as a way for the United States and other nations to perpetuate dreams of unending growth, whatever the cost to the climate and the human and nonhuman communities. Like the construction of multipurpose dams in the West, Stegner would see climate geoengineering as an act of hubris and a failure to recognize nature's limits.

Stegner, like many writers and scholars after him, saw the hundredth meridian as the border between the dry West and the wet East. But with climate change, this seemingly natural, unchanging border is now in motion. Today Stegner would need to retitle his famous book about John Wesley Powell as *Beyond the Ninety-Eighth Meridian*. The arid West is moving northward and eastward. Over the past forty years, warmer temperatures have dried the soil and altered rainfall and snowfall across the area, pushing the arid and semiarid region outward, a trend that will continue in the coming decades. If one of the defining features of the West is its aridity, then a warmer climate will leave more of the middle of the United States hotter and drier—in short, more "western."

But today's West is not only more arid than it was during Stegner's time. It's also more combustible. The zone where suburban and exurban communities meet undeveloped public lands is known as the wildland-urban interface.[17] Although Stegner probably never used the term, he had much to say about suburbs and exurbs that comprise this zone. For over forty years Stegner lived in the Los Altos Hills west of Stanford University, a suburban enclave in the southwest part of the Bay Area. Although he is better remembered now for his nonfiction writings about wilderness and public lands, two of his most critically acclaimed and successful novels, *All the Little Live Things*

(1967) and *The Spectator Bird* (1976), are wholly or partially set in the Los Altos Hills. If the wildland-urban interface has a poet laureate, it is Wallace Stegner.

His novels and essays about the Los Altos Hills help us understand what attracted so many twentieth-century westerners to live in the wildland-urban interface and, to lesser degree, how we might adapt to this sort of landscape. When Wallace Stegner and his wife, Mary, moved to the Los Altos Hills in 1945, they were pioneers. "The Peninsula foothills back of Stanford University seemed to us as untouched as New South Wales must have seemed to Captain Cook," he wrote.[18] There were few roads or shops; many homes lacked water or sewer hookups. Now such communities at the border of suburbs and wildlands are commonplace throughout the country, particularly in the western United States. Town and suburban developments in wildland-urban interface areas blossomed through the last half of the twentieth century. Just since 1990 the number of homes in this zone across the country has increased by 40 percent, and the land encompassed by it has increased by 33 percent. Nestled among the trees and brush, these homes are ripe for burning. Climate change, as it has done with so much else, is only worsening the situation in these areas, forcing the residents at the suburbs' edge to confront a growing wildfire menace.[19]

That his suburban pastoral landscape had become a tinderbox would not have surprised Stegner. He also would have recognized that he and his neighbors were partly responsible for their plight. In Stegner's essay "Remnants" he narrates the environmental history of his corner of the Los Altos Hills from the early to late twentieth century. When he first arrived in the mid-1940s, he reveled in the ecological bounty around him. The hills teemed with owls, raccoons, possums, jackrabbits, deer, and coyotes.[20] Over the decades the hills became a lonesome landscape, bereft of most of the animals that originally roamed near the Stegner home. It saddened him. But he acknowledged his own culpability in creating this new world. The native vegetation had retreated to be replaced with new—and combustible—vegetation: pepper trees, eucalyptus, and Monterey pines. A semiwild landscape was what originally drew the Stegners to the hills. Yet by the early twenty-first century, this Los Altos Hills community and thousands like it throughout the western United States faced a precarious future. As the catastrophic Camp Fire in Paradise showed, a blaze could incinerate these suburban idylls in a few hours. Such is life in the wildland-urban interface in the era of climate change.[21]

Indeed, if climate change projections are correct, the aridity Stegner knew in the twentieth century will seem positively lush by the mid-twenty-first century. With this growing aridity will come a massive rearranging of the environment. Recently scientists have constructed "analog maps" to help Americans visualize what the climate will be like in their home cities fifty years from now. Under a high-emissions scenario, the trajectory we are on right now, the Los Altos Hills will have a climate similar to what the foothills of the Los Angeles Basin have today. Other communities in the West are projected to have climates quite different than they do today, with many becoming hotter and more arid in the coming decades.[22]

Stegner, Despair, and Hope

Stegner wrote at length about the need for westerners to adapt to aridity and the problems with trying to circumvent the limits of the dry West through grand hydrologic engineering schemes. Yet he was also concerned with the West as a wellspring for emotions, particularly hope. Stegner famously called the region's wilderness the "geography of hope," and he wanted to help foster a "a society to match its scenery."[23]

Surveying the West in the 1980s, Stegner had ample reason for despair. The Sagebrush Rebellion sought to transfer the vast western federal public lands to the states and allow ranchers as well as mining and fossil fuel companies more influence over these areas.[24] The Reagan administration was hostile to conservation, and the president appointed James Watt as secretary of the interior, one of the most antienvironmental secretaries in the modern history of the Department of the Interior. Given this, it was easy for Stegner to feel despondent about the region's future. Despair and hope were not separate emotions but ones that existed simultaneously within him. His struggle was how to keep these two emotions in balance and not let despair swamp hope entirely.[25]

As the climate crisis has worsened, creative nonfiction writers and filmmakers have begun contending with despair and hope in ways reminiscent of Stegner. Among them is David Wallace-Wells, who draws on cutting-edge climate science but is as concerned with meaning and emotion as with scientific fact. In his book *The Uninhabitable Earth: Life after Warming* (2019), he writes, "Environmental panic is growing, and so is despair."[26] How will climate change alter our culture, the arts, our very psychology? The first line of his book sets the tone: "It's worse, much worse, than you think."[27] He marshals an array of disparate facts culled from the dull, bureaucratic climate assessments produced by the Intergovernmental Panel on Climate Change (IPCC) and other scientific bodies to narrate a devastating picture of our future.[28] He does not focus on the worst-case scenario, the four-degree Celsius trajectory by the end of the century, but the best-case scenario—the "only" two degrees of warming in store for us if we miraculously manage to lower carbon emissions substantially over the coming decades.[29] He depicts a world of inundated coastlines, raging wildfires, and millions of climate refugees, and bereft of coral reefs.

Writer and climate activist Bill McKibben recounts some of the same dismal science in *Falter: Has the Human Game Begun to Play Itself Out?* (2019). As with Wallace-Wells's writing, McKibben's book is an unflinching examination of the predicament in which we find ourselves and the blazing speed with which climate change is reshaping our world. McKibben believes climate change threatens the human experiment—it's in danger of faltering, he contends. But his book is also a sustained attempt to keep despair at bay despite the increasingly dire predictions from climate scientists and other experts on climate change. "A writer doesn't owe a reader hope—the only obligation is honesty," McKibben writes, "but I want those who pick up this volume to know that its author lives in a state of engagement, not despair."[30] He acknowledges that tackling climate change would take enormous effort and quite a bit of luck. "I don't know that we will make these choices.

I rather suspect we won't—we are faltering now, and the human game has begun to play itself out."[31]

Wallace-Wells and McKibben take solace in people's capacity to make better choices. Bad choices caused this predicament. Better choices can rescue us from the brink of climate catastrophe. We have the power to choose otherwise, they argue, and to use nonviolent collective action to demand more from our governments and hold corporations accountable for failing to address the climate crisis. They both support the climate movement, particularly the youth-led segment epitomized by Swedish teenager Greta Thunberg.[32]

Close cousins to despair are grief and mourning, key themes in Stegner's books such as *Wolf Willow* (1955) and *All the Little Live Things*. Laura Paskus also explores these themes in *At the Precipice: New Mexico's Changing Climate* (2020). Paskus is a seasoned investigative journalist, and much of her book is a clear, in-depth discussion of the myriad climate threats facing the state. But in the chapter "Mourning a Mountain," she offers a personal reflection and shares her anguish as, year by year, she watches the state's forests die. New Mexico's hotter, drier climate has stressed ponderosa pine, piñon, and juniper, allowing beetles and insects to penetrate the bark and weaken the trees. Massive fires have raged though these ghost forests, and in their aftermath, heavy rains have scoured the bare slopes of precious soil, leaving behind a denuded landscape. "How do we mourn nude mountains?" Paskus asks. "What do you do with your grief?" In the climate-changed West, new forests are not necessarily returning after fires or insect infestations destroy them. Instead, a new, unfamiliar landscape is emerging in the state, and Paskus wonders if in a couple of generations New Mexicans will "ache for something they don't know is missing." She adds: "One day a new generation wakes up and doesn't remember that a river once flowed through their community. A dry riverbed is no longer something unusual. Rather, it's just another dry rut in the landscape of memory."[33]

By and large, filmmakers have proved less willing to examine climate change in movies. An exception is esteemed writer and director Paul Schrader's *First Reformed* (2017), a haunting meditation on hope and

31. "Hope and despair . . . Holding these two things in our mind is life itself." In *First Reformed* Rev. Ernst Toller (Ethan Hawke) tries to summon hope as he confronts the reality of impending climate apocalypse. Frame capture from *First Reformed*, 2017, dir. Paul Schrader.

despair in a world that seems teetering on the brink of a climate apocalypse.[34] At first glance the film might appear to have little to do with climate change. It is about Reverend Ernst Toller, the pastor of a small, failing church in upstate New York. When we meet him, he is morose and preaching to a dwindling flock indifferent to his sermons. He is approached by Mary, one of his few parishioners, who is worried about her depressed husband, Michael. Revered Toller agrees to meet Michael and learns that he is a climate activist. Knowledge about climate change has left Michael despondent. He recounts for Reverend Toller the state of global warming, drawing on the same sorts of scientific studies that Wallace-Wells, McKibben, and Paskus discuss in such detail: sea level rise, crop failures, drought, and wildfire. "I thought people would change," the young man says. "I thought people would listen." Mary is pregnant, and Michael considers it immoral to bring a child into a world headed for ruin.[35] Reverend Toller is unconvinced. "This is not about your baby," the reverend says. "This is not about Mary. This is about you. And your despair, your lack of hope." He challenges the activist. "Courage is the solution to despair," he tells him. "Wisdom is holding two contradictory truths in our mind simultaneously. Hope and despair. . . . Holding these two things in our mind is life itself."

These two emotions explored in Schrader's film are also at odds in Wallace-Wells's, McKibben's, and Paskus's books. But they are also in tension throughout Stegner's work, particularly his nonfiction books about the American West. Stegner had a clear-eyed view of the West, of the failings of its residents, and of the federal government, too often beholden to business interests. Yet he still mustered hope in spite of these failings and the damage wrought by a century and a half of development in the region. Like these environmental writers, he took solace in the labor of everyday activists holding government and business accountable for the damage they caused. Stegner's wish for a civilization to match the West's scenery is akin to the desire of Wallace-Wells, McKibben, and Paskus for a sane, just, and flourishing world despite the climate crisis.

First Reformed and these books are not about Wallace Stegner, and except for Paskus's *At the Precipice*, they are not even about the West. But the writers and filmmaker Schrader all wrestle with hope and despair as Stegner did in his work. Keeping hope in the face of climate chaos is our great challenge. While Stegner never wrote about climate change, he thought deeply about adaptation and maintaining hope. Adapting to the climate-changed West will be our great ecological test. But summoning hope amid so much loss will be our deeper spiritual challenge. Stegner was a product of the twentieth-century West. Even so, perhaps he can help us negotiate the perilous, warming twenty-first century. If we can find hope in the West—the U.S. region most threatened by climate change—maybe we can find hope elsewhere. If the West can remain living space amid climate chaos, perhaps other, less threatened regions can remain livable, too. And if so, then perhaps Wallace Stegner was right: the West is indeed the native home of hope.

Notes

1. Gary Ferguson, *Land on Fire: The New Reality of Wildfire in the West* (Portland OR: Timber Press, 2017); John T. Abatzoglou and A. Park Williams, "Impact of Anthropogenic Climate Change on Wildfire across Western US Forests," *Proceedings of the National Academy of Sciences* (*PNAS*) 113, no. 42 (2016): 11,770–75; A. Park Williams, John T. Abatzoglou, Alexander Gershunov, Janin Guzman-Morales, Daniel A. Bishop, Jennifer K. Balch, and Dennis P. Lettenmaier, "Observed Impacts of Anthropogenic Climate Change on Wildfire in California," *Earth's Future* 7, no. 8 (2019): 892–910; Lindy West, "We're Choking on Smoke in Seattle," *New York Times*, August 9, 2017; Julie Turkewitz and Matt Richtel, "Air Quality in California: Devastating Fires Lead to a New Danger," *New York Times*, November 16, 2018; Alastair Gee and Dani Anguiano, "Last Day in Paradise: The Untold Story of How a Fire Swallowed a Town," *The Guardian* (UK), December 20, 2018; Ed Struzik, "The Age of Megafires: The World Hits a Climate Tipping Point," *Yale Environment 360*, September 12, 2020.

2. Andrea Woo, Patrick White, Carrie Tait, and Chantelle Lee, "'Like a War Zone': B.C. Village of Lytton Destroyed by Fire," *Globe and Mail* (Toronto), July 1, 2021, https://www.theglobeandmail.com/canada/article -like-a-war-zone-bc-village-of-lytton-destroyed-by-fire/; "Western North American Extreme Heat Virtually Impossible without Human-Caused Climate Change," World Weather Attribution, July 7, 2021, https://www .worldweatherattribution.org/western-north-american-extreme-heat -virtually-impossible-without-human-caused-climate-change/.

3. James Shulmeister, "Climate Explained: What the World Was Like the Last Time Carbon Dioxide Levels Were at 400ppm," *The Conversation*, July 7, 2020, https://theconversation.com/climate-explained-what-the -world-was-like-the-last-time-carbon-dioxide-levels-were-at-400ppm -141784.

4. "Global CO_2 Levels," 2° Institute, accessed August 8, 2022, https://www .co2levels.org/; K. D. Burke, J. W. Williams, M. A. Chandler, A. M. Haywood, D. J. Lunt, and B. L. Otto-Bliesner, "Pliocene and Eocene Provide Best Analogs for Near-Future Climates," *PNAS* 115, no. 52 (2018): 13,288–93; Jaelyn J. Eberle and David R. Greenwood, "Life at the Top

of the Greenhouse Eocene World—A Review of the Eocene Flora and Vertebrate Fauna from Canada's High Arctic," *GSA Bulletin* 124, no. 1/2 (2012): 3–23.

5. Richard White, *The Organic Machine: The Remaking of the Columbia River* (New York: Hill and Wang, 1995), 70.

6. Intergovernmental Panel on Climate Change (IPCC), "Global Warming of 1.5°C: An IPCC Special Report on the Impacts of Global Warming of 1.5°C above Pre-Industrial Levels and Related Global Greenhouse Gas Emission Pathways, in the Context of Strengthening the Global Response to the Threat of Climate Change," 2018, https://www.ipcc.ch/sr15/. For summary and analysis of this pivotal report, see Coral Davenport, "Major Climate Report Describes a Strong Risk of Crisis as Early as 2040," *New York Times*, October 7, 2018; and Bill McKibben, "A Very Grim Forecast," *New York Review of Books*, November 22, 2018.

7. Wallace Stegner, *Where the Bluebird Sings to the Lemonade Springs: Living and Writing in the West* (New York: Random House, 1992), 75.

8. Donald Worster, *Rivers of Empire: Water, Aridity, and the Growth of the American West* (New York: Pantheon, 1985), 7–14.

9. More accurately, this should be called resettlement since the mostly white settlers dispossessed Indigenous peoples from their homelands. On settler colonialism and the American West, see Janne Lahti, "What Is Settler Colonialism and What It Has to Do with the American West?" *Journal of the West* 56, no. 4 (2017): 8–13; Andrew C. Isenberg and Lawrence H. Kessler, "Settler Colonialism and the Environmental History of the North American West," *Journal of the West* 56, no. 4 (2017): 57–67.

10. Stegner, *Where the Bluebird Sings*, 79.

11. Wallace Stegner, *Sound of Mountain Water: The Changing American West* (1969; rpt., New York: Vintage, 1997), 9.

12. Soumaya Belmecheri, Flurin Babst, Eugene R. Wahl, David W. Stahle, and Valerie Trouet, "Multi-Century Evaluation of Sierra Nevada Snowpack," *Nature Climate Change* 6, no. 1 (January 2016): 2015–16; Erica R. Siirila-Woodburn, Alan M. Rhoades, Benjamin J. Hatchett, Laurie S. Huning, Julia Szinai, Christina Tague, Peter S. Nico, et al., "A Low-to-No Snow Future and Its Impacts on Water Resources in the Western United States," *Nature Reviews Earth & Environment* 2 (2021): 800–819.

13. "Lake Mead Keeps Dropping," NASA Earth Observatory, 2022, https://earthobservatory.nasa.gov/images/150111/lake-mead-keeps-dropping; A. Park Williams, Benjamin I. Cook, and Jason E. Smerdon, "Rapid Intensification of the Emerging Southwestern North American Megadrought in 2020–2021," *Nature Climate Change* 12, no. 3 (March 2022): 232–34.

14. For a scientific overview of how climate change is currently affecting the West and how it might affect the region in the future, see Gregg M. Garfin et al., eds., "Southwest," in *Fourth National Climate Assessment*, vol. 2, *Impacts, Risks, and Adaptation in the United States*, ed. D. R. Reidmiller, C. W. Avery, D. R. Easterling, K. E. Kunkel, K. L. M. Lewis, T. K. Maycock, and B. C. Stewart (Washington DC: Government Printing Office, 2018), 1104; Bradley Udall and Jonathan Overpeck, "The Twenty-First Century Colorado River Hot Drought and Implications for the Future," *Water Resources Research* 53, no. 3 (2017): 2404–18; Brad Udall and Jonathan Overpeck, "The Colorado River Is Shrinking Because of Climate Change," *High Country News*, June 15, 2017, https://www.hcn.org/articles/colorado-river-shrinking-climate-change-drought. On the future of dams and reservoirs along the Colorado River, see Elizabeth Kolbert, "The Lost Canyon under Lake Powell," *New Yorker*, August 9, 2021, https://www.newyorker.com/magazine/2021/08/16/the-lost-canyon-under-lake-powell.

15. Universal Ecological Fund (FEU-US), "The Truth behind the Climate Pledges," https://feu-us.org/behind-the-climate-pledges/; David Roberts, "The World's Bleak Climate Situation, in 3 Charts," *Vox*, May 1, 2018, https://www.vox.com/energy-and-environment/2018/4/30/17300946/global-warming-degrees-replace-fossil-fuels.

16. On the science and politics of geoengineering, see Fred Pearce, "Geoengineer the Planet? More Scientists Now Say It Must Be an Option," *Yale Environment 360*, May 29, 2019, http://e360.yale.edu/features/negative-emissions-is-it-feasible-to-remove-co2-from-the-air; Holly Jean Buck, *After Geoengineering: Climate Tragedy, Repair, and Restoration* (New York: Verso, 2019); Elizabeth Kolbert, *Under a White Sky: The Nature of the Future* (New York: Crown, 2021), 141–202; Bill McKibben, "Dimming the Sun to Cool the Planet Is a Desperate Idea, Yet We're Inching toward It," *New Yorker*, November 28, 2022.

17. Tania Schoennagel, Jennifer K. Balch, Hannah Brenkert-Smith, Phillip E. Dennison, Brian J. Harvey, Meg A. Krawchuk, Nathan Mietkiewicz, et al., "Adapt to More Wildfire in Western North American Forests as Climate Changes," *PNAS* 114, no. 18 (2017): 4582–90; Volker C. Radeloff, David P. Helmers, H. Anu Kramer, Miranda H. Mockrin, Patricia M. Alexandre, Avi Bar-Massada, Van Butsic, et al., "Rapid Growth of the US Wildland-Urban Interface Raises Wildfire Risk," *PNAS* 115, no. 3 (2018): 3314–19.

18. Wallace Stegner, "Remnants," in *Natural State: A Literary Anthology of California Nature Writing*, ed. Steven Gilbar (Berkeley: University of California Press, 1998), 177–78.

19. Jackson J. Benson, *Wallace Stegner: His Life and Work* (New York: Penguin Books, 1996), 153–54; Radeloff et al., "Rapid Growth," 3314–19.

20. The Stegners lived in the Los Altos Hills when wildlife populations were at their lowest. Over the past few decades, wildlife have migrated into American suburbs and large cities. On urban wildlife, see Peter S. Alagona, *The Accidental Ecosystem: People and Wildlife in American Cities* (Berkeley: University of California Press, 2022).

21. The former Stegner home is not threatened by wildfire. It was destroyed nearly a decade ago by new owners of the property. They razed the Stegners' modest ranch house and the small cottage where he wrote many of his best-known books and replaced them with a modern, hi-tech home now valued at over $8 million. Sam Whiting, "Wallace Stegner's Studio Destined for Demolition." *SFGate*, May 13, 2011, https://www.sfgate.com /news/article/Wallace-Stegner-s-studio-destined-for-demolition-2371887 .php.

22. Matthew C. Fitzpatrick, and Robert R Dunn, "American Urban Areas in the Late 21st Century," *Nature Communications* 10 (2019): 1–7; "What Will the Climate Feel Like in 60 Years?" University of Maryland, Center for Environmental Science, https://fitzlab.shinyapps.io/cityapp/.

23. Stegner, *Sound of Mountain Water*, 32, 147.

24. R. McGregor Cawley, *Federal Land, Western Anger: The Sagebrush Rebellion and Environmental Politics* (Lawrence: University of Kansas Press, 1993).

25. Wallace Stegner, "Will Reagan Ride with the Raiders?" *Washington Post*, January 20, 1981; Stegner, "If the Sagebrush Rebels Win, Everybody Loses," *Living Wilderness*, Summer 1981, 30–35.

26. David Wallace-Wells, *The Uninhabitable Earth: Life after Warming* (New York: Tim Duggan Books, 2019), 214.

27. Wallace-Wells, *Uninhabitable Earth*, 3. Some prominent climate scientists see Wallace-Wells's deeply pessimistic perspective as an example of "climate doomism," a debilitating view of the future that might paralyze the public instead of rallying them to tackle climate change. See Michael Mann, *The New Climate War: The Fight to Take Back Our Planet* (New York: PublicAffairs, 2021), 179–224.

28. Climate scientist Katherine Hayhoe calls the massive IPCC reports "doorstops of doom." Emily McFarlan Miller, "Evangelical Scientist Katharine Hayhoe Finds Hope in United Nations' Climate Report," *Religion News Service*, March 14, 2022, https://religionnews.com/2022/03/14/evangelical-scientist-katharine-hayhoe-finds-hope-in-united-nations-climate-report/.

29. The most comprehensive accounting of current warming and informed speculation about future warming is found in the Sixth Assessment Report of the United Nations Intergovernmental Panel on Climate Change, *Climate Change 2021: The Physical Science Basis*, https://www.ipcc.ch/report/sixth-assessment-report-working-group-i/. For a clear, thorough summary of key findings in this report, including future climate projections, see Carbon Brief Staff, "In-Depth Q&A: The IPCC's Sixth Assessment Report on Climate Science," *Carbon Brief*, September 8, 2021, https://www.carbonbrief.org/in-depth-qa-the-ipccs-sixth-assessment-report-on-climate-science/. Since *The Uninhabitable Earth* was published in 2019, Wallace-Wells has become somewhat more optimistic about humanity's climate prospects. The future will be far hotter for most of the world but "mercifully short of true climate apocalypse." See David Wallace-Wells, "Beyond Catastrophe: A New Climate Reality Is Coming into View," *New York Times Magazine*, October 26, 2022, https://www.nytimes.com/interactive/2022/10/26/magazine/climate-change-warming-world.html.

30. Bill McKibben, *Falter: Has the Human Game Begun to Play Itself Out?* (New York: Henry Holt, 2019), 3.

31. McKibben, *Falter*, 255.

32. David Wallace-Wells, "It's Greta's World. But It's Still Burning. The Extraordinary Rise of a 16-Year-Old, and Her Hail Mary Climate

Movement," *New York Magazine*, September 17, 2019, http://nymag.com /intelligencer/2019/09/greta-thunberg-climate-change-movement.html.

33. Laura Paskus, *At the Precipice: New Mexico's Changing Climate* (Albuquerque: University of New Mexico Press, 2020), 65, 69, 71.

34. *First Reformed*, dir. Paul Schrader (New York: A24, 2017).

35. While *First Reformed* is a work of fiction, the despair the character expresses and the angst he feels about bringing a child into a climate-changed world is quite common among Generation Z. An article in the *Lancet* medical journal analyzes polling data that shows that over half of young people think humanity is doomed, and four out of ten are reluctant to have children. See Carol Hickman, Elizabeth Marks, Panu Pihkala, Susan Clayton, R. Eric Lewandowski, Elouise E. Mayall, Britt Wray, Catriona Mellor, and Lise van Susteren, "Climate Anxiety in Children and Young People and Their Beliefs about Government Responses to Climate Change: A Global Survey," *Lancet Planetary Health* 5, no. 12 (2021): E863–E873. On climate despair and the relationship between the climate crisis and reproductive anxiety, see Britt Wray, *Generation Dread: Finding Purpose in an Age of Climate Crisis* (New York: Penguin Random House, 2022), 75–102.

Epilogue

Richer for This Sorrow

MARK FIEGE,
MICHAEL J. LANSING,
AND LEISL CARR CHILDERS

There is a sense in which we are all each other's consequences . . .
—Wallace Stegner, *All the Little Live Things*

Wallace Stegner's ninth novel, *All the Little Live Things*, centers on a struggle over different, although not irreconcilable, ways of seeing the world. The book opens with the main character, Joe Allston, meditating on the human condition following the death of his young friend Marian Catlin. Old, hard, cynical, and righteous, Joe had moved to the California countryside hoping to find refuge from the pain of losing his son, but his quest proves illusory. Evil always stalks good, he believes, and much as he cannot rid his property of thistles, poison oak, gophers, and other pests, neither can he escape foolish, naive, self-interested, manipulative people and all of the tragedies and woes that afflict an earnest person's life. Marian's terrifying, agonizing death from cancer at the moment of childbirth and the conjoined demise of her newborn baby confirms his deeply unsettled worldview. Musing over the meaning of it all, he throws the remains of a beloved cherry tree—its life cut short at the moment of its blossoming—onto a burn pile.[1]

Lovely Marian had disagreed with Joe. If Joe saw evil and self-interest forever afflicting the good, Marian saw a world, however imperfect, alive with good and moving in the direction of its fulfillment. Joe's effort to shape nature to his liking and to suit his needs—his killing of gophers and spraying of weeds—was not necessarily illegitimate, but what was wrong with his approach was his Manichaeanism and his

309

reflexive condemnation of gophers, weeds, and certain people and their offensive behavior to the category of evil. "Walk openly," Joe remembers Marian saying. "Love even the threat and the pain, feel yourself fully alive, cast a bold shadow, accept, accept. What we call evil is only a groping toward good, part of the trial and error by which we move toward the perfected consciousness."[2] Joe sees Marian's position, but he never can and never will completely give in to it—the presence of evil is simply too powerful, too manifest. Yet he grudgingly admits that his memory of Marian "keeps driving me into the open," keeps reminding him of "the stupidity of the attempt to withdraw and be free of trouble and harm."[3]

The contributors to this volume embody and express elements of Joe Allston. Like Joe, we want to protect lives, homes, and loved ones. Some of us, if not old, are growing older and, like Joe in his advanced age, show signs of cynicism characteristic of the curmudgeon. Others of us, if not young, are younger and burn with indignation over the wrongs that define the West. Like Joe, all of us see evil. We recognize that the economic and political systems that structure our lives and that enrich the few at the expense of the many have not failed but succeeded. Corporate industrial capitalism—an entrenched system of mass extraction, production, consumption, accumulation, and destruction—fuels poverty and a climate that grows ever more erratic and destructive. A republic and its Constitution gestures to democracy but excludes many voices and enables the most powerful to stop those who demand necessary change. Settler colonialism and the racism and sexism that feed it perpetuate dispossession, compound inequities, and drive the dark and violent impulses of many fellow citizens.

Like Joe, all of the authors see the value and utility of the burn pile. We recognize and embrace the creative—if unsettling—power of combustion. Rot and deadwood surround us, and we want to rid ourselves of it, reduce and recycle it, break it down and return its constituents to the soil. A few of us also see much of Stegner's literary corpus in that light. We are not book burners; we are people of ideas, words, texts, and libraries. That said, we wonder if it is time, figuratively speaking, to toss at least a few of Stegner's worst pieces on the pile. Burning, as the historian Stephen Pyne tells us, sometimes promotes the good and purges the bad.[4]

But, truth be told, all the essays in this book embody and express as much of Marian Catlin as the curmudgeon named Joe Allston. We see the burn pile not as an end in itself but as a means to an end as we grope toward the good. We gather around the pile and stare into the flames, and we recognize that, as Stegner put it, "we are all each other's consequences."[5] We need each other. Solidarity is strength, and individualism is lonely and alienating. Mesmerized, we realize that there is wonder and beauty and power in a democratic, deliberative process that helps us recognize possibilities—the most important of which are the pathways to a future different from the dreadful one that seems to be waiting for us.

We are the people committed to unsettling. We are Alexandra Hernandez, Michael J. Lansing, and Flannery Burke, and we recognize that negation and erasure—of people, places, experiences, emotions, and memories—are prompts to see the settler West in the fullness of its pain and the silences of its prejudices, not just in its stereotyped beauty. We are Michael Childers, Nancy S. Cook, and Michael A. Brown, and we seek to uncover hidden stories of empowering the least among us, not just the stars; of finding in the sludge hidden philosophies of magnanimity and collective action; and, rather like Joe, of wielding an ideal as a club when circumstances call for it. We are Leisl Carr Childers, Adam M. Sowards, Melody Graulich, and Robert B. Keiter, and we insist that our best ideas are works in progress with enduring potential to foster decent human beings and to restore landscapes to sovereign First Peoples for the benefit of all. We are Mark Fiege, and we acknowledge our settler status even as we seek reconciliation and repair. We are Paul Formisano and Robert M. Wilson, for whom hope is not an empty platitude but a sober recognition that we have a chance to find a path forward despite the formidable odds against us—on behalf of our children and our students and all the people, places, and things that matter most.

Evil and darkness are alive and well in the land, Joe thinks to himself as he builds the burn pile. But was Marian not worth knowing? In his sorrow and despair, should he erase his memory of her? Should he throw it on the burn pile and then return to his defensive crouch against anything or anyone that threatens his isolated, lonely refuge in the countryside? "Not for a moment," he concedes. "And so even in the gnashing of my teeth I acknowledge my conversion . . . I shall be richer all my life for this sorrow."[6]

Alive with Marian, we embrace the West and feel our way toward a better if imperfect future in it. Wary, like Joe, we build the burn pile and a keep a bludgeon at the ready. Intimate, interdependent, and in community, we accept the threat and the pain, mourn and anticipate the deaths, and remember that rot, ashes, and alkali flats are but signs of an unsettled world that still holds the potential for a better one to come.[7]

Notes

1. Wallace Stegner, *All the Little Live Things* (New York: Viking, 1967; rpt., New York: Penguin, 1991), 1–12, 340–45.
2. Stegner, *All the Little Live Things*, 342.
3. Stegner, *All the Little Live Things*, 7, 342.
4. Stephen Pyne, *The Pyrocene: How We Created an Age of Fire, and What Happens Next* (Berkeley: University of California Press, 2021), 67.
5. Stegner, *All the Little Live Things*, x.
6. Stegner, *All the Little Live Things*, 344–45.
7. Wallace Stegner, *The American West as Living Space* (Ann Arbor: University of Michigan Press, 1987), 86.

CONTRIBUTORS

MICHAEL A. BROWN is an assistant professor of philosophy at Creighton University.

FLANNERY BURKE is an associate professor of American studies at St. Louis University.

LEISL CARR CHILDERS is an associate professor of history at Colorado State University.

MICHAEL CHILDERS is an associate professor of history at Colorado State University.

NANCY S. COOK is a professor emerita of English at the University of Montana.

MARK FIEGE is a professor of history and the Wallace Stegner Chair in Western American Studies at Montana State University.

PAUL FORMISANO is an associate professor of English at the University of South Dakota.

MELODY GRAULICH is a professor emerita of English at Utah State University.

ALEXANDRA HERNANDEZ is the Intermountain Region Program manager for the National Park Service National Heritage Areas Program.

ROBERT B. KEITER is the Wallace Stegner Professor of Law at the University of Utah.

MICHAEL J. LANSING is a professor of history at Augsburg University.

ADAM M. SOWARDS is a professor emeritus of history at the University of Idaho.

ROBERT M. WILSON is an associate professor of geography and the environment at Syracuse University.

INDEX

Page numbers in italics refer to illustrations.